CLASSICS IN WESTERN CIVILIZATION

A Course of Selected Reading
by Authorities

*

*Particular attention is directed to the
Introductory Reading Guide by*
D. C. SOMERVELL, M.A.

PHILOSOPHICAL LIBRARY, INC.

Published, 1960 *by*
PHILOSOPHICAL LIBRARY, INC.,
15 EAST 40TH STREET, NEW YORK 16, N.Y.

PRINTED IN GREAT BRITAIN
FOR PHILOSOPHICAL LIBRARY
BY R. AND R. CLARK LTD., EDINBURGH

CONTENTS

BOOK I

WHAT IS WESTERN CIVILIZATION?

BOOK II

THE MAKING OF MODERN EUROPE

BOOK III

THE GROWTH OF POLITICAL FREEDOM

BOOK IV

THE CHALLENGE TO WESTERN CIVILIZATION

INTRODUCTORY READING GUIDE

BY

D. C. SOMERVELL, M.A.

_____

I. ORIGINS

WE are told that the human race, *homo sapiens* as it is oddly called,
has existed on the earth for half a million years ; some say longer. Of
something between ninety-eight and ninety-nine per cent of this history
we have no written records. We rely on the evidence of archaeology
and the arguments of anthropology. It does not matter whether we
call this story history or prehistory ; its subject is mankind organized
in what are called primitive societies, before he entered upon the series
of experiments—interesting, fruitful, but, it must be admitted, hitherto
ultimately unsuccessful experiments—which we call civilizations.

Dr. Arnold Toynbee [1] illustrates the human record by means of a
vivid simile from mountaineering. The human race round about 5000
B.C. may be likened to a number of climbers resting upon a ledge.
They have climbed a long way to reach that ledge. Indeed they have
climbed a stiffer pitch than any they have climbed since, for they have
climbed out of the mere animality of sub-man or ape-man into the
state of *sapientia* that has achieved the thousands of elaborately organized social groupings which we call primitive societies. How and
why that climb was made we do not know, nor how long since its
achievement the climbers had rested on the ledge.

Then, some time soon after 5000 B.C., various groups of climbers
began to rouse themselves from the ledge and essayed to climb again
in search of a higher ledge or maybe the top of the mountain. About
twenty such groups have, at various dates since 5000 B.C., undertaken
such an adventure. We call these groups civilizations, or civilized
societies, or (more accurately) societies in process of civilization. None

[1] Dr. Toynbee was asked to write this essay and I am writing it at his suggestion.
I therefore need make no apology for using here and elsewhere material from his
Study of History. That does not mean, of course, that Dr. Toynbee is responsible for
any statements of fact or opinion I may make.

of them has succeeded in its quest of the upper ledge, the next point of stability. About three-quarters of them have long since perished, the civilizations of Egypt and Sumeria for example, or that brilliant Hellenic (or Graeco-Roman) civilization which was the predecessor of our own. Of the remaining quarter—roughly half a dozen societies— several are manifestly failing ; the Islamic civilization, for example, the Hindu, the Far Eastern. One alone is still " going strong ", but whether it is going in the right direction ; whether it is still painfully plodding towards the upper ledge of achieved civilization or, like the Gadarene swine, rushing violently in the opposite direction—that is a matter on which much is being said every day. We are not concerned at present with such topical discussions. We have to get some sort of notion of the shape and the career of this civilization or would-be civilization of ours, this society *in process of* civilization. And first of all for its origins.

It is obvious that, so far as their origins are concerned, our twenty or so civilizations fall into two groups : those which emerged from the levels of primitive societies and those which emerged from the debris of a previous civilization. Why do civilizations emerge at all ? Dr. Toynbee's answer is comprised in his famous formula : challenge and response. They arise because a difficulty has arisen and something new, some special effort, is the only way to overcome it. In the case of the earliest civilizations this challenge has generally been a geo-physical circumstance, a change of climate such as the desiccation of the steppe lands which drove primitive men out of their Afrasian pasture lands into the Nile and Euphrates valleys where the Egyptian and Sumerian civilizations were founded. Our Western civilization is clearly of the other class ; it arose out of the debris of the Hellenic civilization. To that civilization ours is obviously indebted in a great variety of ways. The Latin language, in which most of our business was transacted and most of our books written during the first two-thirds of our civilization's existence, is an obvious example. An even more obvious example is the Christian church. The surplices and cassocks of the priesthood are the flowing garments of Hellenic costume but slightly modified. Every time a priest enters a church and the con-gregation rise in honour of the God he serves, we see, as it were, an emissary of the Hellenic civilization bringing its greatest treasure to the " trousered barbarians ", *Galli bracchati*, our dubiously civilized selves.

Unstable Equilibrium. But what exactly happened in this change-over from one civilization to another ? Let us remember the metaphor of the climbers. Once the stability of the ledge (primitive life) is left behind upward movement becomes obligatory. You can rest on the ledge, but if you try to rest on the cliff face you will fall. A civilization once started must grow or die, and the condition of growth is leadership. Men may be all equal in their rights but they are very unequal in their capacities. The process of civilization is the work of a creative minority, an " aristocracy "—a Greek word which simply means the rule of the best men. The rest will follow in their wake in so far as the creative minority inspire them to do so.

But suppose the creative minority cease to create and inspire. Suppose they become merely an aristocracy in the vulgar sense of the word, a " dominant minority " who are on top through the merits of their ancestors perhaps, but through no merit of their own. In that case the rest will no longer follow their lead though they may be driven to obey. They will become what Dr. Toynbee, borrowing the term from the Communists and giving it a deeper significance, calls a proletariat, a body of people who, though embedded *in* a civilization, are no longer *of* it. Their goal is no longer the achievement of civilization within a society from which they have been alienated but salvation *from* it, generally by means of an other-worldly religion.

The picture is becoming clear, is it not ? The inspired " glory that was Greece " ossified into the oppressive " grandeur that was Rome ". The creative minority lost its way and became merely dominant. In the end it could not even dominate. It broke down and a gap of mere confusion followed when neither the old civilization nor the new one was discernible. When the new one does emerge, somewhere between A.D. 500 and 750 let us say, it is found to be the response of the creative minority of the proletariat of the old civilization to the challenge presented by the breakdown of the Roman Empire. Its essential feature is the church created by that proletariat in the days of its subjection. So far as one can distinguish individual men of genius as the founders of the new civilization, one finds them in such men as St. Benedict (*circa* 500), the chief founder of Western monasticism, and Gregory the Great (*circa* 600) who may be regarded as the first of the popes. The new civilization may in fact be called Western Christendom.

This Western European society, then, with its comparatively recent offshoots overseas, has been in process of civilization for close on fifteen hundred years. We are using the word civilization in two slightly different senses. When we say " Western Civilization " we seem to imply that we, not merely you and I and Einstein and Churchill, but all the millions of our society, are already civilized, an assumption which might be deemed absurd. When we call it a society " in process of civilization " we imply that its civilization is either a goal not yet reached or is the process of striving towards that goal. If we think of our civilization as a goal not yet reached, how do we picture it ? It is almost as difficult to envisage it as to envisage heaven. Perhaps, if our civilization started as a Christendom, and was meant to be a Christendom, then its goal may be equated with that Kingdom of God on earth which Christ came to establish. However that may be, we may be certain that one of the features of civilization, as a goal achieved, will be stability, and this is something from which we are at present very far away.

II. A FOUR-ACT PLAY

Let us leave these problems of the future and consider some features of the history of Western Civilization up to date. When we survey the near fifteen hundred years of its past we find they fall into three chapters and the beginnings of a fourth. They are commonly called the Dark Ages, the Middle Ages, the Modern Age and—here we are in a difficulty ; for it is beginning to be generally agreed that a new chapter opened round about the end of the nineteenth century. Dr. Toynbee occasionally uses the term " Post-Modern Age ", but that is confessedly a makeshift, for " modern " means much the same as contemporary and is a term which we shall have to carry along with us on our journey through time, finding some other descriptive label for the period lasting some four hundred years and now over, which began shortly before 1500.

All these terms are in fact unsatisfactory. " Middle Ages " has a curious history. The term came into use in the seventeenth century and is a product of the movement of the human mind called the Renaissance. The Renaissance was, among other things, a rediscovery of the splendours of the Hellenic Civilization. We exalted those splendours in so thoroughgoing a fashion that we devoted the whole of our higher education to the study of it ; hence the Classical education, which has only very recently been compelled to make way for the claims of modern technology—which may or may not be an improvement. The older generation still living to-day of those who received a higher education at the end of the nineteenth century—in England at any rate—were taught in schools where the Classical education was the normal course, and all else side-shows tolerated for eccentrics. These men of the Renaissance looked back to the Hellenic Age they admired across a great gulf of what seemed to them barely to deserve the name of civilization at all. They called this gulf the Middle Ages.

In the late eighteenth and early nineteenth centuries there came a partial reaction against this view. It manifested itself in many ways, one of its more obvious and superficial manifestations being the Gothic Revival. It was now realised that the latter half of the despised Middle Age produced much that was valuable and beautiful. Some went so far as to exalt its art and its Christian idealism above the showy and shoddy products of modernity. So the term " Middle Ages " was restricted to a period beginning somewhere in the eleventh century and became almost a term of praise, the preceding 500 years being relegated to a deeper contempt than ever under the name of " Dark Ages ".

Foundations. But this will not do either. These 500 years were the time in which the foundations of our civilization were laid. Foundations are laid underground, so that we do not see them, but that does not make them less of an achievement than the superstructure. We do not describe the first few years of a child's life as its Dark Age. During those years the child learns to speak a language with fluency and idiomatic vigour. Considering how few of us in all the remainder of our lives learn to speak any other language with the like fluency and idiomatic vigour, however hard we may try, we might well conclude that we were less " Dark " in our nursery days than we have since become. The only Dark Age is not the first stage of the growth of our civilization but the Gap—date it how you will—between the death of the Hellenic civilization and the starting-point of our own.[1] So let us find new names. Let us call the Dark Ages the period of Foundations, the Middle Ages the period of Papal Christendom, " Modern times " the period of the Great Powers and " Post-modern times " the Future. We are already living in this Future, as we know to our cost, but it has not yet gone far enough to present us with much more than a menace and a note of interrogation.

During the first years of our personal existence we were but small affairs and the same is true of the first centuries of the existence of our Western Civilization. One can measure its geographical extent round about A.D. 800 when it was for a brief space of time more or less united by the military imperialism of the Frankish chieftain we call Charlemagne. Its military headquarters were on the lower Rhine ; its spiritual headquarters in Rome, whose bishops had inherited something of the prestige of the Roman emperors. It included all France ; northern but not southern Italy, which was a battle-ground between the Byzantine empire and Islam ; a strip of northern Spain, the rest

---

[1] Perhaps there is no Gap, but there is certainly a period in which the destruction of the old is more conspicuous than the creation of the new.

of it being occupied by Islam ; Britain which had been reclaimed from barbarism by Christian missionaries ; and Western Germany which was being annexed in a much less satisfactory manner by Charlemagne's armies.

Belloc once described the so-called Dark Ages as a prolonged siege and that is a reminder that our civilization had to struggle with rivals for its very existence. One rival was Islam, and there is a famous passage in which Gibbon, in his *Decline and Fall*, speculates on the possibility that, if the Muslim Arabs had won, in A.D. 732, the battle in central France in which they were defeated by Charlemagne's grandfather, the Koran might have occupied the place of the Bible as the sacred text imposed upon the sometimes reluctant students of eighteenth-century Oxford. Then there was what Toynbee calls the " abortive civilization " (a civilization started but nipped in the bud) of the highly talented barbarians of Scandinavia, the Vikings as we call them, mispronouncing it Vi-kings when we should say Vik-ings, peoples of the viks or fiords (e.g. Narvik). If these peoples with their pagan warrior pantheon had conquered Western Christendom Christianity might have been driven underground as a submerged religion, much as two thousand years earlier, in a similar period of change-over from one civilization to another, the Achaean war bands with their similar warrior pantheon submerged the religion of the preceding Minoan civilization. There were also the fierce and incredibly mobile Mongolian Magyars, whose war bands occasionally penetrated beyond the Rhine in the darkness of the century following Charlemagne.

All these perils were overcome, and why ? We may attribute our survival in part to the superiority of our spiritual inheritance, but if the darkness of the twentieth century has taught one thing more plainly than another it is that superiority of spiritual inheritance is not enough. There must be superiority of physical defence. Why did the old Roman Empire, so mighty and so stable in appearance, crumple up under the onslaught of " barbarians " whereas the infant Western Christendom survived ? Because Western Christendom evolved the fighting technique of feudalism, which C. Delisle Burns has so aptly compared with the Home Guard. We think of feudalism as an incubus on later ages that had outgrown it, but like so many institutions that survived their usefulness it came into existence to meet a dire need, and it met it. It was the first of the great " social inventions " of our civilization, as valuable in its day as parliaments and national insurance services in theirs.

We think of our period of Foundations, our so-called Dark Ages, as something inferior to the rather dreary fag-end of the Hellenic civilization, the period of the Roman Empire. In many respects it marked an improvement. Some aspects of its superiority are summarized in the striking passage in C. Delisle Burns's book *The First Europe*.

" Under the Roman Empire the governing classes were formed by a city life, a literary education, and a generally accepted taste for the refinements of civilized life. They enjoyed baths and well warmed apartments in their country houses. They could read and write. In the Middle Ages, on the other hand, the governing class were country-bred and most of its members were illiterate, skilful only in hunting and fighting, voracious, vigorous, violent. Their residences were dark, cold and damp fortresses. The mediaeval lord, however, was less completely separated from his dependants, whether retainers in his castle or villeins on his estate, than the Roman magnate from his slaves. The heights of civilization had been reduced in the confusion of 500 years, but the general level of intercourse between men was higher. The fine arts were less appreciated by the ruling class, but the general standard of taste in craftsmanship was shared by the poorest men and women."

Charlemagne's empire, never a stable structure, collapsed with his death, and one is tempted to ask whether this was what school history books call, or are said to call, " a good thing ". Would it have been better if our whole society had from the start been politically clamped together under an ever strengthening central government ? It is impossible to give certain answers to these " if " questions. When we consider the appalling wastage of our international " civil wars " in recent centuries, from the Hundred Years War in which an aggressive England tried to conquer France down to the war in which Nazi Germany tried to conquer all her neighbours, one may incline to wish that *Carolus Augustus a Deo coronatus* [1] had indeed proved a second Augustus. But the growth of our civilization has been accomplished almost entirely through diversities of regional experiments and would not such a political centralization have stifled regional originality ? Dr. Toynbee regards the collapse of Charlemagne's empire as a blessing in disguise—very much in disguise, no doubt, so far as the next 200 years were concerned. The unity that we needed then and need now is not that sort of unity but something that the best Hellenic minds envisaged and never achieved under the name of *homonoia*, which we may express under such various terms (all inadequate) as co-operation, federation, partnership.

[1] The title with which he was greeted on the occasion of his " coronation " St. Peter's, Rome, on Christmas Day, A.D. 800.

III. COHESION IN THE MIDDLE AGES

The central theme of the second chapter of the history of our Western Civilization, the "Middle Ages" (say 1050–1500) which I have called the period of Papal Christendom, is a strenuous effort to achieve this very goal of *homonoia* along ecclesiastical lines by the inspiration of a common religion and under the leadership of a series of remarkable men elected by their cabinets (if we may so describe the conclave of cardinals) to the post in which they claimed to be not only the chief executive of the Church, as the American president is the chief executive of the United States, but also the vicar or representative of God on earth. The sceptre which had slipped from the nerveless fingers of the successors of Charlemagne was grasped a little more than two centuries later by the strong and confident hand of the Lombard monk Hildebrand who became Pope Gregory VII.

The difference between the "empire" at which Hildebrand and his successors aimed and empire as conceived by Charlemagne or Napoleon or any other conqueror can be illustrated by a single famous incident which we may call the "battle" of Canossa. Pope Gregory VII made certain demands which may or may not have been reasonable —Dr. Toynbee thinks they were unreasonable—on the German King who had acquired in imitation of Charlemagne the absurd title of Roman Emperor. The king-emperor sent a rude refusal. The Pope retorted with a thunderbolt; he expelled the king-emperor from the Church, and the king-emperor very quickly found that he had better do something about it. He rushed over the Alps in search of the Pope; and at this point the story begins to be so much improved in the telling that we cannot be sure of the details. Was there snow on the ground? How long did the penitent kneel in it before the Pope consented to admit him? That was, in essentials, Canossa, 1077, and it began the "Middle Ages" for Western Christendom in general as decisively as they had been begun for England eleven years earlier by the Norman Conquest, which was itself a papally blessed crusade.

There was much to be said for the possibility and the desirability of this conception of a Christian commonwealth held together by the organization of the Christian Church. We cannot in this context say "commonwealth of nations" or supernational church, for there were as yet no nations or national patriotisms. The treatment of history on national lines misleads us on this point because it suggests national units long before such existed in days when "England" and "France" were little more than terms of geography. Nor must we think of the

Church as something like what churches are to-day, voluntary societies in which one seeks membership if one wishes, as one seeks membership of a club. The Church was all-embracing and performed most of the social functions, in so far as they were performed at all, of the modern state. Its officialdom was more or less conterminous with the educated class and provided the local secular states with their statesmen and their civil service. For a century and more after Hildebrand the control of the Church over the Commonwealth and of the Papacy over the Church grew stronger. It produced the great monastic orders whose abbeys colonized and developed the remoter regions of Christendom, and whose ruins survive in the ruins of the great Cistercian houses of Yorkshire—and " Cistercian " means " of Cîteaux ", which is in France. It produced the great artistic achievements, from the cathedrals to the illuminated manuscripts, the Christian imperialism of the crusades, the Christian evangelism of the mendicant orders, and the universities which are still with us as national and more and more preponderantly technological institutions.

But it was not to be. " All power corrupts," wrote Lord Acton, " and absolute power corrupts absolutely." Perhaps the Church whose Founder said " My kingdom is not of this world " was not designed to serve society after this fashion. Certainly it was corrupted in the process. The function of religion is persuasion : the function of government is compulsion. To serve the purposes of a Gregory VII or an Innocent III the Church required vast material resources, in other words wealth. In the pursuit of wealth for ends which seemed so legitimate it ran up against another text of its Founder, " Ye cannot serve both God and Mammon ". A. L. Smith in his most impressive lectures on " Church and State in the Middle Ages " locates the turning-point in the middle of the thirteenth century when Pope Innocent IV, whom he describes as " consummate politician . . . a cold, unwavering materialist", mobilized all the resources of the Church for a life-and-death military struggle with Frederick II, the last of the great mediaeval "Roman" emperors. Thenceforward the papal experiment had manifestly failed though it was far from clear what other experiment could replace it. In fact it has not been replaced. Throughout the whole of the next chapter, the Modern Age or the period of the Great Powers, we seemed to get along all right without its replacement. That age is over and we are entering on a new period, post-modern or " the Future " in which every sensible person is saying " we must replace it or perish " ; but we have got no further than that.

The so-called Empire failed together with the Papacy and much more obviously. Germany, its centre, fell into a disunity which was only terminated by the " blood and iron " of Bismarck, but elsewhere the national states were coming together under national monarchies, extruding the political power of the Church in the process. England led the way by many centuries. France followed after the extrusion of the English invaders in the fifteenth century. Spain also, with the extrusion of the Islamic power. A fourth great power, Austria, embracing many different language groups or nationalities was established in the same century in south-eastern Germany, and spread down the Danube as the Turkish empire declined. These great powers, England excepted, were for a long time unwieldy semi-feudal affairs in which the central authority with difficulty maintained its authority over the feudal chieftains representing local government.

IV. THE RISE OF NATIONS

Italy failed to become a Great Power after this fashion, partly because the Papacy, not strong enough to establish an Italian national state ruled from the Vatican, was strong enough to prevent any other local Italian power from doing so. None the less, Italy played an important part in the turnover from the mediaeval chapter to the modern chapter of the history of Western civilization. Northern Italy became a land of city states resembling in many respects the city states of fifth-century Greece in which the preceding Hellenic civilization had achieved its finest results. It was these city states which made the rediscovery of their Hellenic compeers which is called the Renaissance, and when the new enthusiasm spread northwards from Italy it was said that Greece crossed the Alps. But something else crossed the Alps besides a devotion to Classical art and letters. The Italian city states, like their Greek compeers, had been a laboratory of political experiments, and these experiments, conducted with ruthless disregard of moral considerations, generally ended in the establishment of tyrannies. The symbolic name here is Machiavelli, who wrote in the first quarter of the sixteenth century, and his name will always (perhaps with some injustice) be associated with the belief that " power politics " has nothing to do with right and wrong. At that date the large lumbering Transalpine powers were trampling the independence of the Italian cities underfoot, but just as, within the Hellenic civilization, " when Rome conquered Greece, Greece led her conqueror captive ", so now the Transalpine governments were Italianized.

The Origin of Politics. This Italianization is revealed in the incredible and senseless duplicity of the international diplomacy of the Tudor

Age. Shakespeare makes his good old Duke of York in *Richard II*, a man of " Victorian " respectability, speak of " fashions of proud Italy, which our tardy apish nation follows after with base imitation ". It was a popular saying that " An Englishman Italianate is the devil incarnate ".

The Italian influence for good and evil was to be corrected in England by the Puritan reaction. In France it reached its finest flowering in the grand monarchy of Louis XIV, which was simply Machiavellian tyranny writ large. This in turn found its imitators in the " enlightened despots " of the eighteenth century, Frederick the Great, for example. The French Revolution might have provided a remedy but instead it produced Napoleon who admired Frederick and greatly improved on him. In Biblical language Louis begat Frederick, and Frederick begat Napoleon, and Napoleon begat Bismarck, and Bismarck begat Hitler and Hitler begat Stalin. Revolutionary dictators are better at the game than hereditary monarchs ever were. We are not yet out of the Machiavellian wood.

England's Contribution. England became a centralized national state under a strong monarchy much earlier than any other part of the Western European society of which she formed a part. Why was this ? Because it is easier to control a small concern than a big one. If one compares England with any of the neighbouring units which subsequently developed into national states one sees that it enjoyed two great advantages, smaller size and more clearly defined frontiers. Along more than three-quarters of its circumference England enjoyed the best of all frontiers, the sea, and it is a significant fact that it was the local chieftains of the remaining sections of the frontier, the Scottish and Welsh borders, which longest remained formidable to the central authority. Only a Mortimer from the Welsh border or a Percy or a Neville from the Scottish border could overturn the English throne in the fourteenth and fifteenth centuries.

It is because England was so early welded into unity that she was the only nation that made a success of that widespread mediaeval institution, the assembly of estates, lords and commons, to advise and control the crown by discussion in " parliament ". Everywhere else, in France, Spain, Austria, it faded out as the crown grew despotic and " Italianized ". It might have suffered the same fate under the English Tudors but they found it convenient and made full use of it. The powers it acquired under the Tudors it used against the Stuarts and by the end of the seventeenth century England had achieved one of the major social inventions of Western Civilization, parliamentary government. Exactly contemporary with this achievement came the wars of Louis XIV, in which the military genius of Marlborough gave parliamentarized England the leadership of the coalition which over-threw the attempt of France to dominate Europe.

We may say that seventeenth-century England played a part similar to that of fifteenth-century Italy. It was the laboratory in which was fashioned the political technique of the immediate future, and just as in the sixteenth century all the Transalpine governments are found aping " the fashions of Proud Italy ", so the eighteenth and nineteenth centuries are the age, politically, of what the French called anglomania. John Locke, with his philosophic exposition of parliamentarism, plays the part of Machiavelli in the earlier stage. The French revolution was, in its first phase, an attempt to anglicize the French monarchy. From that sprang " liberal " movements elsewhere. Whatever the party name Liberal (which we borrowed from France who borrowed it from Spain) may have meant in England where we already had parlia-mentary government, in countries not blessed with this institution liberals were simply " anglomaniacs " asking for the fashionable English technique.

It proved a mixed or dubious blessing, as we know. Parliamentary government may be the best but it is also the most difficult to work without long practice and traditional acceptance of its conventions. We had that long practice. Moreover, we learnt to work parliament as an aristocratic institution for centuries before we made the experiment, from 1832 onwards, of very cautiously and gradually democratizing it. Our continental imitators had already gone democratic by the time they had gone parliamentarian. Thus they doubled their difficulties.

V. MODERN "DRIVES"

The mention of democracy brings us down towards the end of the third chapter of the history of our Western Civilization, the " modern age " or period of the Great Powers, and leads us to peer into the fourth. We have already suggested that the characteristics of each successive " chapter " are, as it were, fashioned locally in the latter part of the preceding chapter. What are the forces that have brought to an end the age in which, after the failure of unity or co-operation (*homonoia*) under the leadership and control of the Church, it was none the less quite tolerable for Machiavellianly-minded national states to rub along side by side, indulging in the collisions called wars when they felt inclined ? There have been two such forces, for which Dr. Toynbee provides admirable names, the Drive of Democracy and the

Drive of Industrialism. Picture the pre-democratic and pre-industrial state of affairs as a comfortable jog-trot low-powered locomotive. Picture these two " drives " as powerful electric currents switched on to the old mechanism. It rushes all over the place, knocking itself and its occupants to pieces. The new electric currents are good in themselves, but unless we harness them to a new machine they will not serve us but electrocute us. We have not yet got that new machine.

We are here on the verge of subjects that are both vast and all too familiar and it is not the purpose of this essay to make the remarks that can be read in a hundred newspaper articles and heard in a hundred radio talks. Let us consider, however briefly, the parts played by these two " drives ". They came into the world almost simultaneously, the gospel of James Watt and the gospel of Jean-Jacques Rousseau. The first steam-driven cotton-mill started work in Manchester in the same year as the French Revolution. Yet the two " drives " have in origin nothing to do with one another. They might have come in altogether different periods of history, 500 years apart, let us say. Each of them is capable of great good and also of great evil. Sometimes we see them working in opposite directions. At the time of the foundation of the United States (1789 again, the date of the opening of Washington's presidency), itself one of the first great manifestations of the drive of democracy, it was generally supposed that negro slavery in U.S.A. was a moribund institution. Then came the drive of industrialism and tuned it up. Then came a second drive of democracy and fought the bloodiest civil war in history to secure its abolition.

More often, however, they have worked in the same direction, and what has produced the intolerable situation in which we find ourselves to-day is the effect of these two drives upon war, patriotism and propaganda. They have given us what we call total war and totalitarian propaganda.

Militarism. One might incline to regard the drive of industrialism as the major villain of the piece ; but so far as war is concerned it is plain that the drive of democracy entered first. The first wars on the modern scale were those of the French Revolution. Napoleon was, as it were, the first Hitler ; and the new industrial techniques contributed almost nothing to his methods. If Marlborough had watched the battle of Austerlitz he would have had no surprises in the technological field. What enabled the raw levies of the French Revolution to cut through the matured and " respectable " array of the monarchies of the ancien régime like a knife through butter, several years before Napoleon contributed his genius to their direction, was the new élan, the new devilry, of the democratic drive.

No perverse activity has done so much to destroy civilizations as militarism : it is suicidal. Defeat is defeat, but so in the long run is victory. So it is interesting, and even amusing, to note that it was the victories of Napoleon, not his defeat, which deprived France for ever of its primacy among the continental Great Powers. We have spoken of the modern age as the period of the Great Powers, but it was not until the end of the nineteenth century that it became almost exclusively such. Over a large belt of central Europe, from the North Sea down through Switzerland to Italy, another system prevailed, a system of petty principalities, city states, prince bishoprics and the like—what an English nineteenth-century writer called " a mosaic of political curiosities ". The strength of Bourbon France had largely rested on the fact that she was separated on her landward frontier from Austria, her nearest Great Power neighbour, by this broad belt. Napoleon's victories swept all these anachronisms away and after his defeat they could never be recovered from the dustbin. Into their place after a brief interval strode Prussia, the new Germany.

The effect of the " drives " on patriotism and propaganda hardly needs illustration. The drive of democracy has given us totalitarian nationalism and a system of semi-education which has shaken our traditional religious beliefs to their foundations, substituting tribal patriotisms for a religion of universal brotherhood, and the popular press for the Bible as the domestic oracle. The drive of industrialism has given dictators the means of intensive propaganda by radio. In the earlier chapters of the history of Western Civilization governments were too weak : they are now too strong.

VI. EXPANSION

In its earliest days Western Civilization occupied but a small space on the map, confined on the south by the Muslim Caliphate in Spain, on the north by the Vikings, on the east by the not yet included half of Germany, the Slavs and the Magyars. In the course of 1500 years it had expanded. The Muslims had been extruded, the Scandinavians, the rest of the Germans, the Magyars and the most westerly Slavs, such as the Poles and the Czechs, had been included : and the Russians ? We will postpone consideration of them for the moment. But the expansion was much more than European. From the end of the fifteenth century onwards Western Civilization had crossed the oceans and established itself in the Americas, South Africa, Australia, New Zealand. One of the overseas establishments has now developed into a mightier power than any of the old Great Powers of the homeland.

We might be tempted to go further and to say that the whole world has, more or less, been brought within the framework of our civilization, but this would be rather less than a half truth. The extent of a particular civilization can be measured by various standards, economic and technological, political and cultural. Economically and technologically, no doubt, all the world is now one. Trade is world-wide. Our industrial gadgetry is in use everywhere. " Their wiseacres have seen the electric light in the West and are come to worship ", says Robert Bridges in *The Testament of Beauty*. But this is a superficial standard. The Chinaman does not become a Westerner by illuminating his streets with our electric light or killing his neighbours with our machine-guns any more than we have become Chinese by drinking tea, or Arabic by drinking coffee, or Amerindian by eating chocolate and smoking tobacco.[1]

Politically it looked in the latter half of the nineteenth century as if the whole world would be parcelled out among the Western empires ; that China, for example, would go the way of India. We have seen that this forecast was mistaken. It is India that has thrown off Western political control and resumed the status of China. It is now plain that the only parts of the world outside Europe that will remain permanently within a " Western " political system are those parts in which European man has established himself and created " Western " communities. None the less, a temporary imperialism appears to be leaving a permanent legacy. The English language has become for educated Indians what Latin was for the educated Europeans until recent centuries, and our conceptions of democracy, parliamentary government and military dictatorship are almost as popular in Asia as our motor-cars and match-boxes.

Culturally, however, a different picture is presented. Match-boxes and parliaments may girdle the earth but Islam, Hinduism and the fundamental ways of life of the non-Western civilizations remain but little affected. It is conceivable that some day there will be a single world culture, and that will mean a single world civilization, and it may be that that culture and civilization will be on Western lines ; but the prospect is remote.

[1] Curious that all these minor pleasures should have come to us from remote civilizations or from barbarians. They have quite eclipsed, for most English-speaking peoples at any rate, the Hellenic gift of wine. Yet such is the Hellenic prestige that our poets can still wax eloquent about wine, which most of us could get on very well without whereas a rhapsody on tea would fail to maintain what Matthew Arnold called " high seriousness ". Bacchus still remains a god but neither Cadbury nor Player has yet become one. There is food for reflection here.

VII. RUSSIA

We have kept Russia out of the picture until the end of the story, but now we must bring it in. And first of all, is Russia to be regarded as being, or having at any time been, within the circumference of Western Civilization ? It, or the older and more populous half of it, is certainly within what geography calls Europe, but there was never a more meaningless conception than that which drew a line down the long range of lumpy hills called the Ural mountains and declared that west of it was one continent and east of it another. It is all one vast continent, Eurasia, within which can be articulated certain sub-continents such as Western Europe and India and a central mass which is mostly Russia and China.

Dr. Toynbee treats Russia as the Great Power of a civilization distinct from ours. It is a civilization more closely connected with ours than is any other, for it is like ours an offspring of the Hellenic. It stems from Constantinople and the Byzantine empire as ours stems from Rome. Like ours it was cradled in the Christian religion though not in the same Christian Church, for the Orthodox Church drifted apart from the Catholic in the course of the so-called Dark Ages. Within the last few centuries Russia, mainly through the initiative of its rulers, and particularly Peter the Great (1689–1725), adopted a number of Western ideas and techniques, but so also at a later date did Japan and Turkey and other non-Western peoples. The most significant of its recent borrowings is Communism, which Bernard Shaw called a " British Museum product ", for the Bible of Communism, Marx's *Capital*, was mostly written by a Jewish exile from Germany in the library of that institution.

Russian communism is very obviously a product of the combined drives of democracy and industrialism. The early prophets of demo-cracy were manifestly pre-industrial. Rousseau's democratic gospel was derived, through Plutarch, from idealized pictures of Hellenic city states ; his *bête noire* was not the industrial capitalist but the privileged feudal landowner. Jefferson, the exponent of American democratic idealism, thought in agrarian terms and would have kept urban develop-ment, commerce and industry out of his country if he could. The French Revolution of 1789 had no distinctively economic message. It was Marx who, taking industrialism for granted, put forward a scheme in which its organization would be turned upside down and the pro-letariat replace the capitalist. The much modified communism-in-

action of the Russian dictatorship, Kremlinism as it is conveniently
called, has been a policy of aggressive industrialization and imperialism.
In a shorter period than most outsiders deemed possible, the primitive
and inefficient Russia of the Tsars which had crumpled up before the
German onslaught of 1915–17 was converted into the industrialized
Russia of 1941–45 which held a far more powerful German assault at
bay and drove it back all the way to Berlin.   In its subsequent phase of
imperialist expansion the Kremlin has found that an old-fashioned
idealistic communism is a very useful bait for its destined victims.   If
one could ask a Russian leader for his private opinion of this idealistic
communism he might reply in words attributed to one of the sceptical
Popes of the Renaissance : " How much we owe to this Jewish fable ".

VIII. THE FUTURE

The original fount and centre of our Western Civilization is now
in a sad plight, a group of unstable secondary states uneasily poised
between the only two Great Powers left in the world ; and it is not
much consolation to find that this sort of thing has happened before.
The cultural centre of a civilization is apt to become crowded with
little states while the states on the outer rim, whose culture is derivative,
have room to expand.   The cultural centre and source of the Hellenic
civilization was in the Greek city states who continued to quarrel among
themselves until they were politically swallowed by the ruder great
powers that developed on the periphery, first by Macedon and then by
Rome.   The city states of northern Italy were in the fifteenth century
the vanguard of our Western Civilization but they too continued to
quarrel among themselves till they were swallowed first by France and
then by Spain, from whom they were by a dynastic arrangement transferred to Austria.   Similarly the relatively petty states of western
Europe find themselves overshadowed by Russia on one side and the
United States of America on the other.   Most of their citizens look to
America as their patron and Russia as their enemy though a minority,
varying in size from state to state, hold the opposite view and regard
Russia as their patron and America as their enemy.   But, patron or
enemy, there is no doubt about the overshadowing : the Dollar Gap is
a problem only less menacing than the Iron Curtain.

Demosthenes told the Greek city states that if they did not federate
they would be swallowed up by Macedon ; but they did not listen to
him.   Machiavelli told the Italian states that if they did not federate

they would be swallowed up by one or other of the " barbarian "
powers from outside ; but they did not listen to him. Various people
are telling the peoples of Western Europe to-day that if they do not
federate they will be swallowed up by Kremlin imperialism. Will
history repeat itself ?

LEADING QUESTIONS

How does Western Civilization differ from all others ?

Refer to page 11.

What does it owe to Greece and Rome ?

Pages 21, 25 *and* 36.

Why did Western Civilization continue to develop while the Far East stood still ?

Page 44.

How does one culture affect another ?

Page 30.

What great changes in Western Civilization followed the Renaissance and the Reformation ?

Pages 58 *and* 113.

How did Magna Carta lay the foundations of political liberty ?

Page 127.

How was Parliamentary rule, that " major social invention " of the English-speaking peoples, firmly established ?

Pages 143 *to* 192.

How was the first outpost of Western Civilization founded in America ?

Pages 169 *and* 193.

What has led in recent years to " the dwarfing of Europe " ?

Page 243.

How do Western ideals compare with Communism ?

Pages 270 *and* 302.

What political philosophy represents the best in Western Civilization ?

Pages 281 *to* 302.

Can our Civilization survive ?

Page 4.

BOOK I

WHAT IS WESTERN CIVILIZATION?

B

WHAT IS WESTERN CIVILIZATION?

CAN our civilization survive? That is a doubly important question for us all. In the first place it is important because our way of life, or at least that of our children, depends on the answer. And in the second place it is important because that answer may well be, " It depends on us ".

The score or so of other civilizations, large and small, which have originated and developed on this earth have all decayed or crashed. They grew and flourished so long as their rulers could find a satisfactory solution for each great problem as it arose. They failed when the problem proved too big for the man in power. Our Western Civilization, however, is different from most of its predecessors in one important factor : it is based on democracy. We cannot blame our rulers if we follow the downward path, because our fate is in our own hands. It is we who select the rulers.

It is most important, therefore, that we should see the problems of to-day in the clearest light. They are probably bigger by far than any problems of past ages, and their solution depends, in part, on us. D. C. Somervell has pointed out—and all the authorities agree with him—that no civilization can remain static. It must either grow or decay ; either make progress or slip backwards. If we might retain the climbing parable of our brochure, our own civilization to-day seems to be rushing madly along a ledge. Sometimes the ledge seems to be broadening out, sometimes it grows perilously narrow ; sometimes it seems to be leading upwards, sometimes downwards. All we do know is that it is leading us round a corner, and we cannot be certain what lies ahead. Add to this the fact that we climbers are now all roped together with a two-strand cord in which democratic institutions and economic interdependence are closely woven, and it will be seen that, whatever we are heading for, it is bound to affect every man and woman in every country of the world.

Can our civilization survive? We should be better able to answer this question after reading this volume, but in our first lecture Professor Toynbee gives us grounds for hope. He tells us how every other civilization has perished, and a diagnosis of the disease is at least one important step on the way to a cure. Dr. Toynbee, one of the greatest of modern historians, has, in Sir Ernest Barker's words, " the most ingenious mind and the most encyclopædic range of our generation ".

ARNOLD J. TOYNBEE

CIVILIZATION ON TRIAL

CIVILIZATION on trial! That is perhaps rather a new idea, and a strange one. For most of us, I suppose, the word " civilization " stands for just the opposite of something that is on trial. Before the last war—or at any rate before the first war—we used to think of civilization as being as good as gold and as safe as houses. Our forefathers might have had to work in building our civilization up, but there could be no danger, so we thought, of our losing this fine thing that they had handed down to us.

It is natural, I suppose, to take for granted the world one has been born and brought up in. Certainly English people of my own age, who were just grown up before 1914, did take for granted our modern western civilization. We had no notion then that this civilization might be on trial— that it might be weighed in the balance and found wanting. And, even after two world wars, this is still a startling idea to many people, I expect. All the same, this notion that our civilization might come to grief seems now to be in the air. In America, where I spent three months last spring, I found this weighing on people's minds, and of course that makes an impression on a visitor from Europe. The Americans seem to us nowadays to be standing on a pinnacle of power and riches and prosperity. Yet the American middle class is perhaps more anxious and apprehensive at this moment than we are, though we happen to live on what is surely the less safe side of the Atlantic.

The Americans are more upset than we are because they have had a greater disappointment. The Americans had imagined that, in migrating across the Atlantic, they had jumped clear of history; and now history has pursued them and caught them up. History is no joke, because she has skeletons in her cupboard—not just one skeleton, but perhaps about twenty of them. They are the skeletons of civilizations that have come to grief in the past. So long as we had no misgivings about the future of our own civilization, these death's heads did not upset us ; but they do upset us to-day, when our confidence has been shaken by the frightful disasters, and still more by the horrible crimes and cold-blooded cruelties that we have been witnessing in our world in our lifetime. We are wondering what these terrible experiences mean. Do they mean that our own civilization may be going to go the same way as those dead civilizations whose skeletons are preserved for us in history's cupboard ?

The first dead civilization that comes into our minds is, I suppose, the civilization of the Greeks and Romans. Its breakdown and collapse come home to us rather closely, because our own civilization arose out of its ruins. The decline and fall of the Roman Empire ! Is something like that going to happen now to us ? And what was it that did happen when the Roman Empire fell ? Why do we think of its fall as having been such a catastrophe ? If one looks into the fall of the Roman Empire and the break-up of the Greek and Roman civilization, one finds that there were several sides to it. There was a fall in the material standard of living, which means a good deal to us nowadays. There was a decline in rationalism—a return of ignorance and superstition. There was a lowering of standards of behaviour and a set-back to public law and order—a return of barbarism.

For the people who had to live through these painful experiences I fancy that the fall in the material standard of living was the easiest to bear. In the late Roman world people were finding property a burden—not because they did not like having constant hot water and plenty of service ; it is human to like those things and to dislike losing them ; but it is also human to kick against paying too high a price even for things that one values ; and the price that property-owners had to pay in late Roman times was the burden of being regimented in all the petty details of ordinary life. In our world in our time we are having some experience of this, but in the later Roman Empire the burden of it was far heavier, and it came to a point at which people were ready to sacrifice a great deal to escape from it. Spiritually minded people got rid of this burden by giving their goods away to the poor and becoming monks and hermits; aggressive-minded people got rid of it by becoming renegades and running away to seek their fortune with the barbarians. When, at last, the whole complicated material structure of later Greek and Roman civilization fell with a crash, on the whole this was probably a relief to most people concerned.

The dreadful thing was not the loss of material comfort; for this had its compensation in the simplification of life and relief from the worries that are the price of a complicated civilization. The dreadful thing was, not the material crash, but the moral one; the triumph of ignorance, superstition, lawlessness, and cruelty over the moral standards which Greek civilization, in its better days, had so laboriously built up. That is what is terrifying in the fall of a civilization; and it is, I believe, the fear of a return to moral barbarism that is haunting us to-day. We have been warned : in the heart of our western world, in our lifetime, we have suffered the appalling moral disaster of national socialism in Germany. If one of the great nations of the western world could succumb to that, it is obvious that the moral standards of the western world are insecure. If that has happened in Germany, how can we be sure that it will not happen to the rest of us ? The moral breakdown is the real tragedy in the decline and fall of a civilization.

But do we need to worry over the possibility of its happening to us ? That depends on whether the decline and fall of the Greek and Roman civilization was an isolated and abnormal event, or whether it was one instance of something that has happened often enough to make it look as though it were the regular order of nature—something to be reckoned with as part of our normal expectations. When we read in the newspaper the report of a railway accident, or of a house being burnt down, we do not expect that our own house will be burnt over our heads to-night, or that the train we ourselves are going to travel in will be wrecked to-morrow, because we know that accidents like these, awful though they are, are exceptional. The news in the paper would upset us much more, though, if there were reports of accidents of this kind in our own street or on our own railway, every other day. So the first thing we have to ask ourselves about the downfall of the Greek and Roman civilization is this : Was this great social disaster an exceptional event in history, or have there been others of the kind ? The answer to this question is, I am afraid, an unpleasant one. If we look again at history, with this in mind, we do find a number of other examples.

We have called to mind the Greek and Roman case first, because it happens to be the one most familiar to us. Our own civilization, as I was reminding you just now, had sprouted out of the Roman Empire's ruins. The Greek and Roman civilization sprang, in much the same way, out of the wreckage of an earlier civilization than itself. This pre-Greek civilization, the Minoan, perished so utterly that even its Greek successors had lost almost all memory of it. It was re-discovered, towards the end of last century, by a great English archæologist, Sir Arthur Evans, who dug up the material remains of this forgotten Minoan civilization in the island of Crete. We have not yet learnt to read the Minoan writing, but the ruins excavated by our modern archæologists tell their own tale. They tell us that the Minoan civilization was overtaken by a decline and fall, like the Greek and Roman civilization after it.

And these are only the first two cases on the list. We have stumbled on these two by going backwards in time into the historical background of our own western civilization. But if we carry our exploration into other parts of the world we shall find further instances. Look at the history of the Far East, which till lately has lived a life of its own, independent of ours. You will find the same phenomenon there. The ancient Chinese civilization had its own decline and fall, which also came to a head in the break-up of a great empire round about A.D. 200. The ancient Chinese Empire broke up some 200 years before the break-up of the Roman Empire. I can think of about twenty other examples if, besides the civilizations that are dead and buried, one adds in those that, while still alive, are now unmistakably in decline. The result of this count is rather disconcerting. As far as I can see, the only living civilization about which we cannot say for certain that it is in decline already is our own civilization of the modern western world.

If these are the facts, we do find ourselves to-day in a rather uncanny position. We are like someone standing in a room in which there are a number of dead bodies lying about, and also a number of people who, though still alive, are obviously very sick. The one person who is still on his feet in this death-chamber, and is in a position to observe what is going on, can tell the symptoms of the disease that the dead people there have died of, and he can see that the sick people have the same symptoms and are probably going to die of the same disease. He is bound to wonder whether he himself can really be a solitary exception to so general a rule. Is he not bound, in his turn, to go the way of all flesh? Perhaps he too already shows the fatal symptoms. So he starts looking to see whether he is coming out in a rash, and keeps taking his temperature to make sure he is not feverish. He is so bothered about it—and no wonder—that he is in danger of dying of worry if he does not die of the plague. That, I should say, is the state of mind of a great and perhaps growing number of people in our western world to-day.

Now if we have carried our inquiry to this point, we can hardly afford to leave it here. We cannot be content to rest on a question mark when the question is one of life and death. We must try to make out what bearing these rather alarming precedents from past history really have on our civilization's prospects. Is our own civilization doomed? I will give you my own personal answer to that at once. Personally, I do not believe it is doomed; and I do not believe that any of these civilizations that have unmistakably broken down have been fated, either, to suffer the disaster which has eventually overtaken them. So do not let us jump to the conclusion that we are doomed, and then wait, with our heads bowed, for the guillotine blade of Fate to fall on our necks. If we were as faint-hearted and as wrong-headed as that, we should really almost deserve to have our heads cut off.

But haven't you, you may ask me, as good as told us that we are doomed when you have said that about twenty civilizations have broken down already, and that we, and we only, are left? No, not at all, is my answer, and I can give you two good reasons. For one thing, twenty cases of breakdown is far too small a number to draw any exact conclusion from, and, for another thing, human affairs are full of unknown quantities that may turn up at any point and change the whole outlook. One new factor, making for our salvation, might be the psychological effect on us of realizing the danger in which we find ourselves. Suppose that, instead of despairing and resigning ourselves to death, we were stimulated to fight for our lives, that in itself might give a new turn to our prospects.

Let us ask ourselves what the dead civilizations died of, and then see if we cannot avoid making the same fatal mistake. I believe they all died of war. In the history of each of these other civilizations, there were wars of ever-increasing severity between local sovereign states, and, though a civilization that has been killing itself in this way has generally managed, in the last chapter of the story, to get rid of the malady of war, the remedy to which it has resorted has been almost worse than the disease. In the past, civilizations have got rid of war by getting rid of the local states between whom the wars have been fought. They have got rid of these states by a knock-out blow, by which one surviving Great Power has destroyed all its competitors and has then imposed a world-wide peace—the peace imposed on the ancient Greek world by the Roman Empire is the example that is most familiar to us, but the same kind of peace has been established in the same kind of way in China and in other parts of the world. The weak points about a Roman peace are that it comes too late and costs too much. It does not come till the wars between the local states have been fought out to the bitter end and have inflicted mortal wounds on the stricken society. So a peace arrived at in this way does not last. It merely delays the final break-up of a dying civilization; it does not save its life.

The practical question facing our own civilization to-day is this : Are we going to get rid of war by the old-fashioned Roman method of the knock-out blow ? Or are we going to find some cure for war that is not just a peace of exhaustion ? Since the first world war we have been looking for some way of bringing unity and peace to our world by mutual consent and co-operation, as an alternative to the old way of force and conquest. If we could make a success of this, we should have accomplished something that has not been achieved by any other civilization before ours, and this might open quite a new chapter in the history of mankind. So let this be our answer to the challenge of decline and fall. Do not let us shut our eyes to the danger, and do not let us be daunted when we face it; let us take it in the opposite way, which I suggest is the way of salvation. Let us be roused by it to save ourselves by opening a new way forward for ourselves and for the whole human race. We are not doomed; our fate is in our own hands; it is up to us.

What is this Western Civilization which we may have to defend and preserve ? No simple answer to this question can be given. Civilization is not something which is achieved once for all by any age; it is a

process and a continuous process. Indeed, the best way of forming a
clear idea of what Western Civilization means, is to trace very briefly
its development and to see what it has assimilated from various sources.
But first of all let us ask François Guizot to give at least a partial answer
to the question. This extract, like that which follows a little later, is
taken from the second of his lectures on the History of Civilization in
Europe.

A statesman of the first rank as well as an historian, Guizot had a
full share of the prevalent nineteenth-century belief in the inevitability
of social progress in Western Civilization. His lectures at the Sorbonne
were attended, not by a few students, but by large and fashionable
audiences, whose enthusiastic applause paid a well-deserved tribute both
to the eloquence and to the intellectual power of the lecturer.

F. GUIZOT

THE COMPLEXITY OF WESTERN CIVILIZATION

WHEN we regard the civilizations which have preceded
that of modern Europe, whether in Asia or elsewhere,
including even Greek and Roman civilization, it is impossible
to help being struck with the unity which pervades them.
They seem to have emanated from a single fact, from a single
idea ; one might say that society has attached itself to a
solitary dominant principle, which has determined its institutions, its customs, its creeds, in one word, all its developments.

In Egypt, for instance, it was the theocratic principle
which pervaded the entire community ; it reproduced itself
in the customs, in the monuments, and in all that remains
to us of Egyptian civilization. In India, you will discover
the same fact ; there is still the almost exclusive dominion
of the theocratic principle. Elsewhere, society will be the
expression of the democratic principle ; it has been thus
with the commercial republics which have covered the coasts
of Asia Minor and of Syria, in Ionia, in Phœnicia. In short,
when we contemplate ancient civilizations, we find them

stamped with a singular character of unity in their institutions, their ideas, and their manners ; a sole, or, at least, a strongly preponderating force governs and determines all.

I do not mean to say that this unity of principle and form in the civilization of these states has always prevailed therein. When we go back to their earlier history, we find that the various powers which may develop themselves in the heart of a society have often contended for empire. Among the Egyptians, the Etruscans, the Greeks themselves, etc., the order of warriors, for example, has struggled against that of the priests ; elsewhere, the spirit of clanship has struggled against that of free association ; the aristocratic against the popular system, etc. But it has generally been in ante-historical times that such struggles have occurred ; and thus only a vague recollection has remained of them. . . .

The result of this has been a remarkable simplicity in the majority of ancient civilizations. This simplicity has produced different consequences. Sometimes, as in Greece, the simplicity of the social principle has led to a wonderfully rapid development ; never has any people unfolded itself in so short a period with such brilliant effect. But after this astonishing flight, Greece seemed suddenly exhausted ; its decay, if it was not so rapid as its rise, was nevertheless strangely prompt. It seems that the creative force of the principle of Greek civilization was exhausted ; no other has come to renew it.

Elsewhere, in Egypt and in India, for instance, the unity of the principle of civilization has had a different effect ; society has fallen into a stationary condition. Simplicity has brought monotony ; the country has not been destroyed, society has continued to exist, but motionless, and as if frozen.

It is to the same cause that we must attribute the character of tyranny which appeared in the name of principle and under the most various forms, among all the ancient civilizations. Society belonged to an exclusive power, which would

allow of the existence of none other.   Every differing tendency
was proscribed and hunted down.   Never has the ruling
principle chosen to admit beside it the manifestation and
action of a different principle. . . .

It has been wholly otherwise with the civilization of
modern Europe.   Without entering into details, look upon it,
gather together your recollections : it will immediately appear
to you varied, confused, stormy ; all forms, all principles of
social organization coexist therein ; powers spiritual and
temporal ; elements theocratic, monarchical, aristocratic, democratic ; all orders, all social arrangements mingle and press
upon one another ; there are infinite degrees of liberty,
wealth, and influence.   These various forces are in a state of
continual struggle among themselves, yet no one succeeds in
stifling the others, and taking possession of society.   In
ancient times, at every great epoch, all societies seemed cast
in the same mould : it is sometimes pure monarchy, sometimes
theocracy or democracy, that prevails ; but each, in its turn,
prevails completely.   Modern Europe presents us with
examples of all systems, of all experiments of social organization ; pure or mixed monarchies, theocracies, republics, more
or less aristocratic, have thus thrived simultaneously, one
beside the other ; and, notwithstanding their diversity, they
have all a certain resemblance, a certain family likeness, which
it is impossible to mistake.

In the ideas and sentiments of Europe there is the same
variety, the same struggle.   The theocratic, monarchic, aristocratic, and popular creeds, cross, combat, limit, and modify
each other.   Open the boldest writings of the Middle Ages ;
never there is an idea followed out to its last consequences.
The partisans of absolute power recoil suddenly and unconsciously before the results of their own doctrine ; they perceive
around them ideas and influences which arrest them, and
prevent them from going to extremities.   The democrats obey
the same law.   On neither part exists that imperturb-
able audacity, that blind determination of logic, which show

themselves in ancient civilizations. The sentiments offer the same contrasts, the same variety; an energetic love of independence, side by side with a great facility of submission; a singular faithfulness of man to man, and, at the same time, an uncontrollable wish to exert free will, to shake off every yoke, and to live for oneself, without caring for any other. The souls of men are as different, as agitated as society. . . .

On all sides, then, this predominant character of modern civilization discovers itself. It has, no doubt, had this advantage, that, when we consider separately such or such a particular development of the human mind in letters, in the arts, in all directions in which it can advance, we usually find it inferior to the corresponding development in ancient civilizations ; but, on the other hand, when we regard it in the aggregate, European civilization shows itself incomparably richer than any other ; it has displayed, at one and the same time, many more different developments. Consequently, you find that it has existed fifteen centuries, and yet is still in a state of continuous progression ; it has not advanced nearly so rapidly as the Greek civilization, but its progress has never ceased to grow. It catches a glimpse of the vast career which lies before it, and day after day it shoots forward more rapidly, because more and more of freedom attends its movements. Whilst, in other civilizations, the exclusive, or, at least, the excessively preponderating dominion of a single principle, of a single form, has been the cause of tyranny, in modern Europe, the diversity of elements, which constitute the social order, the impossibility under which they have been placed of excluding each other, have given birth to the freedom which prevails in the present day. Not having been able to exterminate each other, it has become necessary that various principles should exist together—that they should make between them a sort of compact. Each has agreed to undertake that portion of the development which may fall to its share ; and whilst elsewhere the predominance of a principle produced tyranny, in Europe liberty has been the result of the variety of the elements of civilization, and of the state of struggle in which they have constantly existed.

Guizot has pointed out the main differences between Western Civilization and the older cultures, but modern Europe is indeed " the heir of all the ages ", and it owes much to its forerunners. *Where was the cradle of our civilization?* Spengler in his famous book, *The Decline of the West*, points out that " Indian man forgot everything, but Egyptian man forgot *nothing* ". Perhaps this passion for remembering is one of the most potent factors in the production of a progressive civilization. In the following lecture a former Professor of Egyptology gives us a few glimpses of early civilizations round the eastern shores of the Mediterranean.

JAMES H. BREASTED

TRACES OF EARLY CIVILIZATIONS IN THE MIDDLE EAST

IT has often been remarked that the outstanding trait of the untrained mind is credulity. The rationalization of man's views of the world has been a very slow process and it is still very far from a completed process. It has commonly been thought to have begun with the Greeks, but its origin must be sought in the Orient in a period long before Greek civilization had arisen. The Edwin Smith Medical Papyrus, acquired in 1906 by the New York Historical Society, discloses the inductive process of scientific investigation already in operation in the seventeenth century before Christ. For example, this document contains the earliest occurrence of the word "brain" anywhere appearing in surviving records of the past. The word is unknown in Old Testament Hebrew, in Babylonian, Assyrian, or any of the ancient languages of Western Asia. The organ itself therefore was evidently discovered, and the recognition of its various functions was begun, for the first time by these physicians of early Egypt in the thousand years preceding the seventeenth century B.C. The observations recorded in the Medical Papyrus show that its author had already observed that control of the members and limbs of the body was localized in different sides of the brain ; and the recognition of localization of functions in the brain, mostly the work of modern surgeons and others within the past generation or two, had already begun in the seventeenth century B.C., at a time when all Europe still lay in savagery or barbarism.

There is in existence part of an original transit instrument, made, as stated by the inscription upon it, by no less a king than Tutankhamen, in the fourteenth century B.C. It did not come from the tomb of Tutankhamen, but was apparently made by him for the tomb of his (or his wife's) great-grandfather, Thothmes IV (fifteenth century B.C.). This and another such piece at Berlin are the oldest scientific instruments of any kind now known to us. It was used for determining meridian time, especially at night, in order that the observer might then set his water-clock, with its 24-hour divisions, a division of the day which thence passed over into Europe in Hellenistic times, whence it was transmitted to us.

Now Herodotus reports a tradition current in his day (fifth century B.C.), that the Greeks were greatly indebted to Egyptian knowledge. This tradition has in recent times been universally rejected ; but it would seem that there was much truth in the tradition transmitted to us by Herodotus, and that its complete rejection by classical prejudice is unjustifiable.

The fact that the early Egyptian scientific worker employed an inductive method so far back as the seventeenth century B.C. does not, however, mean that he had completely banished from his mind all belief in magic or in supernatural forces. This truth has been well demonstrated for later ages by Professor Lynn Thorndyke in his monumental volumes on *The History of Magic and Experimental Science.* Undoubtedly the Greek took the longest step in freeing his mind from inherited religious and traditional prepossessions. Using astronomical observations undoubtedly drawn from Babylonia, Thales predicted a solar eclipse in 585 B.C. Astonishing as it seemed to the Greeks, there is little probability that this feat was an unprecedented achievement. What was unprecedented, however, was the revolutionary generalization which Thales based upon his ability to make such a prediction. For he banished the erratic whims of the gods from the skies and discerned the sway of natural law throughout the celestial world. To tear away and fearlessly to trample under foot beliefs and superstitions which had been sanctified by age-long religious veneration demanded dauntless loyalty to his own intelligence. This first supreme enthronement of the human mind was probably the greatest achievement in the career of man.

We can pay no greater tribute to such Greek thinkers than to recognize that although they put credulity to rout they could not banish it altogether. It has survived with extra-ordinary persistence even to the present day. In modern times it was of course the tremendous significance of the discoveries of Galileo which most impressively re-proclaimed the supremacy of natural law and the sovereignty of the human mind in discerning that law.

From Galileo's struggle with the Church to Huxley's debate with Gladstone, the heavy guns of natural science have dealt tradition one destructive blow after another. It has been under this destructive attack at the hands of natural science that historical criticism has grown up in modern times since Niebuhr. Indeed it has been no accident that the first serious discussion of the Old Testament narratives in Genesis and Exodus was written by Thomas Cooper, who was the associate of Priestley in the discovery of oxygen.

The critical scalpel which had not spared Hebrew tradition was equally unsparing in its treatment of the cherished classical heritage from Greece and Rome. The tales of Romulus and Remus, the Trojan war, and the entire cycle of legends which were linked with it, were shorn away. A critical attitude of

C

universal negation arose.   It included the whole Mediterranean and Oriental world : Rome, Greece, Hebrews, Babylonians, Assyrians, and Egyptians.   Historical criticism would not allow that early man at the beginning of the age of writing had ever heard and transmitted an echo from earlier ages, which, because they possessed no writing, could only send on their story in the form of oral traditions.   This attitude of the historical critic may be compared with that of an observer who stands on a mountain peak, and, looking off across a distant landscape to a dim horizon shrouded in mists and cloud, insists that the intermittent glimpses of mountain profiles which vaguely emerge on the far-away skyline cannot correspond to any reality.   In short, without ever having been himself on the ground to investigate, he denies the existence of the phantom mountains on the horizon.

Critical negation was supreme when, fifty years ago, archæology began to reveal with startling vividness the facts and the daily equipment of human life in the very ages with which the rejected traditions dealt.   In the 'seventies of last century the excavations of an untrained observer from the outside disclosed an astonishing vision of pre-Greek civilization at Mycenæ and Troy.   The incredulity with which these discoveries of Heinrich Schliemann were greeted by the classicists was highly characteristic.   His excavations recovered and exhibited to the incredulous eyes of the destructive critics the whole material equipment of daily life from the very age of the Trojan war (or wars), and from the very city in and around which it was waged.

Similar revelations, involving far earlier periods of time, rapidly disclosed the successive stages of the human career from a remote antiquity, reaching well back of the beginnings of the world as dated by an alleged " Biblical " chronology. In dealing with the traditions of these earlier ages the Orientalists soon developed a similar school of negative criticism. Such traditional accounts were promptly thrown into the discard.   Maspero's bulky history of the Oriental peoples, still a standard work on most modern library shelves, tells us that Menes, the first king of the First Dynasty of Egypt, was a purely mythical or legendary figure. Nevertheless we now possess his tomb, and in Chicago we have a piece of his personal ornaments, a gold bar bearing his name in hieroglyphic—the oldest piece of inscribed jewellery in existence. Since 1894, thousands of prehistoric graves have been excavated along the margin of the Nile valley, revealing to us the successive stages of human advance for many centuries before the once legendary Menes.

Much the same process is going on in the investigation of Babylonian history. Even the mythical hero Gilgamesh, the original of the European Hercules, bids fair to emerge at last as a remote city king of early Babylonia, who gained a reputation for his prowess in war, until he became the typical and pro-verbial strong man of all ages.

The crowning disclosure in this unprecedented series of unexpected revelations has recently come from Asia Minor. Nearly twenty years ago the German Assyriologist, Hugo Winckler, visited the mounds of Boghaz (or Boghaz Koi—" Boghaz village ") in central Asia Minor. As he walked over the ruins he kicked up with his boot-heel several cuneiform tablets, lying practically on the surface. Below were piled the clay tablet archives of the Hittite " Foreign Office ", the earliest of which had been lying there at the capital of the Hittite Empire since the middle of the second thousand years before Christ. The result has been the decipherment of ancient Hittite, or rather a whole group of Hittite dialects.

One of these tablets reports a war of Atreus, king of Achaia, against the king of Caria at about the middle of the thirteenth century, that is, about 1250 B.C. There can be no doubt that in this tablet we have a contemporary reference to the cycle of Trojan wars—a reference which must be regarded as an irreproachable historical source, as old as the events which it records. Thus out of the lost Oriental background of Greek history in Asia Minor comes a written document confirming a

Greek tradition, born in an age when the Greeks themselves still lacked writing. Because writing reaches further back in the Orient by nearly three thousand years than it does in Greece we are able to confirm Greek tradition out of contemporary written sources.

It has long been recognized that in the early development of Greek civilization the cities of Asia Minor took the lead. It is also evident that the inland background of Oriental culture contributed much to this early development of Greek civilization on the western fringes of Asia. It is out of this newly recovered Oriental background that we are slowly regaining the earlier forerunners of Greek civilization.

This contemporary reference to the Trojan war is an epoch-making revelation, which must react powerfully upon our treatment of early human traditions. It at once demonstrates that such traditions must not be thrown to the scrap-heap, but rather carefully divested of gods and goddesses, prodigies and wonders, and then examined from the nucleus of sober fact upon which the legendary tale has been built up.

As we look back upon our earliest historical horizon, we now know that the men who stood there in the grey dawn of the age of writing were able to hear echoes of a remoter past, transmitted in the form of oral tradition, of which some portion was then committed to writing and thus survived. In our modern effort to recover and reconstruct the story of man's past career, we have thus rehabilitated a new body of sources, however cautious it behoves us to be in making use of them. Not credulity alone, but also historical method, demands that we recognize these traditions, or the nucleus of fact to be drawn from them, as a body of sources to be restored to their proper chronological position in the past career of man on earth.

It is quite possible that all civilizations can be traced back to that which arose on the banks of the Nile. Certainly the Greeks borrowed freely from Egypt, even if they did transform what they borrowed. And in ancient Greece there is already a clear promise, or even more than a promise, of that future progress which was to set Western Civilization apart from all others. The promise lay in the Greek delight in an active and wide-ranging curiosity. *What has Western Civilization borrowed from ancient Greece?* The brilliance of the culture which developed so rapidly on the shores of the Ægean has rather dazzled the eyes of scholars, but in the following lecture, given at a summer school, on " The Unity of Western Civilization ", a former Waynflete Professor of Mental and Moral Philosophy at Oxford gives a brief and sober account of the main contributions.

J. A. SMITH

GREEK GIFTS TO CIVILIZATION

THE first and most obvious achievement of the Greek mind was the deliverance of itself in the sphere of imagination.

Behind the fair creations of Greek art lies a dark and ugly background, but it does lie behind them. That was its first conquest. Under the magic spell of Art the hateful and terrifying shapes of barbarous religion retreated and the world of imagination was peopled with gracious and attractive figures. The Greek Pantheon is, for all its defects, a world of dignified and beautiful humanity. " No thorn or threat stains its beauty bright." On the whole, the gods which are its denizens are humanized and humane, the friends and allies of men, who therefore feel themselves not abased or helpless in their relations with them. " Of one kind are gods and men ", and their common world is one in which men feel themselves at home. Dark shadows there are, but they hide no mysteries to appal and unman. The imagination is free to follow its own laws, and so to create what is lovely and lovable. Language is no longer a tyrant but a willing and dexterous servant, and the Greek language reflecting, as all language does, the spirit of its users, is the most perfect instrument that the human mind has ever devised for the expression of its dreams. The works which were then created have ever since haunted the mind of Europe like a passion, and we are right in speaking of them as immortal, " a joy for ever ".

In such a manner the Greek mind humanized its world, and in doing so humanized itself, or rather divinized itself, without stretching to the breaking-point the strands which bound itself to its world. But it did not stop there, and we do it wrong if we dwell too exclusively on its triumphant achievements in literature and art. For " speech created thought, which is the measure of the universe ".

The Greeks were not only supreme artists but also the pioneers of thought. They first took the measure of the Universe in which they lived, asserting the mind of man to be its measure, and it amenable and subject to reason. The world they lived in was not only beautiful to the imagination, it was also reasonable, penetrable, and governable by the intellect. The ways of it and everything in it were regular and orderly, predictable, explicable ; not eccentric, erratic, baffling, and inscrutable. Not only was Nature knowable ; it was also through knowledge of it manageable, a realm over which man could extend his sway, making it ever a more and more habitable home. In it and availing himself of its offered aid he built his households and his cities, dwelling comfortably in his habitations. But the thought which enabled him to lay a secure basis, economic and social or political, for his life had other issues and promised other fruit. The Greek mind became interested in knowledge for its own sake and in itself as the knower of its world.

The second and more important creation of the Greek mind was Science or the Sciences. In no earlier civilization can we trace anything but the faintest germs of this, while in Greek civilization it comes almost at once to flower and fruit. First and foremost we have to think of Mathematics, of Arithmetic and Geometry and Optics and Acoustics and Astronomy, but we must not forget also their later and perhaps not wholly so successful advances in Physics and Chemistry, in Botany and Zoology, in Anatomy and Physiology. Doubtless, especially in the case of the Sciences where experiments are required and have proved so fertile in the extension of our knowledge, there were grave defects and too much trust was placed in mere observations and hasty speculation ; but what they accomplished in Science is not less but more marvellous than what they accomplished in Art. The idea of Science was there, disengaged from the limiting restrictions of practical necessities, the idea of free and therefore all the more potent Science. The whole physical—and much more than the physical—environment of human life was proclaimed permeable to human thought and therefore governable by human will or at any rate already amicable and amenable to human purposes.

But yet a third advance was made. The Greek mind became conscious of itself as the knower and therefore the lord and master of its world. Turning inward upon itself it discovered itself as the centre of its universe and set itself to explore this new inner realm of being. In the consciousness of itself it found inexhaustible interest and strength. Thus it created Philosophy, its last and greatest gift to humanity. In so doing it freed itself from the trammels even of Science, which thus became its servant and not its master—at the same time finally liberating itself from the narrowing and blinding influences of passion and imagination and all the shackles of merely practical needs and disabilities. Here too it fixed the idea or the ideal. " Life without reflection upon life, without self-examination and self-study and self-knowledge, is a life not worth living by man." In doing so it revealed a self deeper than the physical being of man and an environment wider and more real—more stable and permanent—than the physical cosmos, finding in the one and the other something more enduring, substantial, and precious than shows itself either to Science or the economic and political prudence, yet which alone gives meaning and worth to the one and the other.

Thus for the first time arose before the mind of man the conception of a life not sunk in nature and practice, but superior to them and the end or meaning of their existence—a life of intense activity, of unfailing interest, of inexhaustible and eternal value.

This life was, throughout the duration of Greek thought, too narrowly conceived. It was frequently thought and spoken of as the life of a spectator or bystander or onlooker, as a life withdrawn or isolated, cut off from what we should call ordinary human business and concerns, a life into which we, or at least a few of us, could escape or be transported at rare intervals and under exceptionally favourable circumstances. Yet in principle it was open to all, and certainly not confined to those privileged by birth or wealth or social position. It was not the reward of magical favour or ascetic exercises, it was reached by the beaten path of the loyal citizen and the resolute student. There was about it no esoteric mystery or other-worldliness. And if to reach it was a high privilege, its attainment brought with it the imperative duty of a descent into the ordinary world to instruct, to enlighten, to comfort and help and console, to play a part in the great business and work of human civilization. In a sense this was, and is, the most permanent and fruitful gift of Greece to the European world.

These, then, were the three ideas or ideals which the Greeks wrought into the very texture and substance of the modern mind, the idea of Art, the idea of Science, the idea of Philosophy; in all three introducing and still more deeply implanting the ideas of Freedom as the motive and end of civilized life and of Knowledge as its guide and ally. It may be thought that I have dwelt too much on theory, and have not said enough of the specific contribution of Greece as working out in practice a certain type or types of corporate life such as the City State ; but the fact is that in Greek civilization theory continually outran practice and that it endowed mankind much more with ideals than with practical illustrations or models for our imitation. Yet again we must not exaggerate or imagine these ideas as merely Utopian or such stuff as dreams are made of. The ferment which they set up burst the fabric of Greek social and political institutions, but it clarified and steadied down, as the enthusiasms of youth may do, into the sober designs of grave and energetic manhood.

Greek gifts to art, to science, and to philosophy have been mentioned by Professor Smith, and it is indeed difficult to imagine what life would be like without any of these. Another Greek gift is that of democracy or political liberty. *Where did Democracy begin?* It was certainly a Greek invention, and if we may believe Pericles, the city of Athens deserves the credit. Here is his famous funeral speech over the Athenian soldiers killed in the first year of the Peloponnesian War, 431 B.C. This oration has an additional importance, since we find in it, as Whitehead has pointed out, " the first explicit defence of social tolerance, as requisite for high civilization. . . . It puts forth the conception of the organized society successfully preserving freedom of behaviour for its individual members." Our translation is a free one which tries to produce the spirit rather than the literal meaning of the original, and one or two passages are summarized rather than translated.

PERICLES

THE FUNERAL ORATION

OUR ancestors have long thought it right that those who died in battle should be honoured in a speech like this. For myself I would rather see their noble deeds commemorated by our actions than by any words. But I submit to law and custom.

I will begin with our ancestors, for it is meet and right on an occasion like this to remember them first. They have always dwelt in this country generation after generation in unbroken succession, and by their valour they have maintained it as the home of freedom. To our fathers even greater praise is due, for they added most of our present empire to the territory which was handed down to them. And we ourselves, by which I mean those of us still in the full vigour of life, have not been slow to do our part. We consolidated our power and made our city independent and self-sufficient both in war and peace.

As regards our achievements in warfare, whether offensive or defensive, I will say nothing, for you know them as well as I do. What I should like to dwell on is the spirit which animates us, and our way of organizing affairs—our institutions, and our system of government—for it is to these that the greatness of our state is due. And it is fitting that these things should be called to mind as we honour those who died in their defence.

For we enjoy a form of government not copied from the laws of any neighbouring state. Rather do other states copy ours. And since our constitution considers not the benefit of the few, but the welfare of the many, we call it a democracy. The state regards all men as equal so far as their private differences are concerned ; but it selects for public honour those who have shown their ability in the public service, nor does poverty prevent any man from showing his worth as a citizen.

Our public administration, then, is liberal, and there is a similar freedom in our daily intercourse with each other. We are above petty jealousy and each man is allowed the right to please himself in his private avocations without being greeted with censorious looks or those petty actions which, though harmless enough, are still unpleasant. While, however, in private matters we live happily together in mutual toleration, our conduct in public matters is governed by a wholesome fear of disobeying those who may be in authority, or of transgressing the laws, and especially two kinds of laws : those which protect the citizen from injury, and those which, though unwritten, still bring disgrace on the transgressor.

We also pay due attention to the recreation of mind and

body by the institution of games and sacrifices throughout the year, and no other city has as much beauty in its public and private buildings to please the eye and uplift the spirit day by day. Moreover, so great is our city that the commodities of all countries in the world are brought hither to be added to the good things of our own land for our enjoyment.

In the study of war we differ from our enemies. Our city is open to all, and we never expel or exclude strangers for fear they might see things of military importance. We trust to our own valour for victory, and not to material preparations or to stratagems. So, too, with education. Other cities have to train their youth in bold manliness by laborious exercises, while we, though living at our ease, advance no less boldly to meet danger. . . . So with careless ease rather than laborious practice we face danger, and this with a courage that is the result of natural disposition rather than discipline, nor do we grow fearful when troubles are coming, but await the event with the same confidence which we show in action. . . . With other peoples ignorance brings daring and consideration brings fear, but the man who is truly brave is he who knows the danger and is not turned aside.

Again, we differ from most men in generosity, for we make friends by giving rather than by receiving. And he that bestows the favour is the better friend because he wants to keep alive the feeling of good-will towards the man he has obliged. But a friendship founded on the receipt of benefits often proves flat and dull because the recipient is too conscious of his indebtedness. We alone freely do good to others, not with an eye to future gain, but in the confiding spirit of generosity.

In brief our city is a model for the whole of Greece. It was for such a city that these men, determined that it should not be taken away from them, nobly fought and died, and it is natural that we who survive them should be ready to give our all in its service.

That is why I have dealt at such length with the city. I

wanted to emphasize what a lot we have to lose; and at the
same time to show how well justified is my praise of the dead.
For if I have sung the glories of the city it was these men,
and others like them, who decked her in those glories. We
cannot overpraise them. Such an end as theirs does indeed
show us what a good life is, from the first days of manhood to
the closing scenes. Even if some among them had had their
moments of weakness or failure, the last brave hour outweighs
all such faults. In it they wiped out evil with good, and the
benefit to the city of their bravery proved far greater than the
loss from any harm they might have done. No rich man
among them was turned aside by the thought of his wealth;
no poor man shirked the danger because he dreamt of future
wealth. All such considerations they put aside; their thoughts
and their arms were for the city. They counted the desire to
avenge her as the greatest of ventures, and leaving Hope, the
uncertain goddess, to send them what she would, they faced
the foe, as the line of battle approached, relying on their
manhood. And when the shock of battle came, they chose
rather to stand and be slain than to prolong their lives by any
weakness. So their memories escaped reproach, while they
bore the brunt of battle, and in a moment of time, in their
finest hour, they were hurried away from this world, their
eyes filled with glory and not with fear.

Such were these men, worthy of their country. As for all
that remain, we can pray for better luck, but we must not be
less resolute against the enemy. Let us draw strength, not
merely from moral maxims about the need for courage in
battle, but from all that we see of our great city. Let our
love for it grow day by day, and remember, when you consider
its greatness, that its fame was built by boldness, and devotion
to duty, and the shunning of dishonour. These men lost
their lives but they did not lose their valour; that is theirs
and their city's for ever. Collectively they gave their lives
for the city, individually they receive that renown which
never grows old, and the most distinguished tomb they could

have—not that in which their bones are laid but the tomb of fame in which their glory is recorded for ever, to be recalled on great occasions all through the ages. For the whole earth is the tomb of illustrious men ; and while in their own land their virtue is recorded by inscriptions on their monuments, in other lands it is kept alive in the memory and in the hearts of men. Let us follow the example of these men and willingly accept the hazards of war, for there can be no happiness without freedom, and no freedom without courage.

It is not the miserable and desperate man who has the best excuse for holding his life cheaply, but he who has most to lose by defeat and a change of fortune. For to a man of spirit the agony of cowardice is far more grievous than the unfelt death which comes suddenly upon him when he is in the fullness of his strength and his hopes are high. So I do not weep with the parents of the dead. Rather will I comfort them. For they know something of the chances of this life, and they will agree that he to whom the best lot falls is to be accounted fortunate. Theirs is the best sorrow ; just as the best death came to those whom we honour to-day, those whose life did not exceed the span of their happiness. I know it is not easy to lighten your sorrow. I know how the sight of other proud fathers will remind you of your loss. I know that something we have long enjoyed and have lost is always dearer than things we have never experienced. But you must keep a brave heart, and hope for other children, those of you who can still do so. Such new-comers will fill the gap in your own circle and will fill the ranks of the city's soldiers and workers. For no man is fit to take part in the councils of our city unless he has a family for whom he must also think and fight. . . .

I have spoken such words as the law requires and the occasion warrants. As for deeds, the graveside offerings to the dead have been made, and henceforth their children will be brought up at the public expense until manhood. Such is the reward which the city holds out to those who make the supreme sacrifice. For where the prize for virtue is highest, there also will you find the most virtuous men contending for it.

And now, when you have finished your mourning for your relatives, you may depart.

The debt of western culture to the ancient world, to Greece and Palestine and Rome, is undoubtedly great, just as were the debts of these cultures to Egypt. But such influence must not be exaggerated. It is true that many characteristics of Western Civilization, like democracy, can be traced right back into ancient Greece, but how they have changed in western hands! And if credit is due to Greece for those things of hers which have been adopted, to whom is credit due for the rejection of those other things which have not been thought worthy of preservation? Let us get this clear. *How does one culture affect another?* It used to be the fashion to talk of influences and to try to trace a continuity of culture from one country to another and one age to another. But Spengler, in that epoch-making *Decline of the West*, which has already been mentioned, gave a truer interpretation. He showed how one culture takes from another just those elements which fit in with its own ideas, just those institutions which match its ways of thought. As a symbol of Western Civilization, Spengler took Faust, with his thirst for knowledge and his desire for power, so the word " Faustian " in the following extract can be regarded as meaning " Western European " just as " Magian " means " Near Eastern ".

OSWALD SPENGLER

THE RELATIONS BETWEEN CULTURES

THE historian who is intent upon establishing causal series counts only the influences that are present, and the other side of the reckoning—those that are not—does not appear. With the psychology of the " positive " influences is associated that of the " negative ". This is a domain into which no one has yet ventured, but here, if anywhere, there are fruits to be reaped, and it must be tackled unless the answer to the whole question is to be left indeterminate ; for if we try to evade it, we are driven into illusory visions of world-historical happening as a continuous process in which everything is properly accounted for. Two Cultures may touch between man and man, or the man of one Culture may be confronted by the dead form-world of another as presented in its communicable relics. In both cases the agent is the man himself. The closed-off act of A can be vivified by B only out of his own being, and *eo ipso* it becomes B's, his inward property, his work, and part of himself.

There was no movement of " Buddhism " from India to China, but an acceptance of part of the Indian Buddhists' store of images by Chinese of a certain spiritual tendency, who fashioned out a new mode of religious expression having meaning for Chinese, and only Chinese, Buddhists. What matters in all such cases is not the original meanings of the forms, but the forms themselves, as disclosing to the active sensibility and understanding of the observer potential modes of his own creativeness. Connotations are not transferable. Men of two different kinds are parted, each in his own spiritual loneliness, by an impassable gulf. Even though Indians and Chinese in those days both felt as Buddhists, they were spiritually as far apart as ever. The same words, the same rites, the same symbol—but two different souls, each going its own way.

Searching through all Cultures, then, one will always find that the continuation of earlier creations into a later Culture is only apparent, and that in fact the younger *being* has set up a few (very few) relations to the older *being*, always without regard to the original meanings of that which it makes its own. What becomes, then, of the " permanent conquests " of philosophy and science ? We are told again and again how much of Greek philosophy still lives on to-day, but this is only a figure of speech without real content, for first Magian and then Faustian humanity, each with the deep wisdom of its unimpaired instincts, rejected that philosophy, or passed unregarding by it, or retained its formulæ under radically new interpretations.

The naïve credulity of erudite enthusiasm deceives itself here—Greek philosophic notions would make a long catalogue, and the further it is taken, the more vanishingly small becomes the proportion of the alleged survivals. Our custom is simply to overlook as incidental "errors" such conceptions as Democritus's theory of atomic images, the very corporeal world of Plato's "ideas", and the fifty-two hollow spheres of Aristotle's universe, as though we could presume to know what the dead meant better than they knew themselves! These things are truths and essential—only, not for us. The sum total of the Greek philosophy that we possess, actually and not merely superficially, is practically nil. Let us be honest and take the old philosophers at their word, not one proposition of Heraclitus or Democritus or Plato is true for us unless and until we have accommodated it to ourselves. And how much, after all, have we taken over of the methods, the concepts, the intentions, and the means of Greek science, let alone its basically incomprehensible terms ? The Renaissance, men say, was completely under the "influence" of Classical art. But what about the form of the Doric temple, the Ionic column, the relation of column to architrave, the choice of colour, the treatment of background and perspective in painting, the principles of figure-grouping, vase-painting, mosaic, encaustic, the structural element in statuary, the proportions of Lysippus ? Why did all this exercise no " influence " ?

Because that which one (here, the Renaissance artist) *wills to express is in him* a priori. Of the stock of dead forms that he had in front of him, he really saw only the few that he wanted to see, and saw them as he wanted them—namely, in line with his own intention and not with the intention of the original creator, for no living art ever seriously considers that. Try to follow, element by element, the "influence" of

Egyptian plastic upon early Greek, and you will find in the
end that there is none at all, but that the Greek will-to-form
took out of the older art-stock some few characteristics that
it would in any case have discovered in some shape for itself.
All round the Classical landscape there were working, or had
worked, Egyptians, Cretans, Babylonians, Assyrians, Hittites,
Persians, and Phœnicians, and the works of these peoples—
their buildings, ornaments, art-works, cults, state forms,
scripts, and sciences—were known to the Greeks in profusion.
But how much out of all this mass did the Classical soul
extract as its own means of expression ? I repeat, it is only
the relations that are *accepted* that we observe. But what of
those that were *not* accepted ? Why, for example, do we fail
to find in the former category the pyramid, pylon, and obelisk
of Egypt, or hieroglyphic, or cuneiform ? What of the stock
of Byzantium and of the Moorish East was *not* accepted by
Gothic art and thought in Spain and Sicily ? It is impossible
to overpraise the wisdom (quite unconscious) that governed
the choice and the unhesitating transvaluation of what was
chosen. Every relation that was accepted was not only an
exception, but also a misunderstanding, and the inner force
of a Being is never so clearly evidenced as it is in this *art of
deliberate misunderstanding*. The more enthusiastically we
laud the principles of an alien thought, the more fundamentally in truth we have denatured it.

Only consider the praises addressed by the West to Plato !
From Bernard of Chartres and Marsilius Ficinus to Goethe
and Schelling ! And the more humble our acceptance of an
alien religion, the more certain it is that that religion has
already assumed the form of the new soul. Truly, someone
ought to have written the history of the " three Aristotles "—
Greek, Arabian, and Gothic—who had not one concept or
thought in common. Or the history of the transformation
of Magian Christianity into Faustian ! We are told in sermon
and book that this religion extended from the old Church
into and over the Western field without change of essence.

D

Actually, Magian man evolved out of the deepest depths of his dualistic world-consciousness a language of his own religious awareness that we call " the " Christian religion. So much of this experience as was communicable—words, formulæ, rites—was accepted by the man of the Late-Classical civilization as a means of expression for his religious need ; then it passed from man to man, even to the Germans of the Western pre-Culture, in words always the same and in sense always altering. Men would never have dared to *improve upon* the original meanings of the holy words—it was simply that they did not know these meanings.

If this be doubted, let the doubter study " the " idea of Grace, as it appears under the dualistic interpretation of Augustine affecting a substance in man, and under the dynamic interpretation of Calvin, affecting a will in man. Or that Magian idea, which we can hardly grasp at all, of the consensus (Arabic *ijma*) wherein, as a consequence of the presence in each man of a *pneuma* [a breath or spirit] emanating from the divine *pneuma*, the unanimous opinion of the elect is held to be immediate divine Truth. It was this that gave the decisions of the early Church Councils their authoritative character, and it underlies the scientific methods that rule in the world of Islam to this day. And it was because Western man did not understand this that the Church Councils of later Gothic times amounted, for him, to nothing more than a kind of parliament for limiting the spiritual mobility of the Papacy. This idea of what a Council meant prevailed even in the fifteenth century—think of Constance and Basel, Savonarola and Luther—and in the end it disappeared, as futile and meaningless, before the conception of Papal Infallibility.

Or, again, the idea, universal in the Early Arabian world, of the resurrection of the flesh, which again presupposed that of divine and human *pneuma*. Classical man assumed that the soul, as the form and meaning of the body, was somehow co-created herewith, and Greek thought scarcely

mentions it.   Silence on a matter of such gravity may be due
to one or the other of two reasons—the idea's not being there
at all, or being so self-evident as not to emerge into consciousness as a problem.   With Arabian man it was the latter.
But just as self-evident for him was the notion that his *pneuma*
was an emanation from God that had taken up residence in
his body.   Necessarily, therefore, there had to be something
from which the human soul should rise again on the Day of
Judgment, and hence resurrection was thought of as ἐκ νεκρῶν,
" out of the corpses ".   This, in its deeper meaning, is utterly
incomprehensible to the West.   The words of Holy Scripture
were not indeed doubted, but unconsciously another meaning
was substituted by the finer minds amongst Catholics; this
other meaning, unmistakable already in Luther and to-day
quite general, is the conception of immortality as the continued existence to all eternity of the soul as a centre of force.
Were Paul or Augustine to become acquainted with our ideas
of Christianity, they would reject all our dogmas, all our
books, and all our concepts as utterly erroneous and heretical.

Spengler goes on to quote Roman Law as an example of " a system
that to all appearance has travelled unaltered through two millennia,
and yet actually has passed through three whole courses of evolution
in three Cultures, with completely different meanings in each ".   His
three cultures are the Classical, the Arabian, and the European, and
the important points are that in the Classical world different laws
applied to different cities ; in the Arabian world different laws applied
to different religions ; but in Western Europe there arose one of those
three great advantages with which, in Whitehead's words, " Europe
started upon its second effort after civilization—its instinct for legal
organization *transcending local boundaries,* derived from the Church,
and the reminiscence of the Empire ".   This legal organization has
been applied to the safeguarding of civil, personal, and political liberties
to a degree unknown in other civilizations.

The first essential in any system is the establishment of the idea of
" law " on some foundation of morality or justice.   Further progress

depends on how far this idea is helped to grow with the growing size and complexity of society. It was in the practical development of a legal code that the Romans excelled. *What was Rome's greatest gift to Western Civilization?* In the following lecture we shall find a brief but scholarly account of what Greece gave to Rome, and what both have handed down to us.

SIR ERNEST BARKER

THE ROMAN CONTRIBUTION TO OUR CIVILIZATION

HISTORY is a continuous process. Little that has ever been achieved is allowed to slip away and to pass into nothingness. The achievements of Greece were the inheritance of Rome—so far, at any rate, as Rome was able to enter into the spirit and to adopt the method of these achievements. But Rome was essentially different from Greece; and being different, she both altered what she received and added to what she altered. It is difficult to find a formula to cover the development of a people. Some, seeking to find a formula for the development of Greece, have hit on the phrase, "from Achilles to Alexander": others, embarked on the same search, but holding science rather than romance to be the Greek note, have suggested the formula, "from Thales to Hipparchus", thinking of Thales as the first figure, and of Hipparchus, the inventor of trigonometry, as the last, in the history of Greek scientific discovery. For the development of Rome we may find a formula more readily. "The history of Rome" it has been said "begins and ends in a code." It begins with the Twelve Tables in 450 B.C.; it ends with the Code of Justinian, about a thousand years later, towards A.D. 550.

The Roman genius was indeed essentially a legal genius. If the Greeks had a passion for truth, and gave to the world the methods of science; if, again, they had a passion for beauty, and gave to the world the canons of art—we may say that the grave Roman had a sense of conduct, and that he gave to the world, in the strength of that sense, a scheme and system of law. There is here an analogy between the Romans and the English; and indeed the world to-day is divided between two systems of law—the one, which we find in Western Europe and in South America, based on the Roman model; the other, which we find in the British Empire and the United States, based on the English.

Along with the gift of law there naturally goes the gift of government; and Rome, just as she devised a code of law, devised also a system of government which culminated in the Roman Empire. Roman law and the Roman system of government both became permanent possessions of the world; and neither of the two perished or disappeared when the history of the ancient world came to an end with the irruption of the Germans into the Empire. Roman law has never ceased, throughout the centuries, to be administered in courts and studied in schools of law.

The scheme of the Roman Empire persisted after the barbarian invasions of the fifth century A.D.; it was adopted in the Middle Ages, under the name of the Holy Roman Empire, as a mode of union (it is true, a very loose union) among the nations of the West; and indeed it was only in 1806 that the last ruler who called himself Roman Emperor finally abdicated. Nor is this all. The Christian Church, as it grew to greatness in the Roman Empire, modelled its government on that of the Empire; and the Roman Church to-day, in its organization under the Papacy, reflects the order of the old Roman world. " The Papacy " wrote Hobbes " is none other than the ghost of the deceased Roman Empire, sitting crowned on the grave thereof."

In emphasizing the peculiar legacy of Rome to the modern world we must not forget the legacy of Greece to Rome. Roman law itself owed much to the Greek speculation which we find in the *Laws* of Plato, and to the actual body of Greek law which was formed in the Hellenistic kingdoms after the death of Alexander. The government of the Roman Empire was formed on the model and in the tradition of the governments established by Alexander's successors. We may say, therefore, that Rome bequeathed to the modern world not only herself, but also Greece—that the inheritance of Rome is Greco-Roman rather than Roman.

This may be seen in the domain of arts as well as in the field of law and government. Roman literature, as we find it in Virgil or Horace, is a blending of Greek forms with a native Italian genius ; and Roman architecture and sculpture have the same quality. Even Roman engineering, with its aqueducts and its triumphs of applied mechanics, finds its parallels and its inspiration in the achievements of the Hellenistic period. Priene, a little Hellenistic city of 4000 inhabitants, had an aqueduct which brought water from the hills ; and metal water pipes carrying water under the streets from house to house were also known in Hellenistic cities. Alexandria in 300 B.C. had a great lighthouse, 370 feet high, so strongly built that it lasted 1600 years.

We cannot really dispute about the respective contributions of Greece and Rome to civilization. We cannot separate Greece and Rome in order to measure their separate contributions. The whole Greek development flowed into Rome —the Hellenic as well as the Hellenistic, but more particularly the latter ; and the gift of Rome to the future was the whole inherited past—the whole sum of Greco-Roman civilization.

Religion has played a large part in every culture, and the time has now come to ask, *What did Christianity bring to Western Civilization ?* The influence of Christianity has persisted through the centuries, changing to some extent with changing conditions, as will be seen from later lectures, but in the following pages Guizot shows how the Christian Church helped to keep alive the light of civilization when Europe entered the " Dark Ages ".

F. GUIZOT

THE CONTRIBUTION OF CHRISTIANITY

THESE are the elements which Roman has transmitted to European civilization ; upon one hand, the municipal system, its habits, rules, precedents, the principle of freedom ; on the other, a general and uniform civil legislation, the idea of absolute power, of sacred majesty, of the emperor, the principle of order and subjection.

But there was formed at the same time, in the heart of the Roman society, a society of a very different nature, founded upon totally different sentiments, a society which was about to infuse into modern European society elements of a character wholly different ; I speak of the *Christian Church.* I say, the Christian Church, and not Christianity. At the end of the fourth and at the beginning of the fifth century, Christianity was no longer merely an individual belief, it was an institution ; it was constituted ; it had its government, a clergy, an hierarchy calculated for the different functions of the clergy, revenues, means of independent action, rallying points suited for a great society, provincial, national and general councils, and the custom of debating in common upon the affairs of the society. In a word, Christianity, at this epoch, was not only a religion, it was also a church.

Had it not been a church, I cannot say what might have happened to it amid the fall of the Roman Empire. I confine myself to simply human considerations ; I put aside every element which is foreign to the natural consequences of natural facts : had Christianity been, as in the earlier times, no more than a belief, a sentiment, an individual conviction, we may believe that it would have sunk amidst the dissolution of the empire, and the invasion of the barbarians. In later times, in Asia, and in all the north of Africa, it sank under an invasion of the Moslem barbarians ; it sank then, although it subsisted in the form of an institution, or constituted church. With much more reason might the same thing have happened at the moment of the fall of the Roman Empire. There existed, at that time, none of those means by which, in the present day, moral influences establish themselves or offer resistance, independently of institutions ; none of those means whereby a pure truth, a pure idea obtains a great empire over minds, governs actions, and determines events. Nothing of the kind existed in the fourth century to give a like authority to ideas and to personal sentiments. It is clear that a society strongly organized and strongly governed, was indispensable to struggle against such a disaster, and to issue victorious from such a storm.

I do not think that I say more than the truth in affirming that at the end of the fourth and the commencement of the fifth centuries it was the Christian church that saved Christianity ; it was the church with its institutions, its magistrates, and its power, that vigorously resisted the internal dissolution of the empire and barbarism ; that conquered the barbarians and became the bond, the medium, and the principle of civilization between the Roman and barbarian worlds. It is, then, the condition of the church rather than that of religion, properly so-called, that we must look to, in order to discover what Christianity has, since then, added to modern civilization, and what new elements it has introduced therein. What was the Christian church at that period ?

When we consider, always under a purely human point of view, the various revolutions which have accomplished themselves during the development of Christianity, from the time of its origin up to the fifth century ; if, I repeat, we consider it simply as a community and not as a religious creed, we find that it passed through three essentially different states.

In the very earliest period, the Christian society presents itself as a simple association of a common creed and common sentiments ; the first Christians united to enjoy together the same emotions, and the same religious convictions. We find among them no system of determinate doctrines, no rules, no discipline, no body of magistrates.

Of course, no society, however newly born, however weakly constituted it may be, exists without a moral power which animates and directs it. In the various Christian congregations there were men who preached, taught, and morally governed the congregation, but there was no formal magistrate, no recognized discipline ; a simple association caused by a community of creed and sentiments was the primitive condition of the Christian society.

In proportion as it advanced—and very speedily, since traces are visible in the earliest monuments—a body of doctrines, of rules, of discipline, and of magistrates, began to appear ; one kind of magistrates were called *ancients*, who became the priests ; another, *inspectors* or superintendents, who became bishops ; a third *deacons*, who were charged with the care of the poor and with the distribution of alms.

It is scarcely possible to determine what were the precise functions of these various magistrates ; the line of demarcation was probably very vague and variable, but what is clear is that an establishment was organized. Still, a peculiar character prevails in this second period : the preponderance and rule belonged to the body of the faithful. It was the body of the faithful which prevailed, both as to the choice of functionaries, and as to the adoption of discipline, and even doctrine. The church government and the Christian people were not as yet separated. They did not exist apart from, and independently of, one another ; and the Christian people exercised the principal influence in the society.

In the third period, all was different. A clergy existed who were distinct from the people, a body of priests who had their own riches, jurisdiction, and peculiar constitution ; in a word, an entire government, which in itself was a complete society, a society provided with all the means of existence, independently of the society to which it had reference, and over which it extended its influence. Such was the third stage of the constitution of the Christian church ; such was the form in which it appeared at the beginning of the fifth century. The government was not completely separated from the people ; there has never been a parallel kind of government, and less in religious matters than in any others ; but in the relations of the clergy to the faithful, the clergy ruled almost without control.

The Christian clergy had, moreover, another and very different source of influence. The bishops and the priests became the principal municipal magistrates. You have seen that, of the Roman empire, there remained, properly speaking, nothing but the municipal system. It had happened, from the vexations of despotism and the ruin of the towns, that the *curiales*, or members of the municipal bodies, had become discouraged and apathetic ; on the other hand, the bishops and the body of priests full of life and zeal, offered themselves naturally for the superintendence and direction of all matters. We should be wrong to reproach them for this, to tax them with usurpation ; it was all in the natural course of things ; the clergy alone were morally strong and animated ; they became everywhere powerful. Such is the law of the universe. . . .

You perceive what prodigious power was thus obtained by the Christian church, as well by its own constitution, as by its influence upon the Christian people, and by the part which it took in civil affairs. Thus, from that epoch, it powerfully assisted in forming the character and furthering the development of modern civilization. Let us endeavour to sum up the elements which it, from that time, introduced into it.

And first of all there was an immense advantage in the presence of a moral influence, of a moral power, of a power which reposed solely upon convictions and upon moral creeds and sentiments, amidst the deluge of material power which at this time inundated society. Had the Christian church not existed, the whole world must have been abandoned to purely material force. The church alone exercised a moral power. It did more : it sustained, it spread abroad the idea of a rule, of a law superior to all human laws. It proposed, for the salvation of humanity, the fundamental belief, that there exists, above all human laws, a law which is denominated, according to periods and customs, sometimes reason, sometimes the divine law, but which, everywhere and always, is the same law under different names.

In short, with the church originated a great fact, the separation of spiritual and temporal power. This separation is the source of liberty of conscience ; it is founded upon no other principle but that which is the foundation of the most perfect and extended freedom of conscience. The separation of temporal and spiritual power is based upon the idea that physical force has neither right nor influence over souls, over conviction, over truth. It flows from the distinction established between the world of thought and the world of action, between the world of internal and that of external facts. Thus this principle of liberty of conscience for which Europe has struggled so much, and suffered so much, this principle which prevailed so late, and often, in its progress, against the inclination of the clergy, was enunciated, under the name of the separation of temporal and spiritual power, in the very cradle of European civilization ; and it was the Christian church which, from the necessity imposed by its situation of defending itself against barbarism, introduced and maintained it.

The presence, then, of a moral influence, the maintenance of a divine law, and the separation of the temporal and spiritual powers, are the three grand benefits which the Christian church in the fifth century conferred upon the European world.

The cardinal fact which differentiates the West from the East is that the West continued to progress ; the East for a long time stood still. In the Dark Ages the Arabians were far in advance of the Europeans. But they made little further progress, while the West seemed to be granted a new lease of life, and forged ahead, slowly at first, and then with ever-increasing speed. In the two vitally important fields of technology—the "know how" of commerce and industry—and of political organization, the West was soon unrivalled. Civilization depends on the triumph of man over his environment, or the triumph of man over nature, always remembering that man is part of nature, so that this triumph must include the disciplining of man's lower instincts.

Why did Western Civilization continue to progress while the East stood still ? The following answer to this question will also go a long way towards summing up the essential differences between our own and all other civilizations. It is taken from a paper by A. N. Whitehead in his *Adventures of Ideas*—" a study of the concept of civilization ". Whitehead points out that civilized communities must struggle with two great groups of problems : the satisfaction of physical needs, such as food, warmth, and shelter ; and the co-ordination of social activities. If there is to be any upward evolution, this co-ordination must be achieved more and more by persuasion and less and less by force. In this lecture the word " commerce "—an excellent example of the power of persuasion in civilized societies—is used in its widest sense to imply any friendly intercourse between peoples.

A. N. WHITEHEAD

FROM FORCE TO PERSUASION

NATURE is plastic, although to every prevalent state of mind there corresponds iron nature setting its bounds to life. Modern history begins when Europeans passed into a new phase of understanding which enabled them to introduce new selective agencies, unguessed by the older civilizations. It is a false dichotomy to think of Nature *and* Man. Mankind is that factor *in* Nature which exhibits in its most intense form the plasticity of nature. Plasticity is the introduction of novel law. The doctrine of the Uniformity of Nature is to be ranked with the contrasted doctrine of magic and miracle, as an expression of partial truth, unguarded and unco-ordinated with the immensities of the Universe. Our interpretations of experience determine the limits of what we can do with the world.

For the purpose of understanding how it happened that European life escaped the restrictions which finally bound China, India, and the Near East, it is important to recapture the attitude towards Commerce prevalent in various epochs. I do not mean records of trade, but records of the kinds of mentality governing commercial relations. We can only understand a society by knowing what sort of people undertook what sort of functions in that society. It must be remembered that China and Bagdad, at the height of their prosperity, exhibited forms of human life in many ways more gracious than our own. They were great civilizations. But they became arrested, and the arrest is the point of our inquiry. We have to understand the reasons for the greatness and the final barriers to advancement. Of course, such an ambitious design is absurd. It would mean the solution of the main problem of sociology. What can be done is to note some indications of relevant tones of mind apparently widely spread in various districts at different epochs.

There is ample evidence of active Commerce in China and the Near East in ancient times, contemporary with the pre-Hellenic and Hellenic periods of the Ægean Basin. There are Codes of Law which determine commercial problems. Also among the early inscriptions recovered from Babylon and Nineveh there are a mass of records of private transactions between merchants. Three thousand years ago the importance of credit would have been no news either in Mesopotamia or in China. Also there was foreign trade beyond the boundaries of the Near East. There are evidences of ocean-borne trade between India and Egypt, perhaps even between China and Egypt, with Ceylon as an intermediary. Also Central Asia was nearing its last phase of prosperity before it faded out into desert. It seems to have provided the route for a flourishing overland trade between China and the Near East. Thus these great civilizations were supported by internal trade and by external trade with each other. Also there was the whole coastline of semi-barbarous Europe—the shores of the Black

Sea, the shores of the Western Mediterranean, the Atlantic coasts of Europe.

Having regard to relative backwardness of the art of navigation then, compared with the same art in the fifteenth and sixteenth centuries after Christ, the boldness of the Phœnician sailors and the enterprise of their traders at least equals that in any of the later feats. It is impossible to be more than absolutely fearless : and considering the dim geographic knowledge possessed by the ancients, the Phœnicians must be allowed the fame of having displayed the extremity of courage. The Greeks were bold sailors, but the Phœnicians led the way. There is no reason to believe that in later times a Greek or a Roman vessel ever saw a coastline not previously visited by Phœnician traders. Also, remembering Hanno's voyage in the sixth century before Christ, the whole oceanic coastline of Africa was explored by the men of the Near East, where Western Europeans did not venture till the lapse of nigh two thousand years. In the last few hundred years, European races have been apt to forget the greatness of the Near East, whose populations, with no predecessors to guide them, carried mankind from the stage of semi-barbarism only half erect from the soil, to peaks of civilized life, in art, in religion, and in adventure, which remain unsurpassed. Their civilization in its prime was founded on Expanding Commerce, Development of Technology, and Discovery of Empty Continents. But in this list one item has been omitted, the Souls of Men.

The vigour of the Near East survived the first effort to establish a widespread European civilization. This European attempt was embodied in the western portion of the Roman Empire. It was sustained during four hundred and fifty or five hundred years. The limits of this period may be approximately assigned from Cæsar and Augustus at the commencement down to the taking of Rome by Alaric in the year A.D. 410. The failure did not consist in the decline and fall of its political institutions. Such state systems are transient expedients upon the surface of civilization. The real failure consists in the fact that in the year A.D. 600, Western Europe was less civilized than in the year A.D. 100, and was far behind the Eastern Mediterranean during the third and fourth centuries before Christ. Pope Gregory the Great would have been poor company for Sophocles, Aristotle, Eratosthenes, or Archimedes. Gregory was the man for his time. But the delicacies of civilization—in art, or in thought, or in human behaviour— were then at a discount.

In every sense of the term, the Western Empire had lacked expansive force. Across the Rhine and the Danube the northern forests were impenetrable. On the west, the Atlantic Ocean was trackless. With the minor exception of the conquest of Britain, all attempt at physical expansion ceased after Varus lost the legions of Augustus. The Western Empire in all its ramifications was a purely defensive institution, in its sociological functionings, and in its external behaviour. Its learning lacked speculative adventure. In no sense, however we stretch the metaphor, did it discover a New World. Unfortunately life is an offensive, directed against the repetitious mechanism of the Universe. It is the thesis of this discussion that a policy of sociological defence is doomed to failure. We are analysing those types of social functioning which provide that expansion and novelty which life demands. Life can only be understood as an aim at that perfection which the conditions of its environment allow. But the aim is always beyond the attained fact. The goal is some type of perfected things, however lowly and basically sensual. Inorganic nature is characterized by its acceptance of matter of fact. In nature the soil rests while the root of the plant pursues the sources of its refreshment. In the Western Empire there was no pursuit. Its remnants of irritability were devoid of transcendent aim.

Of course Christianity was a tremendous exception. But on the whole, in its immediate effect it was a destructive agency. Its disregard of temporal fact, based on apocalyptic prophecy, was too extreme. It was not till its first few centuries were passed that it began to acquire a fortunate worldliness. Indeed the translation of Eastern modes of thought—Semitic, Greek, and Egyptian—to Western Europe had the unfortunate effect of making the ideal side of civilization appear more abstract than it was in the lands and the epochs of its origin. It had this effect in the Near East itself when, by the lapse of time, circumstances altered. For the early Hebrews, their God was a personage whose aims were expressible in terms of the immediate political and social circumstances. Their religious notions had singularly slight reference to another World. The absorption of the Greek philosophers in the city life of their times is evident. But in other times and, still more, in other lands, such thoughts and ideals took on an abstract tinge. They had lost their practical application. The notion arose that the man of culture and the man of ideal aim was a stranger in the busy world. It is true that such a notion haunted Plato. But it dominated Augustine. Yet in Augustine's age, towards the close of the century after Constantine, the mission of the Church for the reformation of this World was in its first phase. The obstinate survival of the present World was upsetting the unworldly tactics of the early Christians.

But the civilization of the Near East, including its Byzantine fringe, contained other sources of vigour, preserving it from the decadence of its Western offshoot. The true successors of Alexander, the men who realized his fabled dream of extending the Near Eastern civilization from the Tigris to the western shores of the Mediterranean, belonged to the age of Justinian and to the age of Mahometan expansion. Justinian's success was incomplete. It was a false dawn. But the Mahometans represent the complete triumph of the Near East, after it had absorbed the novel ingredients introduced by Hellenism and Hebrewism, its two great offshoots destined to re-create civilization. Thus there are two peaks to the Near Eastern Culture. The earlier is embodied in the first known examples of high civilization in Babylon and Egypt. The metaphor of a peak here fails; for this earlier type of life maintained itself for long ages. The advent of the Persians represents a transitional period. They almost antedated the Mahometans. But the times were not ready.

The distinction separating the Byzantines and the Mahometans from the Romans is that the Romans were themselves deriving the civilization which they spread. In their hands it assumed a frozen form. Thought halted, and literature copied. The Byzantines and the Mahometans were themselves the civilization. Thus their culture retained its intrinsic energies, sustained by physical and spiritual adventure. They traded with the Far East; they expanded westward; they codified law; they developed new forms of art; they elaborated theologies; they transformed mathematics; they developed medicine. In this final period of Near Eastern greatness the Jews played the same part as did the Greeks during the Persian epoch. Finally, the Near East as a centre of civilization was destroyed by the Tartars and the Turks.

Luckily for Europe, the more northern thrust of the Tartars across Russia seems to have been checked by the forests of Poland and the more southern hills and mountains. These conquerors of the Near East were never civilized in any effective sense of the term. During the later centuries, the Turkish pressure on Europe constituted merely the threat of Europe produced by a lower civilization, an ingenious compound of primitive brutality and decadent refinement. In the eighteenth and nineteenth centuries much history was written under the impression that the Turks were the authentic representatives of the previous Near Eastern civilization. Thus the early Greeks were staged as its opponents and not as its derivatives. In fact the long pupilage of Europe to the Near East was entirely misrepresented.

At the close of the Dark Ages Europe started upon its second effort after civilization with three main advantages:

E

its Christian ethics ; its instinct for legal organization transcending local boundaries, derived from the Church and the
reminiscence of the Empire ; and thirdly, its wider inheritance
of antecedent thought, gradually disclosing itself as Hebrew,
Greek, and Roman literatures. The total effect was the
increased sense of the dignity of man as man. There has
been a growth, slow and wavering, of respect for the preciousness of human life. This is the humanitarian spirit, gradually
emerging in the slow sunrise of a thousand years.

The creation of the world—said Plato—is the victory of
persuasion over force. The worth of men consists in their
liability to persuasion. They can persuade and can be persuaded by the disclosures of alternatives, the better and the
worse. Civilization is the maintenance of social order, by its
own inherent persuasiveness as embodying the nobler alternative. The recourse to force, however unavoidable, is a disclosure of the failure of civilization, either in the general
society or in a remnant of individuals. Thus in a live civilization there is always an element of unrest. For sensitiveness
to ideas means curiosity, adventure, change. Civilized order
survives on its merits, and is transformed by its power of
recognizing its imperfections.

Now the intercourse between individuals and between
social groups takes one of two forms, force or persuasion.
Commerce is the great example of intercourse in the way of
persuasion. War, slavery, and governmental compulsion
exemplify the reign of force. The weakness of the Near
Eastern civilizations consisted in their large reliance upon
force. The growth of persuasive intercourse within the
texture of society became halted. These civilizations never
eradicated a large reliance upon the sway of conquerors over
conquered populations, and upon the rule of individual
masters over slaves. This habit of dominance spread its
infection beyond these limits. A rule of men over women
remained an established feature of highly civilized societies.
It survived as a hang-over from barbarism. But its demoraliz-

ing effects increased with civilization. This inequality of men and women seems to have been based upon physical superiorities, and the absorption of women in the birth and care of children. Anyhow it issued in the degradation of women below the level of the males. Thus these Eastern races entered upon the fatal experiment of maintaining themselves at two levels of culture, and of dominating subject populations at yet a third level. The enjoyment of power is fatal to the subtleties of life. Ruling classes degenerate by reason of their lazy indulgence in obvious gratifications.

Commerce followed upon the gradual acquirement of means for easy locomotion in small groups. Whole communities had wandered, gradually shifting to other environments. But travel and return, undertaken by small groups or even by individual men is an enterprise of entirely different character. It requires either open country, free from forest barriers, or the navigation of rivers and seas. The strangers arrive in small groups. They are thus under no temptation to dominate, and excite no fear. Commerce may stabilize itself into a steady, traditional routine. This halt in progress has happened over large areas for long periods of time. But on the whole, Commerce is unstable. It brings together groups of men with different modes of life, different technologies, and different ways of thought. Apart from Commerce, the mariner's compass, with the vast theory which it has suggested, would never have reached the shores of the Atlantic, and printing would not have spread from Pekin to Cairo.

The expanding Commerce of mediæval and modern Europe was promoted in the first place by the great roads which were the legacy from the Roman Empire, by the improving art of navigation which enabled the indented coastline to be utilized, and by the sense of unity promoted by the Catholic Church and Christian ethics. There were pirates and feudal wars, and rough sporadic disorder. But men from different regions, of different races, and of different occupations were meeting together on the basis of free persuasion. Even the feudal castle, though it often harboured men with the mentality of gangsters, was more apt for defence than for offence. Also feudal levies, with their short periods of service, were mostly effective as defensive forces. In later times the evils of this system outweighed its merits. But in its origin it can be compared to the modern police, quite as aptly as to the modern army. Of course it differed from both. The point is that the feudal castle was mostly a sensible mode of self-protection for a peaceful district. The merit of Commerce lies in its close relation to technology. The novelty of experience promoted by Commerce suggests alternatives in ways of production. Again European technology was fertilized from another source. The art of clear thinking, of criticism of premises, of speculative assumption, of deductive reasoning —this great art was discovered, at least in embryo, by the Greeks, and was inherited by Europe. Like other inventions, it has often been disastrously misused. But its effect on intellectual capacity can only be compared with that of fire and iron and steel for the production of the blades of Damascus and Toledo. Mankind was now armed intellectually as well as physically.

Curiosity was now progressive. The static wisdom of the proverbs of Solomon and of the Wisdom Books of the Bible, has been supplanted by Euclid's Elements, by Newton's Physics, by the modern epoch in industry. " All the rivers run into the sea ; there is nothing new under the sun ", was the final judgment of the Near East. When we have allowed for all its brilliance and for its many modes of activity, this great civilization finally sank under the barren criticism of disillusioned sensualists. It is the Nemesis of the reign of force, of the worship of power, that the ideals of the semi-divine rulers centre upon some variant of Solomon's magnificent harem of three hundred wives and seven hundred concubines. The variation may be towards decency, but it is equally decadent. Christianity has only escaped from the Near East with scars upon it.

In this rapid survey of the rise and fall of civilizations, we have noted four factors which decisively govern the fate of social groups. First, there stands the inexorable law that, apart from some transcendent aim, the civilized life either wallows in pleasure or relapses slowly into a barren repetition with waning intensities of feeling. Secondly, there stands the iron compulsion of nature that the bodily necessities of food, clothing, and shelter be provided. The rigid limits which are thereby set to modes of social existence can only be mitigated by the growth of an understanding by which the interplay between man and the rest of nature can be adjusted. Thirdly, the compulsory dominion of men over men has a double significance. It has a benign effect so far as it secures the co-ordination of behaviour necessary for social welfare. But it is fatal to extend this dominion beyond the barest limits necessary for this co-ordination. The progressive societies are those which most decisively have trusted themselves to the fourth factor, which is the way of persuasion. Amidst all the activities of mankind there are three which chiefly have promoted this last factor in human life. They are family affections aroused in sex relations and in the nurture of children, intellectual curiosity leading to enjoyment in the interchange of ideas, and—as soon as large-scale societies arose—the practice of Commerce. But beyond these special activities a greater bond of sympathy has arisen. This bond is the growth of reverence for that power in virtue of which nature harbours ideal ends, and produces individual beings capable of conscious discrimination of such ends. This reverence is the foundation of the respect for man as man. It thereby secures that liberty of thought and action required for the upward adventure of life on this Earth.

BOOK II

THE MAKING OF MODERN EUROPE

THE MAKING OF MODERN EUROPE

THE main features of this Western Civilization have been outlined, and we can see it now as the creation of a restless, dynamic, curious, and ambitious spirit, strongly opposed to the static fatalism of the East. We shall see this spirit at work throughout the centuries, at first in Europe, and then in those countries beyond the seas where it found a suitable home. We can trace only its main manifestations, and a suitable starting-point will be the end of the Middle Ages and the rapid and sometimes painful transformation into the era of modern life.

It will be remembered that Western Civilization started on its second attempt to scale the heights equipped with three great advantages. These factors, and especially the first and third, the Christian ethic and the heritage of Greek, Hebrew, and Latin literature played a vital part in the two great movements which completely transformed the face of Europe, and which changed the mediæval into the modern world.

The Renaissance came before the Reformation, but no one can say just when and where either of these movements started. Certain dates stand out, like 1440, which is the approximate date for the invention of printing; or 1453, when the Turks captured Constantinople and sent its scholars fleeing into Europe; or 1517, when Luther nailed his theses to the church door at Wittenberg, but the spirit of change had been active long before these dates, and the movements would have worked themselves out to their fulfilment if Gutenberg and Constantinople and Luther had never existed.

The Renaissance was a rebellion rather than a rebirth, a revolt against the barriers built by authority in every walk of life, in every field of thought. Its name is justified if we think of it as a rebirth of mental energy. Walter Pater has summed it up : " For us the Renaissance is the name of a many-sided but yet united movement, in which the love of the things of the intellect and the imagination for their own sake, the desire for a more liberal and comely way of conceiving life, make themselves felt, urging those who experience this desire to search out first one and then another means of intellectual or imaginative enjoyment, and directing them not only to the discovery of old and forgotten sources of this enjoyment, but to the divination of fresh sources thereof—new experiences, new subjects of poetry, new forms of art ". *Why was this Renaissance like a spiritual springtime?* The answer is given by our greatest British authority on this subject in the following extract from his standard seven-volume *Renaissance in Italy*.

JOHN ADDINGTON SYMONDS

THE SPIRIT OF THE RENAISSANCE

THE word Renaissance has of late years received a more extended significance than that which is implied in our English equivalent—the Revival of Learning. We use it to denote the whole transition from the Middle Ages to the Modern World ; and though it is possible to assign certain limits to the period during which this transition took place, we cannot fix on any dates so positively as to say—between this year and that the movement was accomplished. To do so would be like trying to name the days on which spring in any particular season began and ended. Yet we speak of spring as different from winter and from summer. The truth is, that in many senses we are still in mid-Renaissance. The evolution has not been completed. The new life is our own and is progressive. As in the transformation scene of some great Masque, so here the waning and the waxing shapes are mingled ; the new forms, at first shadowy and filmy, gain upon the old ; and now both blend ; and now the old scene fades into the background ; still, who shall say whether the new scene be finally set up ?

In like manner we cannot refer the whole phenomena of the Renaissance to any one cause or circumstance, or limit them within the field of any one department of human knowledge.

If we ask the students of art what they mean by the Renaissance, they will reply that it was the revolution effected in architecture, painting, and sculpture by the recovery of antique monuments.

Students of literature, philosophy, and theology see in the Renaissance that discovery of manuscripts, that passion for antiquity, that progress in philology and criticism, which led to a correct knowledge of the classics, to a fresh taste in poetry, to new systems of thought, to more accurate analysis, and finally to the Lutheran schism and the emancipation of the conscience.

Men of science will discourse about the discovery of the solar system by Copernicus and Galileo, the anatomy of Vesalius, and Harvey's theory of the circulation of the blood. The origination of a truly scientific method is the point which interests them most in the Renaissance.

The political historian, again, has his own answer to the question. The extinction of feudalism, the development of the great nationalities of Europe, the growth of monarchy, the limitation of the ecclesiastical authority and the erection of the Papacy into an Italian kingdom, and, in the last place, the gradual emergence of that sense of popular freedom which exploded in the Revolution ; these are the aspects of the movement which engross his attention.

Jurists will describe the dissolution of legal fictions based upon the False Decretals, the acquisition of a true text of the Roman Code, and the attempt to introduce a rational method into the theory of modern jurisprudence, as well as to commence the study of international law.

Men whose attention has been turned to the history of discoveries and inventions will relate the exploration of America and the East, or will point to the benefits conferred upon the world by the arts of printing and engraving, by the compass and the telescope, by paper and by gunpowder ; and will insist that at the moment of the Renaissance all these instruments of mechanical utility started into existence to aid the dissolution of what was rotten and must perish, to strengthen and perpetuate the new and useful and life-giving.

Yet neither any one of these answers taken separately, nor indeed all of them together, will offer a solution of the problem. By the term Renaissance, or new birth, is indicated a natural movement, not to be explained by this or that characteristic, but to be accepted as an effort of humanity for which at length the time had come, and in the onward progress of which we still participate. The history of the Renaissance is not the history of arts, or of sciences, or of literature, or even of nations. It is the history of the attainment of self-conscious freedom by the human spirit manifested in the European races. It is no mere political mutation, no new fashion of art, no restoration of classical standards of taste. The arts and the inventions, the knowledge and the books, which suddenly became vital at the time of the Renaissance, had long lain neglected on the shores of the Dead Sea which we call the Middle Ages. It was not their discovery which caused the Renaissance. But it was the intellectual energy, the spontaneous outburst of intelligence, which enabled mankind at that moment to make use of them. The force then generated still continues, vital and expansive, in the spirit of the modern world.

How was it, then, that at a certain period, about fourteen centuries after Christ, to speak roughly, the intellect of the Western races awoke, as it were, from slumber and began once more to be active ? That is a question which we can but imperfectly answer. The mystery of organic life defeats analysis ; whether the subject of our inquiry be a germ-cell, or a phenomenon so complex as the commencement of a new religion, or the origination of a new phase in civilization, it is alike impossible to do more than to state the conditions under which the fresh growth begins, and to point out what are its manifestations. In doing so, moreover, we must be careful not to be carried away by words of our own making. Renaissance, Reformation, and Revolution are not separate things, capable of being isolated ; they are moments in the history of the human race which we find it convenient to name ; while history itself is one and continuous, so that our utmost endeavours to regard some portion of it independently of the rest will be defeated.

A glance at the history of the preceding centuries shows that, after the dissolution of the fabric of the Roman Empire, there was no immediate possibility of any intellectual revival. The barbarous races which had deluged Europe had to absorb their barbarism ; the fragments of Roman civilization had either to be destroyed or assimilated ; the Germanic nations had to receive culture and religion from the people they had superseded ; the Church had to be created, and a new form given to the old idea of the Empire. It was further necessary that the modern nationalities should be defined, that the modern languages should be formed, that peace should be secured to some extent, and wealth accumulated, before the indispensable conditions for a resurrection of the free spirit of humanity could exist.

The first nation which fulfilled these conditions was the first to inaugurate the new era. The reason why Italy took the lead in the Renaissance was, that Italy possessed a language, a favourable climate, political freedom, and commercial prosperity, at a time when other nations were still semi-barbarous. Where the human spirit had been buried in the decay of the Roman Empire, there it arose upon the ruins of that Empire ; and the Papacy, called by Hobbes the ghost of the dead Roman Empire, seated, throned and crowned, upon the ashes thereof, to some extent bridged over the gulf between the two periods.

Keeping steadily in sight the truth that the real quality of the Renaissance was intellectual, that it was the emancipation of the reason for the modern world, we may inquire how feudalism was related to it. The mental condition of the Middle Ages was one of ignorant prostration before the idols of the Church—dogma and authority and scholasticism. Again, the nations of Europe during these centuries were bound down by the brute weight of material necessities. Without the power over the outer world which the physical sciences and useful arts communicate, without the ease of life which wealth and plenty secure, without the traditions of a civilized past, emerging slowly from a state of utter rawness, each nation could barely do more than gain and keep a difficult hold upon existence. To depreciate the work achieved during the Middle Ages would be ridiculous. Yet we may point out that it was done unconsciously—that it was a gradual and instinctive process of becoming. The reason, in one word, was not awake; the mind of man was ignorant of its own treasures and its own capacities. It is pathetic to think of the mediæval students poring over a single ill-translated sentence of Porphyry, endeavouring to extract from its clauses whole systems of logical science, and torturing their brains about puzzles hardly less idle than the dilemma of Buridan's donkey, while all the time, at Constantinople and at Seville, in Greek and Arabic, Plato and Aristotle were alive but sleeping, awaiting only the call of the Renaissance to bid them speak with voice intelligible to the modern mind.

It is no less pathetic to watch tide after tide of the ocean of humanity sweeping from all parts of Europe, to break in passionate but unavailing foam upon the shores of Palestine, whole nations laying life down for the chance of seeing the walls of Jerusalem, worshipping the sepulchre whence Christ had risen, loading their fleet with relics and with cargoes of the sacred earth, while all the time within their breasts and brains the spirit of the Lord was with them, living but un-recognized, the spirit of freedom which ere long was destined to restore its birthright in the world.

Meanwhile the Middle Age accomplished its own work. Slowly and obscurely, amid stupidity and ignorance, were being forged the nations and the languages of Europe. Italy, France, Spain, England, Germany took shape. The actors of the future drama acquired their several characters, and formed the tongues whereby their personalities should be expressed. The qualities which render modern society differ-ent from that of the ancient world were being impressed upon these nations by Christianity, by the Church, by chivalry, by feudal customs.

Then came a further phase. After the nations had been moulded, their monarchies and dynasties were established. Feudalism passed by slow degrees into various forms of more or less defined autocracy. In Italy and Germany numerous principalities sprang into pre-eminence ; and though the nation was not united under one head, the monarchical principle was acknowledged. France and Spain submitted to a despotism, by right of which the king could say, " L'État, c'est moi ". England developed her complicated constitution of popular right and royal prerogative. At the same time the Latin Church underwent a similar process of transformation. The Papacy became more autocratic. Like the king, the pope began to say, " L'Église, c'est moi ".

This merging of the mediæval State and mediæval Church in the personal supremacy of king and pope may be termed the special feature of the last age of feudalism which preceded the Renaissance. It was thus that the necessary conditions and external circumstances were prepared. The organization of the five great nations, and the levelling of political and spiritual interests under political and spiritual despots, formed the prelude to that drama of liberty of which the Renaissance was the first act, the Reformation the second, the Revolution the third, and which we nations of the present are still evolving in the establishment of the democratic idea.

Meanwhile, it must not be imagined that the Renaissance burst suddenly upon the world in the fifteenth century without premonitory symptoms. Far from that : within the Middle Age itself, over and over again, the reason strove to break loose from its fetters. Abelard, in the twelfth century, tried to prove that the interminable dispute about entities and words was founded on a misapprehension. Roger Bacon, at the beginning of the thirteenth century, anticipated modern science, and proclaimed that man, by use of nature, can do all things. Joachim of Flora, intermediate between the two, drank one drop of the cup of prophecy offered to his lips, and cried that " the Gospel of the Father was past, the Gospel of the Son was passing, the Gospel of the Spirit was to be ". These three men, each in his own way, the Frenchman as a logician, the Englishman as an analyst, the Italian as a mystic, divined the future but inevitable emancipation of the reason of mankind.

Nor were there wanting signs, especially in Provence, that Aphrodite and Phœbus and the Graces were ready to resume their sway. The premature civilization of that favoured region, so cruelly extinguished by the Church, was itself a reaction of nature against the restrictions imposed by ecclesiastical discipline ; while the songs of the wandering students, known under the title of *Carmina Burana*, indicate a revival of Pagan or pre-Christian feeling in the very stronghold of mediæval learning.

We have, moreover, to remember the Cathari, the Paterini, the Fraticelli, the Albigenses, the Hussites—heretics in whom the new light dimly shone, but who were instantly exterminated by the Church. We have to commemorate the vast conception of the Emperor Frederick II, who strove to found a new society of humane culture in the south of Europe, and to anticipate the advent of the spirit of modern tolerance. He, too, and all his race were exterminated by the Papal jealousy. Truly we may say with Michelet that the Sibyl of the Renaissance kept offering her books in vain to feudal Europe. In vain because the time was not yet. The ideas projected thus early on the modern world were immature and abortive, like those headless trunks and zoophitic members of half-moulded humanity which, in the vision of Empedocles, preceded the birth of full-formed man. The nations were not ready. Franciscans imprisoning Roger Bacon for venturing to examine what God had meant to keep secret ; Dominicans preaching crusades against the cultivated nobles of Toulouse ; popes stamping out the seed of enlightened Frederick ; Benedictines erasing the masterpieces of classical literature to make way for their own litanies and lurries, or selling pieces of the parchment for charms ; a laity devoted by superstition to saints and by sorcery to the devil ; a clergy sunk in sensual sloth or fevered with demoniac zeal : these still ruled the intellectual destinies of Europe. Therefore the first anticipations of the Renaissance were fragmentary and sterile.

Then came a second period. Dante's poem, a work of conscious art, conceived in a modern spirit and written in a modern tongue, was the first true sign that Italy, the leader of the nations of the West, had shaken off her sleep. Petrarch followed. His ideal of antique culture as the everlasting solace and the universal education of the human race, his lifelong effort to recover the classical harmony of thought and speech, gave a direct impulse to one of the chief movements of the Renaissance—its passionate outgoing toward the ancient world. After Petrarch, Boccaccio opened yet another channel for the stream of freedom. His conception of human existence as joy to be accepted with thanksgiving, not as a gloomy error to be rectified by suffering, familiarized the fourteenth century with that form of semi-pagan gladness which marked the real Renaissance.

In Dante, Petrarch, and Boccaccio Italy recovered the consciousness of intellectual liberty. What we call the Renaissance had not yet arrived; but their achievement rendered its appearance in due season certain. With Dante the genius of the modern world dared to stand alone and to create confidently after its own fashion. With Petrarch the same genius reached forth across the gulf of darkness, resuming the tradition of a splendid past. With Boccaccio the same genius proclaimed the beauty of the world, the goodliness of youth and strength and love and life, unterrified by hell, unappalled by the shadow of impending death.

It was now, at the beginning of the fourteenth century, when Italy had lost indeed the heroic spirit which we admire in her Communes of the thirteenth, but had gained instead ease, wealth, magnificence, and that repose which springs from long prosperity, that the new age at last began. Europe was, as it were, a fallow field, beneath which lay buried the civilization of the old world. Behind stretched the centuries of mediævalism, intellectually barren and inert. Of the future there were as yet but faint foreshadowings.

Meanwhile, the force of the nations who were destined to

F

achieve the coming transformation was unexhausted; their physical and mental faculties were unimpaired. No ages of enervating luxury, of intellectual endeavour, of life artificially preserved or ingeniously prolonged, had sapped the fibre of the men who were about to inaugurate the modern world. Severely nurtured, unused to delicate living, these giants of the Renaissance were like boys in their capacity for endurance, their inordinate appetite for enjoyment. No generations, hungry, sickly, effete, critical, disillusioned, trod them down. Ennui and the fatigue that springs from scepticism, the despair of thwarted effort, were unknown. Their fresh and unperverted senses rendered them keenly alive to what was beautiful and natural. They yearned for magnificence, and instinctively comprehended splendour. At the same time the period of satiety was still far off. Everything seemed possible to their young energy; nor had a single pleasure palled upon their appetite. Born, as it were, at the moment when desires and faculties are evenly balanced, when the perceptions are not blunted nor the senses cloyed, opening their eyes for the first time on a world of wonder, these men of the Renaissance enjoyed what we may term the first transcendent springtide of the modern world. Nothing is more remarkable than the fullness of the life that throbbed in them. Natures rich in all capacities and endowed with every kind of sensibility were frequent. Nor was there any limit to the play of personality in action. We may apply to them what Browning has written of Sordello's temperament:

> " A footfall there
> Suffices to upturn to the warm air
> Half germinating spices, mere decay
> Produces richer life, and day by day
> New pollen on the lily-petal grows,
> And still more labyrinthine buds the rose."

During the Middle Ages man had lived enveloped in a cowl. He had not seen the beauty of the world, or had seen it only to cross himself, and turn aside and tell his beads and pray. Like St. Bernard travelling along the shores of the Lake Leman, and noticing neither the azure of the waters, nor the luxuriance of the vines, nor the radiance of the mountains with their robe of sun and snow, but bending a thought-burdened forehead over the neck of his mule ; even like this monk, humanity had passed, a careful pilgrim, intent on the terrors of sin, death, and judgment, along the highways of the world, and had scarcely known that they were sightworthy or that life is a blessing. Beauty is a snare, pleasure a sin, the world a fleeting show, man fallen and lost, death the only certainty, judgment inevitable, hell everlasting, heaven hard to win ; ignorance is acceptable to God as a proof of faith and submission ; abstinence and mortification are the only safe rules of life : these were the fixed ideas of the ascetic mediæval Church. The Renaissance shattered and destroyed them, rending the thick veil which they had drawn between the mind of man and the outer world, and flashing the light of reality upon the darkened places of his own nature. For the mystic teaching of the Church was substituted culture in the classical humanities ; a new ideal was established, whereby man strove to make himself the monarch of the globe on which it is his privilege as well as destiny to live. The Renaissance was the liberation of the reason from a dungeon, the double discovery of the outer and the inner world.

" During the Middle Ages man had lived enveloped in a cowl." In that graphic sentence Symonds crystallized the narrowness of mediæval life, but the cowl served for protection as well as blinkers. *What were the powers, the influence, and the privileges of the mediæval Church ?* J. A. Froude, the eminent historian of the fifteen and sixteenth centuries, will answer this question in the following extracts from the first of a series of lectures which he gave at Newcastle on " The Times of Erasmus and Luther ".

JAMES ANTHONY FROUDE

THE CHURCH IN THE MIDDLE AGES

THERE was a time—a time which, measured by the
years of our national life was not so very long ago—when
the serious thoughts of mankind were occupied exclusively by
religion and politics. The small knowledge which they possessed of other things was tinctured by their speculative
opinions on the relations of heaven and earth ; and, down to
the sixteenth century, art, science, scarcely even literature,
existed in this country, except as, in some way or other,
subordinate to theology. Philosophers—such philosophers as
there were—obtained and half deserved the reputation of
quacks and conjurers. Astronomy was confused with astrology.
The physician's medicines were supposed to be powerless,
unless the priests said prayers over them. The great lawyers,
the ambassadors, the chief ministers of state, were generally
bishops ; even the fighting business was not entirely secular.
Half a dozen Scotch prelates were killed at Flodden ; and,
late in the reign of Henry the Eighth, no fitter person could
be found than Rowland Lee, Bishop of Coventry, to take
command of the Welsh Marches, and harry the freebooters
of Llangollen.

Every single department of intellectual or practical life
was penetrated with the beliefs, or was interwoven with the
interest, of the clergy ; and thus it was that, when differences
of religious opinion arose, they split society to its foundations.
The lines of cleavage penetrated everywhere, and there were
no subjects whatever in which those who disagreed in theology
possessed any common concern. When men quarrelled, they
quarrelled altogether. The disturbers of settled beliefs were
regarded as public enemies who had placed themselves beyond
the pale of humanity, and were considered fit only to be
destroyed like wild beasts, or trampled out like the seed of a
contagion.

Centuries have passed over our heads since the time of

which I am speaking, and the world is so changed that we can hardly recognize it as the same.

The secrets of nature have been opened out to us on a thousand lines ; and men of science of all creeds can pursue side by side their common investigations. Catholics, Anglicans, Presbyterians, Lutherans, Calvinists, contend with each other in honourable rivalry in arts, and literature, and commerce, and industry. They read the same books. They study at the same academies. They have seats in the same senates. They preside together on the judicial bench, and carry on, without jar or difference, the ordinary business of the country.

Those who share the same pursuits are drawn in spite of themselves into sympathy and good-will. When they are in harmony in so large a part of their occupations, the points of remaining difference lose their venom. Those who thought they hated each other, unconsciously find themselves friends; and as far as it affects the world at large, the acrimony of controversy has almost disappeared. . . .

Controversy has kept alive a certain quantity of bitterness ; and that, I suspect, is all that it would accomplish if it continued till the day of judgment. I sometimes, in impatient moments, wish the laity in Europe would treat their controversial divines as two gentlemen once treated their seconds, when they found themselves forced into a duel without knowing what they were quarrelling about.

As the principals were being led up to their places, one of them whispered to the other, " If you will shoot your second, I will shoot mine." . . .

If you ask me why I have chosen this subject for my lectures, I fear that I shall give you rather a lame answer. I might say that I know more about the history of the sixteenth century than I know about anything else. I have spent the best years of my life in reading and writing about it ; and if I have anything to tell you worth your hearing, it is probably on that subject.

Or, again, I might say—which is indeed most true—that to

the Reformation we can trace, indirectly, the best of those very influences which I have been describing. The Reformation broke the theological shackles in which men's minds were fettered. It set them thinking, and so gave birth to science. The Reformers also, without knowing what they were about, taught the lesson of religious toleration. They attempted to supersede one set of dogmas by another. They succeeded with half the world—they failed with the other half. In a little while it became apparent that good men—without ceasing to be good—could think differently about theology, and that goodness, therefore, depended on something else than the holding of orthodox opinions.

It is not, however, for either of these reasons that I am going to talk to you about Martin Luther ; nor is toleration of differences of opinion, however excellent it be, the point on which I shall dwell in these Lectures.

Were the Reformation a question merely of opinion, I for one should not have meddled with it, either here or anywhere. I hold that, on the obscure mysteries of faith, every one should be allowed to believe according to his conscience, and that arguments on such matters are either impertinent or useless.

But the Reformation, gentlemen, beyond the region of opinions, was an historical fact—an objective something which may be studied like any of the facts of nature. The Reformers were men of note and distinction, who played a great part for good or evil on the stage of the world. If we except the Apostles, no body of human beings ever printed so deep a mark into the organization of society ; and if there be any value or meaning in history at all, the lives, the actions, the characters of such men as these can be matters of indifference to none of us.

We have not to do with a story which is buried in obscure antiquity. The facts admit of being learnt. The truth, what-ever it was, concerns us all equally. If the divisions created by that great convulsion are ever to be obliterated, it will be when we have learnt, each of us, to see the thing as it really was, and not rather some mythical or imaginative version of the thing—such as from our own point of view we like to think it was. Fiction in such matters may be convenient for our immediate theories, but it is certain to avenge itself in the end. We may make our own opinions, but facts were made for us; and if we evade or deny them, it will be the worse for us. . . .

One caution, however, I must in fairness give you before we proceed further. It lies upon the face of the story, that the Reformers imperfectly understood toleration; but you must keep before you the spirit and temper of the men with whom they had to deal. For themselves, when the movement began, they aimed at nothing but liberty to think and speak their own way. They never dreamt of interfering with others, although they were quite aware that others, when they could, were likely to interfere with them. . . .

Never in all their history, in ancient times or modern, never that we know of, have mankind thrown out of themselves anything so grand, so useful, so beautiful, as the Catholic Church once was. In these times of ours, well-regulated selfishness is the recognized rule of action—every one of us is expected to look out first for himself, and take care of his own interests. At the time I speak of, the Church ruled the State with the authority of a conscience; and self-interest, as a motive of action, was only named to be abhorred. The bishops and clergy were regarded freely and simply as the immediate ministers of the Almighty; and they seem to me to have really deserved that high estimate of their character. It was not for the doctrines which they taught, only or chiefly, that they were held in honour. Brave men do not fall down before their fellow-mortals for the words which they speak, or for the rites which they perform. Wisdom, justice, self-denial, nobleness, purity, high-mindedness—these are the qualities before which the free-born races of Europe have been contented to bow; and in no order of men were such qualities to be found as they were found seven hundred years ago in the clergy of the Catholic Church. They called themselves the successors of the Apostles. They claimed in their Master's name universal spiritual authority, but they made good their pretensions by the holiness of their own lives. They were allowed to rule because they deserved to rule, and in the fullness of reverence kings and nobles bent before a power which was nearer to God than their own. Over prince and subject, chieftain and serf, a body of unarmed defenceless men reigned supreme by the magic of sanctity. They tamed the fiery northern warriors who had broken in pieces the Roman Empire. They taught them—they brought them really and truly to believe—that they had immortal souls, and that they would one day stand at the aweful judgment bar and give account for their lives there. With the brave, the honest, and the good—with those who had not oppressed the poor nor removed their neighbour's landmark—with those who had been just in all their dealings—with those who had fought against evil, and had tried valiantly to do their Master's will—at that great day it would be well. For cowards, for profligates, for those who lived for luxury and pleasure and self-indulgence, there was the blackness of eternal death.

An awful conviction of this tremendous kind the clergy had effectually instilled into the mind of Europe. It was not a PERHAPS ; it was a certainty. It was not a form of words repeated once a week at church ; it was an assurance entertained on all days and in all places, without any particle of doubt. And the effect of such a belief on life and conscience was simply immeasurable.

I do not pretend that the clergy were perfect. They were very far from perfect at the best of times, and the European nations were never completely submissive to them. It would not have been well if they had been. The business of human creatures in this planet is not summed up in the most excellent of priestly catechisms. The world and its concerns continued to interest men, though priests insisted on their nothingness.

They could not prevent kings from quarrelling with each other. They could not hinder disputed successions, and civil wars, and political conspiracies. What they did do was to shelter the weak from the strong. In the eyes of the clergy, the serf and his lord stood on the common level of sinful humanity. Into their ranks high birth was no passport. They were themselves for the most part children of the people ; and the son of the artisan or peasant rose to the mitre and the triple crown, just as nowadays the rail-splitter and the tailor become Presidents of the Republic of the West.

The Church was essentially democratic, while at the same time it had the monopoly of learning ; and all the secular power fell to it which learning, combined with sanctity and assisted by superstition, can bestow.

The privileges of the clergy were extraordinary. They were not amenable to the common laws of the land. While they governed the laity, the laity had no power over them. From the throne downwards every secular office was dependent on the Church. No king was a lawful sovereign till the Church placed the crown upon his head : and what the Church bestowed, the Church claimed the right to take away. The disposition of property was in their hands. No will could be proved except before the bishop or his officer ; and no will was held valid if the testator died out of communion. There were magistrates and courts of law for the offences of the laity. If a priest committed a crime, he was a sacred person. The civil power could not touch him ; he was reserved for his ordinary. Bishops' commissaries sate in town and city, taking cognizance of the moral conduct of every man and woman. Offences against life and property were tried here in England, as now, by the common law ; but the Church Court dealt with sins—sins of word or act. If a man was a profligate or a drunkard ; if he lied or swore ; if he did not come to communion, or held unlawful opinions ; if he was idle or unthrifty ; if he was unkind to his wife or his servants ; if a child was disobedient to his father, or a father cruel to his child ; if a tradesman sold adulterated wares, or used false measures or dishonest weights—the eye of the parish priest was everywhere, and the Church Court stood always open to examine and to punish.

Imagine what a tremendous power this must have been ! Yet it existed generally in Catholic Europe down to the eve of the Reformation. It could never have established itself at all unless at one time it had worked beneficially—as the abuse of it was one of the most fatal causes of the Church's fall.

I know nothing in English history much more striking than the answer given by Archbishop Warham to the complaints of the English House of Commons after the fall of Cardinal Wolsey. The House of Commons complained that the clergy made laws in Convocation which the laity were excommunicated if they disobeyed. Yet the laws made by the clergy, the Commons said, were often at variance with the laws of the realm.

What did Warham reply ? He said he was sorry for the alleged discrepancy ; but, inasmuch as the laws made by the clergy were always in conformity with the will of God, the laws of the realm had only to be altered and then the difficulty would vanish.

What must have been the position of the clergy in the fullness of their power, when they could speak thus on the eve of their prostration ? You have only to look from a distance at any old-fashioned cathedral city, and you will see in a moment the mediæval relations between Church and State. The cathedral *is* the city. The first object you catch sight of as you approach is the spire tapering into the sky, or the huge towers holding possession of the centre of the landscape —majestically beautiful—imposing by mere size amidst the large forms of Nature herself. As you go nearer, the vastness of the building impresses you more and more. The puny dwelling-places of the citizens creep at its feet, the pinnacles are glittering in the tints of the sunset, when down below among the streets and lanes the twilight is darkening. And, even now, when the towns are thrice their ancient size, and the houses have stretched upwards from two storeys to five ; when the great chimneys are vomiting their smoke among the clouds, and the temples of modern industry—the workshops and the factories—spread their long fronts before the eye, the cathedral is still the governing form in the picture—the one object which possesses the imagination and refuses to be eclipsed.

As that cathedral was to the old town, so was the Church of the Middle Ages to the secular institutions of the world. Its very neighbourhood was sacred ; and its shadow, like the shadow of the Apostles, was a sanctuary. When I look at the new Houses of Parliament in London, I see in them a type of the change which has passed over us. The House of Commons of the Plantagenets sate in the Chapter House of Westminster Abbey. The Parliament of the Reform Bill, in 1832, debated in St. Stephen's Chapel, the Abbey's small dependency. Now, by the side of the enormous pile which has risen out of that chapel's ashes, the proud Minster itself is dwarfed into insignificance.

Let us turn to another vast feature of the Middle Ages—I mean the monasteries. . . .

These houses became centres of pious beneficence. The monks, as the brotherhoods were called, were organized in different orders, with some variety of rule, but the broad principle was the same in all. They were to live for others, not for themselves. They took vows of poverty, that they might not be entangled in the pursuit of money. They took vows of chastity, that the care of a family might not distract them from the work which they had undertaken. Their efforts of charity were not limited to this world. Their days were spent in hard bodily labour, in study, or in visiting the sick. At night they were on the stone floors of their chapels, holding up their withered hands to heaven, interceding for the poor souls who were suffering in purgatory.

The world, as it always will, paid honour to exceptional

excellence. The system spread to the farthest limits of Christendom. The religious houses became places of refuge, where men of noble birth, kings and queens and emperors, warriors and statesmen, retired to lay down their splendid cares, and end their days in peace. Those with whom the world had dealt hardly, or those whom it had surfeited with its unsatisfying pleasures, those who were disappointed with earth, and those who were filled with passionate aspirations after heaven, alike found a haven of rest in the quiet cloister. And, gradually, lands came to them, and wealth, and social dignity—all gratefully extended to men who deserved so well of their fellows ; while no landlords were more popular than they, for the sanctity of the monks sheltered their dependents as well as themselves. . . .

Of authority, the religious orders were practically independent. They were amenable only to the Pope and to their own superiors. Here in England, the king could not send a commissioner to inspect a monastery, nor even send a policeman to arrest a criminal who had taken shelter within its walls. Archbishops and bishops, powerful as they were, found their authority cease when they entered the gates of a Benedictine or Dominican abbey. . . .

So the Church was in its vigour : so the Church was *not* at the opening of the sixteenth century. Power—wealth—security—men are more than mortal if they can resist the temptations to which too much of these expose them. . . .

The powers which had been given to the clergy required for their exercise the highest wisdom and the highest probity. They had fallen at last into the hands of men who possessed considerably less of these qualities than the laity whom they undertook to govern. They had degraded their conceptions of God ; and, as a necessary consequence, they had degraded their conceptions of man and man's duty. The aspirations after sanctity had disappeared, and instead of them there remained the practical reality of the five senses. The high prelates, the cardinals, the great abbots, were occupied chiefly in maintaining their splendour and luxury. The friars and the secular clergy, following their superiors with shorter steps, indulged themselves in grosser pleasures ; while their spiritual powers, their supposed authority in this world and the next, were turned to account to obtain from the laity the means for their self-indulgence. . . .

I do not think that, in its main features, the truth of this sketch can be impugned ; and if it be just even in outline, then a reformation of some kind or other was overwhelmingly necessary. Corruption beyond a certain point becomes unendurable to the coarsest nostril. The constitution of human things cannot away with it.

Something was to be done ; but what, or how ? There were three possible courses.

Either the ancient discipline of the Church might be restored by the heads of the Church themselves.

Or, secondly, a higher tone of feeling might gradually be introduced among clergy and laity alike, by education and literary culture. The discovery of the printing press had made possible a diffusion of knowledge which had been unattainable in earlier ages. The ecclesiastical constitution, like a sick human body, might recover its tone if a better diet were prepared for it.

Or, lastly, the common sense of the laity might take the matter at once into their own hands, and make free use of the pruning knife and the sweeping brush. There might be much partial injustice, much violence, much wrong-headedness ; but the people would, at any rate, go direct to the point, and the question was whether any other remedy would serve.

The first of these alternatives may at once be dismissed. The heads of the Church were the last persons in the world to discover that anything was wrong. People of that sort always are. For them the thing as it existed answered excellently well. They had boundless wealth, and all but boundless power. What could they ask for more ? No monk drowsing over his wine-pot was less disturbed by anxiety than nine out of ten of the high dignitaries who were living on the eve of the Judgment Day, and believed that their seat was established for them for ever.

Froude has shown how urgent was the need for reform in the mediæval Church, and he has summarily dismissed the possibility of such reform being brought about by any action of the heads of the Church. But there were people in the fifteenth century who hoped for this. They listened eagerly to men like Savonarola. *How did Savonarola wish to reform the Church?* Below is an example of his colourful oratory, and his vigorous denunciations of the prevalent abuses. He had no desire to reform the doctrine ; he was no scholar like Erasmus. He wished only to purify both Church and State. He warned the people of the wrath to come ; his influence rapidly grew, and when the Medici were driven out of Florence he became supreme. He built a bonfire of vanities : pictures, silken dresses, lace, musical instruments, Boccaccio's *Tales* and Petrarch's *Songs and Sonnets* were burnt to ashes. But fasts and chants instead of feasts and songs could not last for ever in Florence. Savonarola tried the people too hard ; his popularity and his power rapidly waned. The Pope, too, could scarcely regard with favour what was taking place. He called on Savonarola to stop his preaching and his attacks on the Church. Savonarola refused, and he was promptly excommunicated. His doom was rapidly approaching, but, as may be gathered from his sermon, he faced it boldly. Brought to trial in 1498 as an impostor and heretic, he was condemned and hanged ; and his body was burnt not far from where his own bonfire of vanities had been lit.

SAVONAROLA

A PLEA FOR REFORMATION IN THE CHURCH

THE earth teems with bloodshed, yet the priests take no heed, rather by their evil example they bring spiritual death upon all. They have withdrawn from God, and their piety consists in spending their nights in debauchery, and all their days in chattering with choirs ; and the altar is made a place of traffic for the clergy. They say that God hath no care of the world, that all cometh by chance, neither believe they that Christ is present in the sacrament. . . .

Come here thou ribald Church. The Lord saith : I gave the beautiful vestments, but thou hast made idols of them. Thou hast dedicated the sacred vessels to vainglory, the sacraments to simony ; thou hast become a shameless harlot in thy lusts ; thou art lower than a beast, thou art a monster of abomination. Once thou felt shame for thy sins, but now thou art shameless. Once anointed priests called their sons nephews, but now they speak no more of their nephews, but always and everywhere of their sons. Everywhere hast thou made a public place and raised a house of ill-fame.

And what doeth the harlot ? She sitteth on the throne of Solomon, and soliciteth all the world : he that hath gold is made welcome and may do as he will ; but he that seeketh to do good is driven forth. O Lord, my Lord, they will allow no good to be done ! And thus, O prostitute Church, thou hast displayed thy foulness to the whole world. Thou hast multiplied thy fornications in Italy, in France, in Spain, and all other parts. Behold, I will put forth My hand, saith the Lord, I will smite thee, thou infamous wretch ; My sword shall fall on thy children, on thy house of shame, on thy harlots, on thy palaces, and My justice shall be made known. Earth and heaven, the angels, the good and the wicked, all shall accuse thee, and no man shall be with thee ; I will give thee into thy enemy's hand. . . .

O priests and friars, ye whose evil example hath entombed this people in the sepulchre of ceremonial, I tell ye this sepulchre shall be burst asunder, for Christ will revive His Church in His spirit. Think ye that St. Francis, St. Dominic, and the other saints have forgotten their creed and no longer intercede for it ? We must all pray for its renovation.

Write to France and to Germany ; write everywhere to this effect : That Friar ye wot of bids ye all seek the Lord and implore His coming. Haste ye at full speed, O ye messengers !

Think ye that we alone are good ? That there be no servants of God in other places ? Jesus Christ hath many servants, and great numbers of them, concealed in Germany, France, and Spain, are now bewailing this evil. In all cities and strong places, in all manors and convents, there be some inspired with this fire of zeal. They send to whisper somewhat in my ear, and I reply : " Remain concealed until ye hear the summons— *Lazare, veni foras !* " [Lazarus, come forth !] I am here, because the Lord appointed me to this place, and I await His call, but then will I send forth a mighty cry that shall resound throughout Christendom, and make the corpse of the Church to tremble even as trembled the body of Lazarus at the voice of our Lord.

Many of ye say that excommunications will be decreed but I repeat to ye that more than excommunication is intended. For my part I beseech Thee, O Lord, that it may come quickly. What, hast thou no fear ? Not I, for they seek to excommunicate me, because I do no evil. Bear this excommunication aloft on a lance and open the gates to it. I will reply unto it, and if I do not amaze thee, then thou mayst say what thou wilt. I shall make so many faces turn pale, that they will seem to thee a multitude ; and I will send forth a shout that will cause the world to tremble and shake. I know well that there be one, Rome, that striveth against me without cease. But that man is not moved by religious zeal, but only hateth me because he is ever crawling after great lords and potentates. Others say : the Friar hath yielded, he hath sent one of his friends to Rome. I can tell thee that folks there hold not these views ; and that if I wished to play the part of a flatterer, I should not now be in Florence, nor clad in a tattered robe ; and would be able to escape my present danger. But I seek none of these things, O Lord, I seek only Thy Cross : let me be persecuted, I ask this grace of Thee. Let me not die in my bed, but let me give my blood for Thee, even as Thou gavest Thine for me. . . . Meanwhile doubt not, my children, for the Lord will certainly lend us His aid.

Apparently there was little hope at that time of any reforming of the Church from the top, although this did occur later on in the Counter-Reformation. How might the second of Froude's three possible ways have fared? *Could education and literary culture have cured the ills of the Church?* Erasmus, who was probably the greatest intellect of his age, thought they could. Erasmus was a child of the Renaissance. He taught himself Greek when a knowledge of Greek was more rare in Europe than a knowledge of Chinese is to-day. He moved about in restless fashion from one centre of learning to another in the Low Countries, France, England, Switzerland, and Italy, always seeking knowledge, writing his *Colloquies*, his pamphlets, and his books, and those letters which princes and scholars sought so eagerly, and treasured so highly. He printed an edition of the New Testament in Greek, together with his own critical notes and a translation into Latin. This, and similar editions of the early Christian Fathers were eagerly devoured by all thinkers, both clerical and lay. But, while Erasmus delighted in knowledge, he was still more urgent that it should be put to its proper use—to unite rather than to separate men. The following extracts from his letters will show how earnestly he pleaded for toleration in an age when toleration was most often regarded as a criminal weakness. As Drummond said: "From the beginning to the end of his career he remained true to the purpose of his life, which was to fight the battle of sound learning and plain common sense against the powers of ignorance and superstition". Some 3000 of his letters have been preserved, and a most valuable light they throw on the history of his times. Here are two or three of them which show us the man, and his dominant ideas.

ERASMUS

PLEAS FOR A RATIONAL RELIGION

1. From a letter to Colet, Dean of St. Paul's, written in 1505.

I AM rushing at full speed into sacred literature, and look at nothing which keeps me back from it. Fortune wears her old face and is still a difficulty. I hope now that I have returned to France to put my affairs on a slightly better footing. This done, I shall sit down to Holy Scripture with my whole heart, and devote the rest of my life to it. Three

G

years ago I wrote something on the Epistle to the Romans.
I finished four sheets at a burst, and I should have gone on
had I been able. Want of knowledge of Greek kept me back,
but for all these three years I have been working entirely at
Greek, and have not been playing with it. I have begun
Hebrew too, but make small progress owing to the difficulty
of the construction. I am not so young as I was, besides.

I have also read a great part of Origen, who opens out new
fountains of thought and furnishes a complete key to theology.
I send you a small composition of my own on a subject over
which we argued when I was in England. It is so changed
you would not know it again. I did not write to show off my
knowledge. It is directed against the notion that religion
consists of ceremonies and a worse than Jewish ritual.

2. To Fabricius Capito at Basle, written in 1517, following the publication of Erasmus's New Testament, dedicated to the Pope Leo X
and graciously accepted by him.

I am now fifty-one years old, and may be expected to feel
that I have lasted long enough. I am not enamoured of life,
but it is worth while to continue a little longer with such a prospect of a golden age. Learning is springing up all round out
of the soil; languages, physics, mathematics, each department
thriving. Even theology is showing signs of improvement.
Theology, so far, has been cultivated only by avowed enemies
of knowledge. The pretence has been to protect the minds of
the laity from disturbance. All looks brighter now. Three
languages are publicly taught in the schools. The most learned
and least malicious of the theologians themselves lend their
hand to the work. I myself, insignificant I, have contributed
something. I have at least stirred the bile of those who would
not have the world grow wiser, and only fools now snarl at me.

But the clouds are passing away. My share in the work
must be near finished. But you are young and strong ; you
have the first pulpit in Basle ; your name is without spot—
no one dares to reflect upon Fabricius ; you are prudent, too,

and know when to be silent ; you have yourself experienced the disorder, and understand the treatment of it. I do not want the popular theology to be abolished. I want it enriched and enlarged from earlier sources. When the theologians know more of Holy Scripture they will find their consequence undiminished, perhaps increased. All promises well, so far as I see. My chief fear is that with the revival of Greek literature there may be a revival of paganism. There are Christians who are Christians only in name, and are Gentiles at heart ; and, again, the study of Hebrew may lead to Judaism, which would be worse still. I wish there could be an end of scholastic subtleties, or, if not an end, that they could be thrust into a second place, and Christ be taught plainly and simply. The reading of the Bible and the early Fathers will have this effect. Doctrines are taught now which have no affinity with Christ and only darken our eyes.

3. To Cardinal Albert, previously Archbishop of Mayence, written in 1519 at the height of the quarrel between Luther and the papal authorities.

Propositions taken out of Luther's writings have been condemned as heretical which are found in Bernard or Augustine, and from them are received as orthodox and edifying. I warned these Doctors at the beginning to be careful what they were about. I advised them not to clamour to the multitude, but to confine themselves to writing and argument, and above all to censure nothing publicly till they were sure that they had considered and understood it. I said it was indecorous for grave theologians to storm and rage at a person whose private life was admitted to be innocent. I said that topics like secret confession ought not to be declaimed upon before mixed audiences, where there would be many persons present who felt so strongly about it. I supposed I was speaking sense to them, but it only made them more furious. They insisted that I had prompted Luther, and that his work had been conceived and brought forth at Louvain. They stirred such a tragedy as I have never witnessed the like of.

The business of theologians is to teach the truth. These people have nothing in their mouths but violence and punishment. Augustine would not have the worst felon put to death till an effort had been made to mend him. The Louvain theologians may call themselves meek, but they are thirsting for human blood, and demand that Luther shall be arrested and executed. If they wish to deserve to be called divines, let them convert Jews, let them mend the morals of Christendom, which are worse than Turkish. How can it be right to drag a man to the scaffold who has done no more than what the theological schools themselves have always permitted? He has proposed certain subjects for discussion. He is willing to be convinced. He offers to submit to Rome or to leave his cause to be judged by the Universities. Is this a reason for handing him over to the executioners? I am not surprised that he will not trust himself to the judgment of men who would rather find him guilty than innocent. How have all these disturbances risen? The world is choked with opinions which are but human after all, with institutions and scholastic dogmas, and the despotism of the mendicant friars, who are but satellites of the Holy See, yet have become so numerous and so powerful as to be formidable to secular princes and to the Popes themselves. . . . Of course it is an offence to corrupt the truth, but everything need not be made an article of faith. The champions of orthodoxy should have no taint on them of ambition, or malice, or revenge. . . . The less your Eminence listens to such advisers as the monks, the better it will be for your peace.

4. To Conrad Peutinger, Councillor of the Empire, following a conference of men of moderate views summoned by the Council of the Empire to meet at Cologne to discuss the case of Luther. The date is November 9, 1520, a few months before the Diet at Worms.

We have been consulting how this tornado can be quieted. If not wisely handled it may wreck the Christian religion itself.

Fearful consequences have come of lighter causes, and for myself I think, like Cicero, that a bad peace is better than the justest war. The quarrel has gone deeper than I like. It is not yet past cure, but the wound must be so healed that it shall not break out again. Strong measures are wanted. The Pope's authority as Christ's Vicar must be upheld, but in upholding it Gospel truth must not be sacrificed. Leo, I believe, thinks on this as we do.

The question is not what Luther deserves, but what is best for the peace of the world. The persons who are to prosecute, the remedies which are to be applied, must be carefully chosen. Some are for violence, not to defend the Pope, but to keep out light, and in destroying Luther to destroy knowledge along with him. The true cause of all this passion is hatred of learning, and it is on this account that many persons now support Luther who would otherwise leave him. The contagion, we think, has spread far, and the German nation will be dangerous if provoked to active resistance. Force never answers in such cases, and other means must be found.

The reports of the state of morals at Rome have caused vast numbers of men to dislike and even abhor it. On both sides there has been want of discretion. If every word had been true which Luther has said, he has so said it as to grudge truth the victory. If his opponents' case had been the best possible they would have spoilt it by their wrongheadedness. Luther was advised to be more moderate. He wrote more passionately every day. His prosecutors were cautioned too, but they continued so savage that they might have seemed in collusion with him. They are of the sort that fatten on the world's misfortunes and delight in confusion. No good can come till private interests are laid aside. Human devices will come to nought.

It is not for me to judge the Pope's sentence. Some regret the tone of the Bull, but impute it to his advisers, not to himself. The fear is that, if Luther's books are burnt and Luther executed, things will only grow worse. If he is removed others will take his place, and there will first be war and then a schism. Luther's conduct and the causes which led to it ought to be referred to a small committee of good learned men who will be above suspicion. The Pope need not be bound to bow to their authority. It is rather thought that this is the course which he would himself prefer as promising best for peace. Our hopes are in the approaching Diet.

This Luther has pushed our Erasmus out of the limelight, and we must go back a little to see how he has so suddenly become so important. *How far did Luther speak for his age ?* For the answer to this question, and for a most lively account of the events leading up to his trial for heresy we turn again to Froude's lectures, adding a paragraph from one given at Oxford to extracts from the second given at Newcastle.

JAMES ANTHONY FROUDE

LUTHER'S APPEAL TO CONSCIENCE

SIXTEEN years after the birth of Erasmus, therefore in the year 1483, Martin Luther came into the world in a peasant's cottage, at Eisleben, in Saxony. By peasant, you need not understand a common boor. Hans Luther, the father, was a thrifty, well-to-do man for his station in life— adroit with his hands, and able to do many useful things, from farm work to digging in the mines. The family life was strict and stern—rather too stern, as Martin thought in later life. . . .

At seventeen he left school for the University at Erfurt. It was then no shame for a poor scholar to maintain himself by alms. Young Martin had a rich noble voice and a fine ear, and by singing ballads in the streets he found ready friends and help. He was still uncertain with what calling he should take up, when it happened that a young friend was killed at his side by lightning.

Erasmus was a philosopher. A powder magazine was once blown up by lightning in a town where Erasmus was staying, and a house of infamous character was destroyed. The inhabitants saw in what had happened the Divine anger against sin. Erasmus told them that if there was any anger in the matter, it was anger merely with the folly which had stored powder in an exposed situation.

Luther possessed no such premature intelligence. He was distinguished from other boys only by the greater power of his feelings and the vividness of his imagination. He saw in his friend's death the immediate hand of the great Lord of the universe. His conscience was terrified. A lifelong penitence seemed necessary to atone for the faults of his boyhood. He too, like Erasmus, became a monk, not forced into it—for his father knew better what the holy men were like, and had no wish to have a son of his among them—but because the monk of Martin's imagination spent his nights and days upon the stones in prayer; and Martin, in the heat of his repentance, longed to be kneeling at his side.

In this mood he entered the Augustine monastery at Erfurt. He was full of an overwhelming sense of his own wretchedness and sinfulness. Like St. Paul, he was crying to be delivered from the body of death which he carried about him. He practised all possible austerities. He, if no one else, mortified his flesh with fasting. He passed nights in the chancel before the altar, or on his knees on the floor of his cell. He weakened his body till his mind wandered, and he saw ghosts and devils. Above all, he saw the flaming image of his own supposed guilt. God required that he should keep the law in all points. He had not so kept the law—could not so keep the law. One morning he was found senseless and seemingly dead; a brother played to him on a flute, and soothed his senses back to consciousness.

It was long since any such phenomenon had appeared

among the rosy friars of Erfurt. They could not tell what to make of him. Staupitz, the prior, listened to his accusations of himself in confession. " My good fellow " he said " don't be so uneasy ; you have committed no sins of the least consequence ; you have not killed anybody, or committed adultery, or things of that sort. If you sin to some purpose, it is right that you should think about it, but don't make mountains out of trifles. . . ."

Luther too, like Erasmus, was to see Rome ; but how different the figures of the two men there ! Erasmus goes with servants and horses, the polished, successful man of the world. Martin Luther trudges penniless and barefoot across the Alps, helped to a meal and a night's rest at the monasteries along the road, or begging, if the convents fail him, at the farm-houses.

He was still young, and too much occupied with his own sins to know much of the world outside him. Erasmus had no dreams. He knew the hard truth on most things. But Rome, to Luther's eager hopes, was the city of the saints, and the court and palace of the Pope fragrant with the odours of Paradise. " Blessed Rome " he cried, as he entered the gate— " Blessed Rome, sanctified with the blood of martyrs ! "

Alas ! the Rome of reality was very far from blessed. He remained long enough to complete his disenchantment. The cardinals, with their gilded chariots and their parasols of peacock's plumes, were poor representatives of the apostles. The gorgeous churches and more gorgeous rituals, the pagan splendour of the paintings, the heathen gods still almost worshipped in the adoration of the art which had formed them, to Luther, whose heart was heavy with thoughts of man's depravity, were utterly horrible. The name of religion was there : the thinnest veil was scarcely spread over the utter disbelief with which God and Christ were at heart regarded. Culture enough there was. It was the Rome of Raphael and Michael Angelo, of Perugino and Benvenuto ; but to the poor German monk, who had come there to find help for his suffering soul, what was culture ?

He fled at the first moment that he could. "Adieu! Rome" he said; "let all who would lead a holy life depart from Rome. Everything is permitted in Rome except to be an honest man." He had no thought of leaving the Roman Church. To a poor monk like him to talk of leaving the Church was like talking of leaping off the planet. But, perplexed and troubled, he returned to Saxony; and his friend Staupitz, seeing clearly that a monastery was no place for him, recommended him to the Elector as Professor of Philosophy at Wittenberg.

The senate of Wittenberg gave him the pulpit of the town church, and there at once he had room to show what was in him. "This monk" said someone who heard him "is a marvellous fellow. He has strange eyes, and will give the doctors trouble by and by."

He had read deeply, especially he had read that rare and almost unknown book, the New Testament. He was not cultivated like Erasmus. Erasmus spoke the most polished Latin. Luther spoke and wrote his own vernacular German. The latitudinarian philosophy, the analytical acuteness, the sceptical toleration of Erasmus were alike strange and distasteful to him. In all things he longed only to know the truth— to shake off and hurl from him lies and humbug. . . .

We come now to the memorable year 1517, when Luther was thirty-five years old. A new cathedral was in progress at Rome. Michael Angelo had furnished Leo the Tenth with the design of St. Peter's; and the question of questions was to find money to complete the grandest structure which had ever been erected by man.

Pope Leo was the most polished and cultivated of mankind. The work to be done was to be the most splendid which art could produce. The means to which the Pope had recourse will serve to show us how much all that would have done for us.

You remember what I told you about indulgences. The notable device of his Holiness was to send distinguished persons about Europe with sacks of indulgences. Indulgences

and dispensations ! Dispensations to eat meat on fast days—
dispensations to marry one's near relation—dispensations for
anything and everything which the faithful might wish to
purchase who desired forbidden pleasures. The dispensations
were simply scandalous. The indulgences—well, if a pious
Catholic is asked nowadays what they were, he will say that
they were the remission of the penances which the Church
inflicts upon earth; but it is also certain that they would
have sold cheap if the people had thought that this was all
that they were to get by them. As the thing was represented
by the spiritual hawkers who disposed of these wares, they
were letters of credit on heaven. . . .

The Pope had bought the support of the Archbishop of
Mayence, Erasmus's friend, by promising him half the spoil
which was gathered in his province. The agent was the
Dominican monk Tetzel, whose name has acquired a forlorn
notoriety in European history.

His stores were opened in town after town. He entered
in state. The streets everywhere were hung with flags. Bells
were pealed; nuns and monks walked in procession before
and after him, while he himself sate in a chariot, with the
Papal Bull on a velvet cushion in front of him. The sale-
rooms were the churches. The altars were decorated, the
candles lighted, the arms of St. Peter blazoned conspicuously
on the roof. Tetzel from the pulpit explained the efficacy of
his medicines; and if any profane person doubted their
power, he was threatened with excommunication. . . .

Acolytes walked through the crowds, clinking their plates
and crying, " Buy ! buy ! " The business went as merry as a
marriage bell till the Dominican came near to Wittenberg.

Half a century before, such a spectacle would have excited
no particular attention. The few who saw through the imposition would have kept their thoughts to themselves; the
many would have paid their money, and in a month all would
have been forgotten.

But the fight between the men of letters and the monks,

the writings of Erasmus and Reuchlin, the satires of Ulric von Hutten, had created a silent revolution in the minds of the younger laity.

A generation had grown to manhood of whom the Church authorities knew nothing ; and the whole air of Germany, unsuspected by pope or prelate, was charged with electricity.

Had Luther stood alone, he too would probably have remained silent. What was he, a poor, friendless, solitary monk, that he should set himself against the majesty of the triple crown ?

However hateful the walls of a dungeon, a man of sense confined alone there does not dash his hands against the stones.

But Luther knew that his thoughts were the thoughts of thousands. Many wrong things, as we all know, have to be endured in this world. Authority is never very angelic ; and moderate injustice, a moderate quantity of lies, is more tolerable than anarchy.

But it is with human things as it is with the great icebergs which drift southward out of the frozen seas. They swim two-thirds under water, and one-third above ; and so long as the equilibrium is sustained, you would think that they were as stable as the rocks. But the sea-water is warmer than the air. Hundreds of fathoms down, the tepid current washes the base of the berg. Silently in those far deeps the centre of gravity is changed ; and then, in a moment, with one vast roll, the enormous mass heaves over, and the crystal peaks which had been glancing so proudly in the sunlight are buried in the ocean for ever.

Such a process as this had been going on in Germany, and Luther knew it, and knew that the time was come for him to speak. Fear had not kept him back. The danger to himself would be none the less because he would have the people at his side. The fiercer the thunderstorm, the greater peril to the central figure who stands out above the rest exposed to it. But he saw that there was hope at last of a change ; and for himself—as he said in the plague—if he died, he died. . . .

While Tetzel, with his bull and his gilt car, was coming to Wittenberg, Luther, loyal still to authority while there was a hope that authority would be on the side of right, wrote to the Archbishop of Mayence to remonstrate.

The archbishop, as we know, was to have a share of Tetzel's spoils; and what were the complaints of a poor insignificant monk to a supreme archbishop who was in debt and wanted money?

The Archbishop of Mayence flung the letter into his waste-paper basket; and Luther made his solemn appeal from earthly dignities to the conscience of the German people. He set up his protest on the church door at Wittenberg; and in ninety-five propositions he challenged the Catholic Church to defend Tetzel and his works.

The Pope's indulgences, he said, cannot take away sins. God alone remits sins; and He pardons those who are penitent, without help from man's absolutions.

The Church may remit penalties which the Church inflicts. But the Church's power is in this world only, and does not reach to purgatory.

If God has thought fit to place a man in purgatory, who shall say that it is good for him to be taken out of purgatory? Who shall say that he himself desires it?

True repentance does not shrink from chastisement. True repentance rather loves chastisement.

The bishops are asleep. It is better to give to the poor than to buy indulgences; and he who sees his neighbour in want, and, instead of helping his neighbour, buys a pardon for himself, is doing what is displeasing to God. Who is this man who dares to say that for so many crowns the soul of a sinner can be made whole?

These, and like these, were Luther's propositions. Little guessed the Catholic prelates the dimensions of the act which had been done. The Pope, when he saw the theses, smiled in good-natured contempt. "A drunken German wrote them" he said; " when he has slept off his wine, he will be of another mind."

Tetzel bayed defiance ; the Dominican friars took up the quarrel ; and Hochstrat of Cologne, Reuchlin's enemy, clamoured for fire and faggot.

Voice answered voice. The religious houses all Germany over were like kennels of hounds howling to each other across the spiritual waste. If souls could not be sung out of purgatory, their occupation was gone.

Luther wrote to Pope Leo to defend himself ; Leo cited him to answer for his audacity at Rome ; while to the young laymen, to the noble spirits all Europe over, Wittenberg became a beacon of light shining in the universal darkness.

It was a trying time to Luther. Had he been a smaller man, he would have been swept away by his sudden popularity— he would have placed himself at the head of some great democratic movement, and in a few years his name would have disappeared in the noise and smoke of anarchy.

But this was not his nature. His fellow-townsmen were heartily on his side. He remained quietly at his post in the Augustine Church at Wittenberg. If the powers of the world came down upon him and killed him, he was ready to be killed. Of himself at all times he thought infinitely little ; and he believed that his death would be as serviceable to truth as his life.

Killed undoubtedly he would have been if the clergy could have had their way. It happened, however, that Saxony just then was governed by a prince of no common order. Were all princes like the Elector Frederick, we should have no need of democracy in this world—we should never have heard of democracy. The clergy could not touch Luther against the will of the Wittenberg senate, unless the Elector would help them ; and to the astonishment of everybody, the Elector was disinclined to consent. The Pope himself wrote to exhort him to his duties. The Elector still hesitated. His professed creed was the creed in which the Church had educated him ; but he had a clear secular understanding outside his formulas. When he read the propositions they did not seem to him the pernicious things which the monks said they were. " There is much in the Bible about Christ " he said " but not much about Rome." He sent for Erasmus, and asked him what he thought about the matter.

The Elector knew to whom he was speaking. He wished for a direct answer, and looked Erasmus full and broad in the face. Erasmus pinched his thin lips together. " Luther " he said at length " has committed two sins ; he has touched the Pope's crown and the monks' bellies."

He generously and strongly urged Frederick not to yield for the present to Pope Leo's importunacy ; and the Pope was obliged to try less hasty and more formal methods.

He had wished Luther to be sent to him to Rome, where his process would have had a rapid end. As this could not be, the case was transferred to Augsburg, and a cardinal legate was sent from Italy to look into it.

There was no danger of violence at Augsburg. The townspeople there and everywhere were on the side of freedom ; and Luther went cheerfully to defend himself. He walked from Wittenberg. You can fancy him still in his monk's brown frock, with all his wardrobe on his back—an apostle of the old sort. The citizens, high and low, attended him to the gates, and followed him along the road, crying " Luther for ever ! " " Nay " he answered " Christ for ever."

The cardinal legate, being reduced to the necessity of politeness, received him civilly. He told him, however, simply and briefly, that the Pope insisted on his recantation, and would accept nothing else. Luther requested the cardinal to point out to him where he was wrong. The cardinal waived discussion. He was come to command, he said, not to argue. And Luther had to tell him that it could not be.

Remonstrances, threats, entreaties, even bribes, were tried. Hopes of high distinction and reward were held out to him if he would only be reasonable. To the amazement of the proud Italian, a poor peasant's son—a miserable friar of a provincial German town—was prepared to defy the power and resist the prayers of the Sovereign of Christendom. " What ! " said the cardinal at last to him " do you think the Pope cares for the opinion of a German boor ? The Pope's little finger is stronger than all Germany. Do you expect your princes to take up arms to defend *you—you*, a wretched worm like you ? I tell you, No ! and where will you be then—where will you be then ? "

Luther answered, " Then, as now, in the hands of almighty God."

The Court dissolved. The cardinal carried back his report to his master. The Pope, so defied, brought out his thunders ; he excommunicated Luther, he wrote again to the Elector, entreating him not to soil his name and lineage by becoming a protector of heretics ; and he required him, without further ceremony, to render up the criminal to justice.

The Elector's power was limited. As yet, the quarrel was simply between Luther and the Pope. The Elector was by no means sure that his bold subject was right—he was only not satisfied that he was wrong—and it was a serious question with him how far he ought to go. The monk might next be placed under the ban of the empire ; and if he persisted in protecting him afterwards, Saxony might have all the power of Germany upon it. He did not venture any more to refuse absolutely. He temporized and delayed ; while Luther himself, probably at the Elector's instigation, made overtures for peace to the Pope. Saving his duty to Christ, he promised to be for the future an obedient son of the Church, and to say no more about indulgences if Tetzel ceased to defend them.

" My being such a small creature " Luther said afterwards " was a misfortune for the Pope. He despised me too much ! What, he thought, could a slave like me do to him—to him, who was the greatest man in all the world. Had he accepted my proposal, he would have extinguished me."

But the infallible Pope conducted himself like a proud,

irascible, exceedingly fallible mortal. To make terms with the town preacher of Wittenberg was too preposterous. . . .

The Pope issued a second bull condemning Luther and his works. Luther replied by burning the bull in the great square at Wittenberg.

At length, in April 1521, the Diet of the Empire assembled at Worms, and Luther was called to defend himself in the presence of Charles the Fifth.

That it should have come to this at all, in days of such high-handed authority, was sufficiently remarkable. It indicated something growing in the minds of men, that the so-called Church was not to carry things any longer in the old style. Popes and bishops might order, but the laity intended for the future to have opinions of their own how far such orders should be obeyed. . . .

The Emperor's Council were evidently in extreme perplexity. The Pope and the Sacred College were equally at a loss. In better ages they would have burnt Luther at the stake and cleared away the whole business. But these time-honoured methods had grown dangerous. The Vatican thunder and lightning had passed unheeded. The great novelty of the situation—how great we can now hardly realize —was that for the first time for many centuries a spiritual question, hitherto exclusively reserved to Church courts and councils, was to be referred to a Diet where lay barons and representatives would sit as judges and an Emperor would preside. This alone taught Rome caution. Cardinal Campeggio, an old, prudent, accomplished man of the world, was despatched to see what could be done, and mend the blunders of Aleandro and Cajetan. Campeggio naturally applied to Erasmus for help. Erasmus replied in another extremely valuable letter. After regretting that he had been unable to go to Rome and speak in person to the Pope, he gave his own explanation of what had happened, and he attributed the whole convulsion to the religious orders, and especially to the Carmelites and Dominicans.

But it is time for Luther to speak for himself. " If we want truth," said Erasmus in the letter to Campeggio just mentioned by Froude, " every man ought to be free to say what he thinks without fear. If the advocates of one side are to be rewarded with mitres, and the advocates of the other with rope or stake, truth will not be heard." But Erasmus was not of the stuff out of which martyrs are made. Luther was, and he spoke the truth as he saw it, knowing full well that there would be no mitre for him, and willing to risk the stake. *How did Luther justify his part in the Reformation ?*

MARTIN LUTHER

ADDRESS TO THE DIET AT WORMS

IN obedience to your commands given me yesterday, I stand here, beseeching you, as God is merciful, so to deign mercifully to listen to this cause, which is, as I believe, the cause of justice and truth. And if through inexperience I should fail to apply to any his proper title or offend in any way against the manners of courts, I entreat you to pardon me as one not conversant with courts, but rather with the cells of monks, and claiming no other merit than that of having spoken and written with that simplicity of mind which regards nothing but the glory of God and the pure instruction of the people of Christ.

Two questions have been proposed to me : Whether I acknowledge the books which are published in my name, and whether I am determined to defend or disposed to recall them. To the first of these I have given a direct answer, in which I shall ever persist that those books are mine and published by me, except so far as they may have been altered or interpolated by the craft or officiousness of rivals. To the other I am now about to reply ; and I must first entreat your Majesty and your Highness to deign to consider that my books are not all of the same description. For there are some in which I have treated the piety of faith and morals with

H

simplicity so evangelical that my very adversaries confess them to be profitable and harmless and deserving the perusal of a Christian. Even the Pope's bull, fierce and cruel as it is, admits some of my books to be innocent, though even these, with a monstrous perversity of judgment, it includes in the same sentence. If, then, I should think of retracting these, should I not stand alone in my condemnation of that truth which is acknowledged by the unanimous confession of all, whether friends or foes.

The second species of my publications is that in which I have inveighed against the papacy and the doctrine of the papists, as of men who by their iniquitous tenets and examples have desolated the Christian world, both with spiritual and temporal calamities. No man can deny or dissemble this. The sufferings and complaints of all mankind are my witnesses, that, through the laws of the Pope and the doctrines of men, the consciences of the faithful have been ensnared, tortured, and torn in pieces, while, at the same time, their property and substance have been devoured by an incredible tyranny, and are still devoured without end and by degrading means, and that too, most of all, in this noble nation of Germany. Yet it is with them a perpetual statute, that the laws and doctrines of the Pope be held erroneous and reprobate when they are contrary to the Gospel and the opinions of the Fathers.

If, then, I shall retract these books, I shall do no other than add strength to tyranny, and throw open doors to this great impiety which will then stride forth more widely and licentiously than it has dared hitherto ; so that the reign of iniquity will proceed with entire impunity, and, notwithstanding its intolerable oppression upon the suffering vulgar, be still further fortified and established ; especially when it shall be proclaimed that I have been driven to this act by the authority of your serene Majesty and the whole Roman Empire. What a cloak, blessed Lord, should I then become for wickedness and despotism !

In a third description of my writings are those which I have published against individuals, against the defenders of the Roman tyranny and the subverters of the piety taught by men.   Against these I do freely confess that I have written with more bitterness than was becoming either my religion or my profession ; for, indeed, I lay no claim to any especial sanctity, and argue not respecting my own life, but respecting the doctrine of Christ.   Yet even these writings it is impossible for me to retract, seeing that through such retraction despotism and impiety would reign under my patronage, and rage with more than their former ferocity against the people of God.

Yet since I am but man and not God, it would not become me to go further in defence of my tracts than my Lord Jesus went in defence of His doctrine ; who, when He was interrogated before Annas, and received a blow from one of the officers, answered : " If I have spoken evil, bear witness of the evil ; but if well, why smitest thou me ? "   If then the Lord Himself, who knew His own infallibility, did not disdain to require arguments against His doctrines even from a person of low condition, how much rather ought I, who am the dregs of the earth and the very slave of error, to inquire and search if there be any to bear witness against my doctrine ! Wherefore, I entreat you, by the mercies of God, that if there be anyone of any condition who has that ability, let him overpower me by the sacred writings, prophetical and evangelical. And for my own part, as soon as I shall be better instructed, I will retract my errors and be the first to cast my books into the flames. . . .

Since your most serene Majesty and the princes require a simple answer I will give it thus : Unless I shall be convinced by proofs from Scripture or by evident reason—for I believe neither in popes nor councils, since they have frequently both erred and contradicted themselves—I cannot choose but adhere to the Word of God, which has possession of my conscience ; nor can I possibly, nor will I ever make any recantation, since it is neither safe nor honest to act contrary to conscience! Here I stand; I cannot do otherwise; so help me God! Amen.

Luther had gone to the Diet with a safe-conduct, and he was allowed to go free from the meeting in spite of the cries " To the flames with him! " of the Spanish guards. He had, however, a still more effective protection in the friendship of the Elector of Saxony, who had him kidnapped when he was ordered to leave Worms, and removed incognito to the safety of the castle of Wartburg in the Thuringian Forest. A short time afterwards the Emperor signed the Edict of Worms which outlawed Luther and all his followers, and placed a close censorship on the printing presses.

Luther spent his time at Wartburg making a German translation of the Bible, and when this was published in 1522 the demand was so great that the printers could hardly cope with it. Germany was soon flooded with the Scriptures, either complete Bibles or New Testaments, and with the people thus studying the foundations of Christianity for themselves the Reformation swept across the country like wildfire.

A similar movement took place in Great Britain, and a graphic picture of the heated controversies that ensued is given in the last speech of Henry VIII to his Parliament. Henry VIII has been well described by H. A. L. Fisher:

> " Gross, cruel, crafty, hypocritical, avaricious, he was nevertheless a great ruler of men. His grasp of affairs was firm and comprehensive; his devotion to public duty was, at least after Wolsey's fall, constant and sustained by a high and kingly sense of his own virtues and responsibilities. . . . His Government, which depreciated the coinage, flogged vagabonds, broke up the institutions which had provided relief to the poor, burned heretics at the stake, stamped out the old order with ruthless cruelty in many a Yorkshire and Lancashire village, was yet a Government to which, in all the ordinary concerns of life, lowly men might look for even-handed justice; a despotism, furnished with an apparatus of resonant and edifying apologies, but not without enlightenment, conscience, and virtue."

How did the Reformation bring dissension into England? Here is the close of Henry's speech after he had dealt with the business of the session. His manner, one of the onlookers tells us, was unusual; he spoke " so sententiously, so kingly, so rather fatherly " that he was listened to with peculiar emotion.

KING HENRY VIII

LAST SPEECH IN PARLIAMENT

THE present is not the first time that my subjects have allowed me to see their affection for me; I trust that they know that, as their hearts are towards me, so is my heart towards them. One other thing there is, however, in which I must work alone; and I must call upon you all to help me, in the name and for the honour of Almighty God.

I hear that, the special foundation of our religion being charity between man and man, it is so refrigerate as there was never more dissension and lack of love between man and man, the occasions whereof are opinions only and names devised for the continuance of the same. Some are called Papists, some Lutherans, and some Anabaptists; names devised of the devil, and yet not fully without ground, for the severing of one man's heart by conceit of opinion from the other.

For the remedy whereof I desire, first, every man of himself to travail first for his own amendment. Secondly, I exhort the bishops and clergy, who are noted to be the salt and lamps of the world, by amending of their diversions, to give example to the rest, and to agree especially in their teaching—which, seeing there is but one truth and verity, they may easily do, calling therein for the aid of God.

Finally, I exhort the nobles and the people not to receive the grace of God in vain; and albeit, by the instinct of God, the Scriptures have been permitted unto them in the English tongue, yet not to take upon them the judgment and exposition of the same, but reverently and humbly, with fear and dread, to receive and use the knowledge which it hath pleased God to show unto them, and in any doubt to resort unto the learned, or at best the higher powers.

I am very sorry to know and hear how unreverently that precious jewel the Word of God is disputed, rhymed, sung, and jangled in every alehouse and tavern. This kind of man is depraved, and that kind of man : this ceremony and that ceremony. Of this I am sure, that charity was never so faint among you ; and God Himself, amongst Christians, was never less reverenced, honoured, and served.

Therefore, as I said before, be in the charity one with another, like brother and brother. Have respect to the pleasing of God, and then I doubt not that love I spake of shall never be dissolved betwixt us. Then may I justly rejoice that thus long I have lived to see this day, and you, by verity, conscience, and charity between yourselves, may in this point, as you be in divers others, accounted among the rest of the world as blessed men !

Henry VIII has given a picture of England after the Reformation, and in fairness to Scotland a brief description of the sister-kingdom in the fifteenth century should be included. *How did modern civilization come to Scotland ?* Lord Rosebery tells how the lamp of learning was lit at St. Andrews in 1411, and traces its influence over succeeding years. These passages are taken from his Rectorial Address at St. Andrews in 1911.

EARL OF ROSEBERY

OUTLINE OF SCOTTISH HISTORY

IT marks a great week in Scotland, when we celebrate the five hundredth anniversary of the foundation of this University. It is the crowning of St. Andrews with the accumulated glories of centuries. And I would that for such an occasion you could have chosen someone steeped in St. Andrews traditions, accustomed to inhale the keen and piercing St. Andrews air, or that you had at least allowed me to depute one of these experts to deliver this rectorial address.

The University seems to have been obscurely at work in 1410. The charter was no doubt given by Bishop Wardlaw in 1411, but the chronological vicissitudes carried it forward into 1412, and it was not till 1414 that the charter was confirmed by the Pope. No less than five bulls were brought to St. Andrews by Henry Ogilvy, and on a Sunday in February 1414 they were presented with conspicuous pomp to the Bishop as Chancellor of the University.

After that ceremony the inhabitants, learned and unlearned, gave themselves up to revelry and rejoicing. Bonfires blazed and wine flowed. A sort of symposium of this day. Two days afterwards a solemn procession comprising no less than 400 clergy expressed the gratitude of the community for the papal boon.

In the exaltation they triumphed more wisely than they knew, for they were celebrating the greatest and most pregnant fact of Scottish history during that century. The planting of the first Scottish University, in that bleak north, was analogous to the erection of a lighthouse on a rocky and savage coast, only on a higher plane and with a larger scope. That magnetic spark appearing in Fife was the source of illumination for all the darkness of Scotland. Before the foundation of St. Andrews it was scarcely too much to say that, outside the priesthood, there was no higher education in Scotland at all.

The ignorance was past belief. It was calculated that not one of the nobility could sign his name before 1370, forty years before the foundation. Two centuries after the foundation, Patrick, Earl of Orkney, the virtual king of those islands, a noble of royal lineage, was so ignorant that, being scarcely able to repeat the Lord's Prayer, his execution was postponed for a few days so that he could receive a little instruction before he left this life. The foundation of St. Andrews excited wise and generous emulation. Forty years afterwards Glasgow claimed and obtained similar privileges. That University was also founded by a bishop under a bull from a pope, for indeed there was no other way, but without the public spirit of the bishop there would have been nothing to set the papal machine in action, and so no Universities. Let us not then forget the debt we owe to those prelates, though their office has so long been an offence and stumbling-block to zealous Presbyterians.

A like period again elapsed, and Aberdeen in a similar way obtained its University, founded with a view to civilizing the Highland clergy—whose ignorance, as we may well believe, seems to have been formidable. But it was from St. Andrews that the light and inspiration came, and it is St. Andrews which must be hailed as the mother University of Scotland.

It is impossible to over-estimate the blessing which St. Andrews thus conferred upon the ancient Kingdom, for it was not only the Highland priests who needed civilizing : it was the nation itself. We cannot exaggerate the barbarism of our country at that time—the reign of naked violence, of un-blushing cupidity, of relentless cruelty.

Some ten years before the foundation of this University, on the very spot where it was inaugurated, the eldest son of the King, the heir to the crown, was torn or allured from the castle of St. Andrews and carried to Falkland to be murdered by, it was alleged, a death of calculated agony. Twenty-five years afterwards the King of Scots was himself assassinated. We remember the mournful utterance of King Robert the Third in the *Fair Maid of Perth*. " Alas ! reverend Father, there is in Scotland only one place where the shriek of the victim and the threats of the oppressor are not heard ; and that, Father, is the grave."

That is a summary of the state of Scotland at that time. At the very time, indeed, when our University was founded, our King was a prisoner in the Tower of London.

These things, which we can scarcely realize now in this coronation year, when the King and Queen and Heir-apparent have been received with such a frenzy of enthusiasm, sufficiently characterize the epoch, and make it all the more remarkable that at that black and cruel time the first University was being set up in Scotland.

Assassination, indeed, is not the fruit or symbol of any age. It is always with us, but in the very year we are celebrating to-day, the year 1411, there was a stranger sight to be seen, one famous and unique. On July 24—St. James' Eve—there were to be seen by the Water Ury, in Aberdeenshire, some score of miles north of Aberdeen, a Highland and Lowland army arrayed in battle against each other, the one led by the Lord of the Isles and the other by the Earl of Mar. Both fought desperately, but the undisciplined valour of the Highlanders broke in vain on the solid square of their opponents.

It is difficult to believe, as Burton tells us, that the battle of Harlaw was felt in the Lowlands to be a greater deliverance than Bannockburn. The Highlander was not less the enemy than the Southron. To imagine that the Highlander and the Lowlander could be blended into one nation, proud of the union and the common name, would have seemed, in 1411, an insane delusion to either side. This fight decided whether civilization should rule in Scotland.

What a strange spectacle for our infant University. Its pulses must have ceased to beat while the result of the raid remained in suspense, and what a strange collocation of history which marks 1411 with St. Andrews and Harlaw, the beginning of Scottish learning and the final struggle with Scottish barbarism.

Not that Harlaw closed the reign of Scottish violence in the Lowlands or the Highlands. For two centuries after this our domestic annals, if domestic they can be called, record little else. Savage murders, followed by savage vendettas, are found on every page. It is not until the seventeenth century that we see any real note of civilization or any sign of amelioration.

This then was the age of darkness in which our little glow-worm of a University displayed its modest light. These were the conditions with which it had to cope; this was the lump which it had set to leaven.

Nothing could be more unpromising, but mark the results. Now I ask you to remember this, that our University of St. Andrews—for I belong to it and am proud to belong to it— our University of St. Andrews is all that remains of the Scotland of that time with the possible exception of the Convention of Royal Burghs.

All that Scotsmen in 1411 prized and venerated has disappeared like a snow-wreath; only this little University, bleached by time, often poverty-stricken, often all but submerged, lashed by a thousand storms of the ocean of politics, of religion, of circumstance, this alone remains.

Surely this is a notable fact. Before this fair shrine of learning by the Northern Sea the lamp has always been kept alight. And the reason possibly is that, partly from the veneration it inspired, partly from its learned character, partly from its comparative poverty, it has remained outside the political arena. What the acid of party touches, it generally corrodes and often destroys. But this venerable institution, though it has witnessed some of the most stirring and tragic episodes in Scottish history, has kept itself aloof from the political life of the time.

This day we stand looking across the abyss of five centuries, face to face with the University at the moment of its birth. It is wonderful to think how little in outward form it has been changed by the lapse of time when all else has been transformed past recognition.

Now, while considering my double function of celebrating our quincentenary and delivering a rectorial address, a strange, whimsical fancy came into my head. I likened myself to one of the Struldbrugs, the race doomed to immortality, one of the weirdest conceptions that ever proceeded from the powerful brain of Swift in his *Gulliver's Travels*. As a Struldbrug

or an " immortal " Lord Rector I weaved a fanciful picture.
Please imagine with me your first Lord Rector, whoever he
may have been, as an intelligent and remarkable Struldbrug.
He must have lived through five centuries, noting, not without
an occasional spasm, the vast changes that he has witnessed.
I ask you to dream with me, and imagine what such a figure
would have to utter to us to-day. The first rector is alleged
to be Laurence of Lindores, Abbot of Scone, a great theologian,
and, like the theologians of that day, a great persecutor. He
was chosen for his character and authority, and, according to
his hypothesis, watched intelligently the course of events. He
would scarcely, for one thing, have remained a respecter of
persons.

He would have seen a fair proportion of our few archbishops hanged or assassinated. He would have seen dummy
bishops content to collect their lawful incomes for the benefit
of unscrupulous laymen and appointed for no other purpose. He would have seen the Scottish peerage almost
annihilated on a single battlefield. He would have seen five
of his sovereigns die violent deaths and their line eventually
wither and perish in a foreign land. He would have seen the
great Church which had overshadowed Scotland, full of
wealth, power, and renown, fall like the walls of Jericho at the
blast of the trumpet, which would also blast the material
prosperity of St. Andrews. He would have seen the Church
which succeeded it, not less ambitious of power, attempt to
found a theocracy of which they should be the visible instruments, but ultimately confined by the good sense of the
people to its spiritual functions, for its own great advantage,
and for the strengthening of its legitimate action.

He would be told one morning that the chief man in
Scotland, the great Cardinal of St. Andrews, had been
murdered in his bedroom, and would see his ghastly figure
dangling from the castle. He would hear the wail of Flodden.
He would learn with dismay that the young Queen, whom he
had seen a girl of beauty in this city, had been imprisoned and

beheaded in England. He would see her son depart to mount the English throne; and, henceforward, for long generations, his kings would be as nothing to him. He would see much of John Knox, who must have been an awful figure to the old Romanist, sometimes in his vigour " dinging his pulpit to blads," sometimes in his old age tottering about the city, leaning on what was destined to be a great ecclesiastical institution in Scotland, the minister's servant; sometimes suspected, and they may be sure believed by their rector, to be raising the devil in his back garden. He would receive with respectful awe Jerome Carden, the physician of world-wide renown, who came from St. Andrews, led, or at least rewarded, by an enormous fee, to cure the Archbishop, who was saved by his cure, but saved only for the gallows.

He would watch among the students the gay youth of Montrose, and the reserved youth of Argyll, both destined to conspicuous lives and to the scaffold, faced with equal dignity and courage. He would mark the exquisite features of Claverhouse, doomed to a bloody renown and a triumphant death. Later again he would see a sturdy student of Argyll's clan who rose to the woolsack and the seat of Chief Justice by hard work, who enriched our literature with books full of entertainment, the best about himself, and many racy volumes about the other chancellors—I mean Lord Campbell. He comes oddly with Montrose and Claverhouse. He would see Charles I come and go. He would see Cromwell come and go. He would see Charles II and James II come and go.

He would see a firefly flutter of favourites come and go, Albanies, Bothwells, Lennoxes, Anguses, and the like. One favourite, the Chastelard, whom poets still remembered, he would see executed there in St. Andrews. He would bloom or wither, as the case might be, under the long line of ecclesiastics who had adorned or controlled St. Andrews, the Beatons, and the Melvilles, Wardlaw, Kennedy, Knox, Rutherford, Sharpe, Chalmers, and Tulloch. I might also include Buchanan, as a Moderator of the General Assembly, a post to which no layman, not even our chancellor himself, might now aspire. He would see the University sometimes plundered, sometimes ruined, sometimes shivering in dumb decay, but containing an indestructible principle of life which enables it to survive.

And in the material world he would have beheld strange transformations. Æneas Sylvius had marvelled to see the poor at the church-doors depart joyfully on receiving an armful of stones. These stones our rector would have literally seen turned into bread, for these rare coals were the germs of that great industry which has been at the root of so much of Scotland's prosperity. He who had seen the little fleets of Scotland would behold the affluent Clyde developed into one of the greatest shipyards of the world. Near at hand he would see the Forth, arched by a gigantic bridge, and blazing at night with ships of war, a fraction of the imperial armada. He would have seen the barren wolds and moors of Scotland transformed by science and labour into the very models of agriculture. He would have seen developed the mystery of steam, cutting through deserts, ploughing through the ocean, awakening to life the Hebrides and the Orkneys. He would have seen a score of obscure villages transformed into puissant communities, ringing with hammers and machinery and with passionate din of toil. The naked, plundered, harassed Scotland of his youth would he have seen changed into a fervid hive of industry.

And then at last he would come to that hall and deliver a rectorial address, telling them that his one great joy, as the centuries progressed, was to be free from religious intolerance. The next great transformation, which he would contemplate with complacency, would be the supersession of violence by law.

Now, our rector would find not a total absence of violence, far from it, very far, but he would see the excuse for it removed by the way of justice, from the Sheriffs to the High Court, from the High Court to the Higher Court which lurks in the ruins of the House of Lords.

Then, after dwelling on the two greatest changes which had occurred in Scotland in his time, he would, perhaps, condescend to give, in the way of counsel, some positive result of his enormous experience. Well, he would tell them to take large views, not with regard to their trade or profession, or the gaining of their daily bread, or even with regard to their studies, but with regard to the circumstances of their time.

He would show how the Reformation, which was, for the moment, a merciless revolution, which ruined St. Andrews and much else besides, but which roused Scotland into a keener intelligence and a manlier faith, was accompanied by a rapacity on the part of the aristocracy and a brutality of wreckage which must have obscured its benefits, and caused sorrow and alarm to many of its well-wishers. Then he would point out how this manifold reform again degenerated into a spiritual tyranny and a domestic inquisition which, had it been successful, might have crushed and emasculated the nation.

Then came the Union, and my Struldbrug would tell you that it seemed the end of all ; all seemed to disappear but our Universities and frugal colleges, cultivating the humanities on a little oatmeal. The King had long vanished, but now there followed him southwards ministers, Parliament, nobles, and all the waiters upon Providence. The life-blood of the country seemed sucked into England. Some of it went, no doubt. Ay, but the heart remained. The patient peasantry, the doughty lairds, too poor or too proud to go, the parochial divines, the merchants produced and nourished by the Union, remained, and wrought out undisturbed the prosperity and character of the nation, undisturbed by politics and the selfish contention of politicians and nobles which had so long blighted the country. What had seemed ruin was indeed salvation, for it brought about the disappearance of party strife in Scotland. For a century and a quarter after the treaty Scotland was free from politics, a result due to the Union. Outside the pious polemics of the General Assembly there reigned a supreme calm.

Mark, then, adds our eternal rector, how on a large survey

we perceive that what had seemed the wreck and catastrophe of the nation was the direct cause of such wealth, power, and peace as it had never known before. Mark, too, he would add, how little statesmen can do for a strong, reliant race. Scotland rose and throve by neglect. She prospered more in the century during which she was forgotten and ignored by Parliament than in all the centuries before or since. That is a lesson from which many inferences may be drawn, some visible, some occult, which in any case are not likely to be recognized now, but which may be realized hereafter. But this at least may be noted.

We at this time seem to be in some danger of becoming a spoon-fed nation. What is in the spoon it is not for me to say ; the future can only reveal. It may be nourishment, it may be poison, it may be simply some languid and relaxing potion. Whatever it may be, noxious or beneficial, let us at least remember that it was not by such means, or in this way, that the Scottish nation was braced and built up.

By proceeding on our present lines we may produce a nation stronger, nobler, and more self-reliant than it has hitherto been. But it was not by such methods that the strong, noble, and self-reliant Scottish nation, as we have known it, was evolved. How then would our undying rector sum up ? " Be of good cheer " I think he would say " you have gained enormously in my long recollection, much in freedom, much in prosperity, and the admiration of mankind for your race. If there are momentary shadows, remember this, that depression often arises from too limited a view. I entered upon office in mediæval times, forty years before the date of the fall of Constantinople, at which modern history is supposed to begin. I have seen eclipses that seemed eternal, and the rivers as in Egypt, turned to blood. I have seen life and death and glory chasing each other like shadows on a summer sea, and all has seemed to be vanity.

" But I remain in the conviction that though individuals may suffer, when we take stock of a century at its end, we shall find that the world is better and happier than it was at the beginning. Lift up your hearts, for the world is moving onward. Its chariot-wheels may crush for the moment, but it does not move to evil. It is guided from above, and guided, we may be sure, with wisdom and goodness which cannot fail. That is the comfort which even in blackest darkness must afford light. And (so your ancient rector would continue), if I am destined to live through the next five centuries, and behold the millenary of St. Andrews, I shall see, no doubt, a community as different from this as is this from that of 1414, but as much better, happier, and wiser than the University of 1911, as is the last from the first."

To these words, which convey the wisdom of your first rector, his present fleeting successor has nothing to add. He is perhaps not so convinced an optimist as his excellent and fictitious predecessor; he sees the present shadows and distractions more clearly than the ultimate outcome. He, poor mortal, cannot chew the cud of centuries; he cannot see beyond the horizon or discern the silver linings of the clouds. He can only look to the morrow, and scarcely to that. But he believes that the patriarch substantially expresses the historical truth in the crumbs of ripe experience which we have the privilege to gather.

And to those who have ears to hear there will always be a voice from these old walls which will speak as a second conscience, calling on you to aim high and follow the right, where the light cannot be discerned, bidding you, in the words of your own motto, "Be foremost and excell", and exhorting you to face the necessary storms and tribulations of life with the same patient strength which has enabled your ancient University to endure and survive the revolutions of five centuries.

The Renaissance and the Reformation, as was said earlier, mark the transition to modern times, and H. A. L. Fisher has summed up the implications of this change in an admirable sentence. "A society divided between lay and cleric gave place to one divided into rich and poor, an atmosphere hostile to free inquiry to one in which science could live and mature." It is, indeed, with the Reformation that capitalism begins its modern development, and the success of the Reformation was in large part due to the fact that it met the growing needs of commerce. What we might call the " economic theory " of the mediæval Church was well suited to a feudal society, in which the rich man's wealth consisted chiefly of claims on the services of his vassals ; but in its condemnation of such things as usury it did not promote trade or industry. The Reformation conscience, allowing the individual to judge (rightly or wrongly) what might be permissible in the way of business, allowed for the development of a middle class far more interested in goods than in services. A further impulse to capitalist development was given in all Calvinist countries by their acceptance of an austere mode of life which allowed for the accumulation of wealth and its employment in foreign trade. But there were other changes brought about by the two great movements, so let us ask H. A. L. Fisher to tell us: *What were the first fruits of the Renaissance and the Reformation ?* Fisher was eminent as a historian and a statesman. He lectured for many years at Oxford, and his *History of Europe*, from which the following extract is taken, is an acknowledged masterpiece.

H. A. L. FISHER

THE NEW EUROPE

TO this Roman and clerical outlook upon the world, the sixteenth century, the first age which may be regarded as distinctively modern, offers the sharpest contrast. The lay mind, fortified by the free use of the vernacular languages and by the full recovery of Greek and Hebrew, had come into its own. The close interrogation of nature, which was to lead to the development of modern science, had begun. Painters examined the human frame, surgeons dissected it. Verrocchio, the sculptor, was also an anatomist. The discovery made by Copernicus, a Polish astronomer, that the earth revolved

I

round the sun, steadily secured adherents. A new lay culture, aristocratic in origin, for it had chiefly grown up in the luxurious courts of the Italian despots, was made a general possession through the invention of printing. Strong and continuous as were the theological interests, they were now balanced by an exciting body of new knowledge, having no connexion with the theology, and the fruit of mental processes which theology was unable to turn to account. With a sharp gesture of impatience Europe turned away from the vast literature of commentaries and glosses, which the pedants of the later Middle Ages had inscribed "in letters of opium on tablets of lead ".

An important part of this new knowledge was geographical. The Portuguese conquest of Ceuta on the African coast in 1415 had been the first step in that long and wonderful series of marine adventures which led to the circumnavigation of Africa by Vasco da Gama, to the foundation of the Portuguese Empire in the east, and to the discovery by Christopher Columbus, the Genoese sailor, of the new world beyond the Atlantic. The Mediterranean ceased henceforth to be the centre of the civilized world. The sceptre of commerce passed from the cities of Italy to the nations having easy access to the Atlantic Ocean, first to Portugal, then in succession to Spain, the Netherlands, France, and England. A civilization which had sprung up in the river basins of the Euphrates and the Nile, and had spread round the littoral of the Mediterranean, was now carried far and wide on ocean-going ships to distant lands. Europe began to enter into that new phase of its existence, which is marked by the foundation of colonies and empires beyond the ocean, and by the gradual spread of European influences throughout the habitable globe.

The discovery of the new world, coinciding with the swift diffusion of printed books, taught the Europeans that " Truth " in Bacon's noble phrase " is the daughter not of authority but of time ". The inhabitants of this continent had long known that the earth was round, and that if they sailed far enough to the west they would find the Indies. Nothing, however, had prepared them for the emergence of an intermediate land-mass of incalculable vastness and resources. If their expectations of the shape of the planet were confirmed, their estimate of its size was rudely overthrown. The world was far bigger than they had thought. The old notions of geography, taught for centuries by learned clerks and believed in all the universities, were suddenly shown to be in sharp contradiction to established facts.

The consequences were farther reaching than the additions to positive knowledge resulting from the geographical discoveries. Insensibly mankind acquired a new attitude towards knowledge itself. Authority no longer went unchallenged. The past was no longer supreme. As the planet unfolded its unending wonders, generations grew up for whom truth was not a complete thing already given in ancient books, but a secret yet to be retrieved from the womb of time. . . .

Meanwhile the political framework of the mediæval Empire had given way before the growth of national states. A universal monarchy, supported by a universal church, though it corresponded to the aspirations of Europe during many centuries, was never closely adjusted to its needs or respected by its observance. The Empire had never secured a general allegiance. The claims of the Papacy had often been countered by the will of princes. By slow and painful steps, as feudal licence was brought under the control of central power, national states were formed, first of all in England, where the conditions were favourable, then in the Christian states of the Iberian peninsula, in France, and in the larger principalities of the German federation. By the end of the fifteenth century national governments had been established, not without the assistance of the new invention of gunpowder, in England, France, and Spain. In England the suicide of the old feudal nobility in the Wars of the Roses was the prelude to the establishment of Tudor rule.

Framed against the background of mediæval licence, the

type of government which was now coming into vogue was remarkable for strength ; judged by modern standards it was pitiably weak. The resources, moral, intellectual, and material, at the disposal of the most powerful monarchs of the sixteenth century were indeed paltry when we measure them against the disciplined social conscience, the organized national education, the powerful instruments for the accumulation and concentration of knowledge, the great military and naval establishments and vast revenues which support the fabric of a modern state. The papers which nourished the machine of English government during the whole reign of Queen Elizabeth would probably be outweighed in a month by the accumulations of the least important of our modern government offices. The strongest army put into the field by Francis I would have withered away before a single division of the army of Pétain or Foch. Even in the most advanced states of the sixteenth century the government lived from hand to mouth, improvising armies and navies to suit particular occasions, and driven to the most desperate expedients for finance. To recruit, to pay, to feed a national army were feats not only beyond the power of any government to execute, but beyond the scope of any statesman to conceive. Charles VII of France had asked of every parish in France that it should maintain an archer for the wars. The scheme broke down at once. His successor, Louis XI, fell back on a force of foreign mercenaries. The chronic insolvency of Charles V, judged to be the most powerful monarch of his time, is symptomatic of a weakness which afflicted all governments alike.

Nevertheless it is to this age, which witnesses the disruption of Latin Christianity, that we may ascribe the clear emergence of that more efficient form of social and political communion which claims the free yet disciplined loyalties of a nation. In the sixteenth century Europeans began, in larger measure than before, to think in nations, to act in national groups, and to render to the head of the national state some part of the loyalty which had previously been paid to the undivided Church. Roger Ascham, the schoolmaster and educational reformer who taught Queen Elizabeth, is a typical figure in the new lay educational movements which gave support to vernacular literature and national pride.

The formation of the strong continental monarchies ushers in a period of acute diplomatic rivalry which was governed by the conception of the balance of power. While the mediæval sense of a common European interest had faded away, no country had acquired a measured estimate of its own strength and resources. Romantic ambitions, the legacy of the Roman and Carolingian ages, filled the minds of rulers who would have been better occupied in attending to the welfare of their subjects. Statecraft was still immature, political economy had not been invented, and the art of domestic comfort was neither understood nor intelligently pursued. In the absence of exact statistics the vaguest notions prevailed as to the wealth and population of the European States. It was a common belief that dazzling conquests might still be made and held within the old framework of European society. . . .

Money, which has always been a power in human affairs, had become more plentiful in the later Middle Ages, and was destined to become more abundant still through the importation of Peruvian silver before the sixteenth century had run its course. In all the progressive countries of the west the growth of trade and commerce, which had received its first important stimulus during the Crusades, had created an influential middle class whose material interests were opposed to the continuance of feudal disorder. Capital was coming into its own. Great merchants and bankers, a Jacques Cœur of Bourges, a Fugger of Augsburg, a Dick Whittington of London, a Roberto Strozzi of Florence, out-topped many a great feudal noble in their command of free capital, and rose to positions of political influence. For many years the Empire was financed from Augsburg, while the Italian enterprises of France depended upon the support of the Strozzi Bank of Florence, with its branches in Lyons, Venice, and Rome. Capital, then, must be counted as a force in aid of those monarchical nation states whose consolidated power is one of the new facts distinguishing the Europe of the sixteenth century from the conditions of the feudal age.

Upon such a Europe, kindled by new knowledge and new horizons, and charged with the spirit of national pride and independence, fell the spark of the Protestant Reformation. A challenge to Roman doctrine was no new thing. It had been made by Wycliffe in England and by Hus in Bohemia. The problem how best to reform the manifest abuses of the Church had, ever since the first schism, engaged the attention of serious minds throughout Christendom. Councils had met, deliberated, and dispersed, without effecting any serious improvement. The Pope, for whose sovereign authority no menace seemed to be more formidable than the recognition of a General Council as a regular and established organ of Church government, had been able to circumvent the conciliar movement by entering into separate and direct concordats with national governments. The ill-organized and tumultuous deliberations of an international assembly, whose members were divided from one another by race, language, and allegiance, were no match for the experienced diplomacy of the Roman *curia*. A combination of the Papacy on the one hand, and the temporal powers on the other, might always be relied on to frustrate the endeavours of an œcumenical council. The Protestant Reformation, however, was neither initiated nor assisted by councils of the Church. It arose out of a passionate sense of the contrast between the simplicity of the Apostolic age and the wealth and fiscal exactions of the Roman Church ; it was sheltered by the help and assisted by the appetites of certain temporal princes. And finally, in those regions of northern Europe in which it succeeded in securing a foothold, it was protected against the forces of Catholic reaction by a widespread confiscation of abbey lands and the creation of a vested interest in the spoils of the plundered church, which was, in certain regions, so deeply rooted that neither war nor revolution was able to disturb it.

The rise of a national spirit, as Fisher has pointed out, is one of the features of the new Europe. This is well illustrated in the case of England. *How did the new spirit of patriotism find expression in Elizabethan England?* We have, on the one hand, the great popularity of Shakespeare's historical plays, and the magnificent eulogy which he put into the mouth of his John of Gaunt :—

> " This royal throne of kings, this scepter'd isle,
> This earth of majesty, this seat of Mars,
> This other Eden, demi-paradise ;
> This fortress built by Nature for herself
> Against infection and the hand of war ;
> This happy breed of men, this little world ;
> This precious stone set in the silver sea,
> Which serves it in the office of a wall,
> Or as a moat defensive to a house,
> Against the envy of less happier lands. . . ."

And on the other hand we have the following brief speech of Queen Elizabeth to her Parliament in 1593, when the country was at war with Spain, and Philip was threatening to build a new Armada to revenge the defeat of the first one.

QUEEN ELIZABETH

THE WAR WITH SPAIN

MY Lords and Gentlemen,
This kingdom hath had many wise, noble, and victorious princes ; I will not compare with any of them in wisdom, fortitude, or any other virtues ; but saving the duty of a child, that is not to compare with his father in love, care, sincerity, and justice, I will compare with any prince that ever you had, or shall have.

It may be thought simplicity in me, that, all this time of my reign, I have not sought to advance my territories, and enlarge my dominions ; for opportunity hath served me to do it. I acknowledge my womanhood and weakness in that respect ; but though it hath not been hard to obtain, yet I doubted how to keep the things so obtained ; and I must say, my mind was never to invade my neighbours, or to usurp over any ; I am contented to reign over my own, and to rule as a just princess.

Yet the King of Spain doth challenge me to be the quarreller, and the beginner of all these wars ; in which he doth me the greatest wrong that can be, for my conscience doth not accuse my thoughts, wherein I have done him the least injury ; but I am persuaded in my conscience, if he knew what I know, he himself would be sorry for the wrong that he hath done me.

I fear not all his threatenings ; his great preparations and mighty forces do not stir me ; for though he come against me with a greater power than ever was his invincible navy, I doubt not (God assisting me, upon whom I always trust) but that I shall be able to defeat and overthrow him. I have great advantage against him, for my cause is just.

I heard say, when he attempted his last invasion, some upon the sea-coast forsook their towns, and flew up higher into the country, and left all naked and exposed to his entrance : but, I swear unto you, if I knew those persons, or any that should do so hereafter, I will make them know and feel what it is to be so fearful in so urgent a cause.

The subsidies you give me, I accept thankfully, if you give me your good wills with them ; but if the necessity of the time, and your preservations, did not require it, I would refuse them ; but let me tell you that the sum is not so much, but that it is needful for a princess to have so much always lying in her coffers for your defence in time of need, and not be driven to get it, when we should use it.

You that be lieutenants and gentlemen of command in your counties, I require you to take care that the people be well armed, and in readiness upon all occasions. You that be judges and justices of the peace, I command and straightly charge you, that you see the laws to be duly executed, and that you make them living laws, when we have put life into them.

The independent spirits who questioned religious authority were not always content to stop there. " If you have religious doubts " said Chateaubriand two and a half centuries later " you will soon have political doubts as well." Luther, on this question, was on the side of established authority, but among his followers there were many who harboured " political doubts as well ". Prominent among these was John Knox, the founder of the Presbyterian Church. " It is evident " said Knox " that the sword of God is not committed to the hand of man to use as it pleases him, but only to punish vice and maintain virtue." Thus he first asserted the divine right of the subject to pass judgment on the exercise of the divine right claimed by kings. *How did John Knox justify his attacks on absolute monarchy?* Here is an example of his pulpit oratory, some passages from a sermon delivered in Edinburgh in 1565 on Isaiah xxvi, 13-16. They lead up to the theme of the next book, the rise of political freedom.

JOHN KNOX

AGAINST TYRANTS

THESE are the chief points of which, by the grace of God, we intend more largely at this present to speak :
First, the prophet saith, " O Lord our God, other lords besides thee have ruled us ".

This, no doubt, is the beginning of the dolorous complaint, in which he complains of the unjust tyranny that the poor afflicted Israelites sustained during the time of their captivity. True it is that the prophet was gathered to his fathers in peace, before this came upon the people : for a hundred years after his decease the people were not led away captive ; yet he, foreseeing the assurance of the calamity, did beforehand indite and dictate unto them the complaint, which afterward they should make. But at the first sight it appears that the complaint has but small weight; for what new thing was it that other lords than God in His own person ruled them, seeing that such had been their government from the beginning? For who knows not that Moses, Aaron, and Joshua, the judges Samuel, David, and other godly rulers, were men, and not God; and so other lords than God ruled them in their greatest prosperity?

For the better understanding of this complaint, and of the mind of the prophet, we must, first, observe from whence all authority flows; and second, to what end powers are appointed by God: which two points being discussed, we shall better understand what lords and what authority rule beside God, and who they are in whom God and His merciful presence rules.

The first is resolved to us by the words of the Apostle, saying: "There is no power but of God". David brings in the eternal God speaking to judges and rulers, saying: "I have said ye are gods, and sons of the Most High". And Solomon, in the person of God, affirmeth the same, saying: "By me kings reign, and princes discern the things that are just". From which place it is evident that it is neither birth, influence of stars, election of people, force of arms, nor, finally, whatsoever can be comprehended under the power of nature, that makes the distinction betwixt the superior power and the inferior, or that establishes the royal throne of kings; but it is the only and perfect ordinance of God, who willeth His terror, power, and majesty, partly to shine in the thrones of kings, and in the faces of judges, and that for the profit and comfort of man. So that whosoever would study to deface the order of government that God has established, and allowed by His holy word, and bring in such a confusion that no difference should be betwixt the upper powers and the subjects, does nothing but avert and turn upside down the very throne of God, which He wills to be fixed here upon earth.

The end and cause, then, why God imprints in the weak and feeble flesh of man this image of His own power and majesty, is not to puff up flesh in opinion of itself; neither yet that the heart of him that is exalted above others should be lifted up by presumption and pride, and so despise others, but that he should consider he is appointed lieutenant to One, whose eyes continually watch upon him, to see and examine how he behaves himself in his office. St. Paul, in few words, declares the end wherefore the sword is committed to the powers, saying: " It is to the punishment of the wicked doers, and unto the praise of such as do well."

Of which words it is evident that the sword of God is not committed to the hand of man to use as it pleases him, but only to punish vice and maintain virtue, that men may live in such society as is acceptable before God. And this is the true and only cause why God has appointed powers in this earth. . . .

The first thing, then, that God requires of him who is called to the honour of a king, is, the knowledge of His will revealed in His word.

The second is, an upright and willing mind, to put in execution such things as God commands in His law, without declining to the right, or to the left hand.

Kings, then, have not an absolute power to do in their government what pleases them, but their power is limited by God's word; so that if they strike where God has not commanded, they are but murderers; and if they spare where God has commanded to strike, they and their throne are criminal and guilty of the wickedness which abounds upon the face of the earth, for lack of punishment.

BOOK III

THE
GROWTH OF POLITICAL FREEDOM

THE GROWTH OF POLITICAL FREEDOM

THIS book will deal with what Western Civilization has made of the Greek idea of democracy. We shall watch, in Whitehead's words, " a growth, slow and wavering, of respect for the preciousness of human life—the humanitarian spirit, gradually emerging in the slow sunrise of a thousand years ".

After the fall of Rome the rule of law established itself again in Europe through the feudal system, but this system tended to leave far too much arbitrary power in the hands of each baron or lord of the manor. There was a danger, to borrow a golfing analogy, of too many " local rules ", and not sufficient knowledge of, or respect for, the laws of golf. Feudalism was leavened, however, by that " instinct for legal organization transcending local boundaries " of which we have read, and this worked in a variety of ways. It led, for example, in England, to the signing of Magna Carta. *Why is Magna Carta regarded as the foundation of British liberty?* Professor Maitland said that the importance of Magna Carta lay in its affirmation that " the king is, and shall be, below the law ". This brings out again the fundamental difference between our Western Civilization and the eastern despotisms where the will of the ruler, in Sir Ernest Barker's words, " fell like an indiscriminate rain " on just and unjust alike, and there was no security either for property or for life. William Penn appealed to the liberties granted by Magna Carta when he was arrested for preaching without permission in the London streets.

WILLIAM PENN

PRINCIPLES OF MAGNA CARTA

WE have lived to an age so debauched from all humanity and reason, as well as faith and religion, that some stick not to turn butchers to their own privileges and conspirators against their own liberties. For however Magna Carta had once the reputation of a sacred unalterable law, and few were hardened enough to incur and bear the long curse that attends the violators of it, yet it is frequently objected now, that the benefits there designed are but temporary, and therefore liable to alteration, as other statutes are. What game such persons play at may be read in the attempts of Dionysius, Phalaris, etc., which would have will and power to be the people's law.

But that the privileges due to Englishmen, by the Great Charter of England, have their foundation in reason and law ; and that those new Cassandrian ways to introduce will and power deserve to be detested by all persons professing sense and honesty, and the least allegiance to our English Government, we shall make appear from a sober consideration of the nature of those privileges contained in that charter.

1. The ground of alteration of any law in government (where there is no invasion) should arise from the universal discommodity of its continuance, but there can be no profit in the discontinuance of liberty and property, therefore there can be no just ground of alteration.

2. No one Englishman is born slave to another, neither has the one a right to inherit the sweat and benefit of the other's labour, without consent ; therefore the liberty and property of an Englishman cannot reasonably be at the will and beck of another, let his quality and rank be never so great.

3. There can be nothing more unreasonable than that which is partial, but to take away the liberty and property of any, which are natural rights, without breaking the law of nature (and not of will and power) is manifestly partial, and therefore unreasonable.

4. If it be just and reasonable for men to do as they would be done by, then no sort of men should invade the liberties and properties of other men, because they would not be served so themselves.

5. Where liberty and property are destroyed, there must always be a state of force and war, which, however pleasing it may be unto the invaders, will be esteemed intolerable by the invaded, who will no longer remain subject in all human probability than while they want as much power to free them-

selves as their adversaries had to enslave them ; the troubles, hazards, ill consequences, and illegality of such attempts, as they have declined by the most prudent in all ages, so have they proved most uneasy to the most savage of all nations, who first or last have by a mighty torrent freed themselves, to the due punishment and great infamy of their oppressors ; such being the advantage, such the disadvantage which necessarily do attend the fixation and removal of liberty and property.

We shall proceed to make it appear that Magna Carta (as recited by us) imports nothing less than their preservations :

" No freeman shall be taken or imprisoned, or be disseized of his freehold, or liberties, or free customs, or be outlawed, or exiled, or any other ways destroyed ; nor we will not pass upon him nor condemn him, but by lawful judgment of his peers, etc.

" A freeman shall not be amerced for a small fault, but after the manner of the fault, and for a great fault after the greatness thereof, and none of the said amercement shall be assessed, but by the oath of good and lawful men of the vicinage."

1. It asserts Englishmen to be free ; that's liberty.

2. That they have freeholds ; that's property.

3. That amercement or penalties should be proportioned to the faults committed, which is equity.

4. That they shall lose neither, but when they are adjudged to have forfeited them, in the judgment of their honest neighbours, according to the law of the land, which is lawful judgment.

It is easy to discern to what pass the enemies of the Great Charter would bring the people.

1. They are now freemen ; but they would have them slaves.

2. They have now right unto their wives, children, and estates, as their undoubted property ; but such would rob them of all.

K

3. Now no man is to be amerced or punished but suitably to his fault ; whilst they would make it suitable to their revengeful minds.

4. Whereas the power of judgment lies in the breasts and consciences of twelve honest neighbours, they would have it at the discretion of mercenary judges ; to which we cannot choose but add that such discourses manifestly strike at this present constitution of government ; for it being founded upon the Great Charter, which is the ancient common law of the land, as upon its best foundation, none can design the cancelling of the charter, but they must necessarily intend the extirpation of the English Government ; for where the cause is taken away the effect must consequently cease. And as the restoration of our ancient English laws, by the Great Charter, was the sovereign balsam which cured our former breaches, so doubtless will the continuation of it prove an excellent prevention to any future disturbances.

But some are ready to object that " The Great Charter consisting as well of religious as civil rights, the former having received an alteration, there is the same reason why the latter may have the like ".

To which we answer that the reason of alteration cannot be the same ; therefore the consequence is false. The one being a matter of opinion, about faith and religious worship, which is as various as the unconstant apprehensions of men ; but the other is matter of so immutable right and justice, that all generations, however differing in their religious opinions, have concentrated, and agreed to the certainty, equity, and indispensable necessity of preserving these fundamental laws ; so that Magna Carta hath not risen and fallen with the differing religious opinions that have been in this land, but have ever remained as the stable right of every individual Englishman, purely as an Englishman.

So heinous a thing was it esteemed of old to endeavour an enervation or subversion of these ancient rights and privileges, that Acts of Parliament themselves (otherwise the most sacred with the people) have not been of force enough to secure or defend such persons from condign punishment, who, in pursuance of them, have acted inconsistent with our Great Charter. Therefore it is that great lawyer, the Lord Coke, doth once more aggravate the example of Empson and Dudley (with persons of the same rank) into a just caution, as well to Parliaments as judges, justices, and inferior magistrates, to decline making or executing any act that may in the least seem to restringe or confirm this so often avowed and confirmed Great Charter of the liberties of England, since Parliaments are said to err when they cross it ; the obeyers of their acts punished as time-serving transgressors, and that kings themselves (though enriched by those courses) have, with great compunction and repentance, left among their dying words their recantations.

Therefore most notable and true it was, with which we shall conclude this present subject, what the King pleased to observe in the speech to the Parliament about 1662, namely : " The good old rules of law are our best security ".

Magna Carta was the work of the barons, and in a country where serfdom was the rule it concerned itself only with the rights of free men. But there was another influence at work, slowly transforming the whole social structure of Europe. *How did England come to be a land of free men ?* The social revolution is briefly described in the following lecture by Robert Vaughan, sometime Professor of History in London University. Much the same process took place in all countries of Europe, the date depending on how quickly they were touched by the magic wand of commerce, Russia being among the last. Indeed the " collective farm " of the communist seems to have something in common with the ancient serfdom in so far as it pins the peasant down to his land ; and the new tyrannies of the communist countries resemble the older Eastern despotisms in their disregard for the rights of the individual. Vaughan shows how the rise of industry helped the decay of serfdom, and led to the emergence of a nation of free men, " claiming the right to take their labour to the market that should be most to their advantage ".

ROBERT VAUGHAN

INDUSTRY COMES TO ENGLAND

THE progress of the industrial arts, by adding so much to the population and importance of the towns, made them a refuge to multitudes who were not at ease under the harsh treatment of the baron or the manorial landlord. Even the slave, as we have seen, if he could only manage to retain his footing for a year and a day in a town, became free. Additions were thus constantly made to the constantly increasing numbers in such places who would be born free. In the meanwhile the causes which had long tended to increase the number of comparatively free labourers, and free tenants, upon the soil, had therein increased the class of persons who would be sure to direct their thoughts, more or less, towards town life, as towns became distinguished by intelligence, wealth, and comfort. Even the abbey lands, in this view, became a normal school for citizens. The wars, too, of our Norman kings, especially those of Edward I and Edward III, carried on as they were in a foreign land, disturbed all those feudal relations which had connected the people of England so immediately with its soil, and brought about a large amount of virtual manumission. Military life and feudal serfdom, or even feudal villeinage, were little compatible. The service of the soldier, which took him from his home, and often out of the kingdom, detached him of necessity from predial servitude ; and the service of the sailor was always felt, for the same reason, to be that of the freeman. In the fourteenth century this constant drifting of the population from the country to the town had so diminished the number of agricultural labourers, that great complaint arose on that ground ; and when in 1349 the great pestilence diminished the hands left for such labour still more, the parliament began to take the question of employer and employed under its consideration, as the great question of the time.

The course taken by the parliament was, to fix the wages

for all kinds of husbandry and handicraft, and to make it penal in any man to refuse to do the work required from him on the prescribed terms. At the same time, severe regulations were adopted against all begging by able-bodied men. To work for a given wage or to starve, was the alternative which these laws were intended to place before every working man. At first, wages were thus fixed wholly irrespective of the varying price of commodities. But subsequently, either better knowledge or better feeling disposed the legislature to amend its proceedings in this particular. But to the last, our parliaments, during this period, never seemed to doubt that they were more competent to judge than the parties themselves, concerning what the relation would be between master and man.

It was found, however, to be more easy to issue regulations on this subject than to secure obedience to them. The spirit of resistance appears to have been general and determined. Hence, in 1360, ten years later, the Statute of Labourers enjoined that no labourer should quit his abode, or absent himself from his work, on pain of imprisonment fifteen days, and of having the letter F fixed upon his forehead with a hot iron. It was further provided in this statute, that the town refusing to deliver up a runaway labourer should forfeit ten pounds to the king, and five pounds to the employer. In 1378 the Commons repeat their lamentation over the general disregard of this statute. Husbandmen, they say, continue to fly to the great towns, where they become seamen, artificers, and clerks, to the great detriment of agriculture. After another ten years, we find the same assembly deploring the same evil, in the same terms, and endeavouring to correct it by new penalties. So far did our parliaments carry their meddling in such things in those days, that they determined the kinds of food the labourer should eat, and the quality of the cloth that he should wear.

These facts are all significant. They not only show us what were the notions of political economy prevalent with our legislators in those days, but, what is much more material, they show us that the great mass of working men in town and country had now come to be free men, claiming the right to take their labour to the market that should be most to their advantage. In this fact we have a great social revolution.

Our House of Commons does not appear to advantage in their manner of dealing with this question. It should have seen, that to become a party to such laws in relation to industry, was to become a mere tool in the hands of the Upper House. The rod of feudalism was visibly broken, and these commoners belonged to the class of men who had broken it. Consistency required that they should have done their best to strengthen the work of their own hands. But, in common with many timid reformers, they appear to have become alarmed at their own success. It was this middle-class caution which disposed them to take the side of the barons, when they should have taken the side of their dependants.

Not that the rate of wages in those times, as compared with the price of commodities, was such as to constitute a serious ground of complaint. Indeed, it is hardly to be doubted that the working men of England in the fourteenth century were better able to sustain a family by their earnings than the same class of men among ourselves. If the most competent judges are right, in supposing the population of England in those times to have been less than three millions, we have only to remember the drain that was made on that population by almost ceaseless wars, and by occasional pestilence, to feel assured that labour must then have been a commodity of high value. This fact may suggest that the condition of the industrial classes in England under our Norman kings, could hardly have been so degraded as it is sometimes said to have been, and may suffice to explain how the people of this country came to be distinguished by that feeling of independence, and that passion for freedom, which is so variously, and so generally attributed to them by ancient writers. In such a state of society, the servile class would be too valuable as property, not to be on the whole well treated, and everything would naturally tend to hasten the extinction of such service.

So, by slow degrees, the children of the soil of England rose in influence, and in the consciousness of possessing it. The Saxon element again became ascendant in our history, and the feudal element declined. It was the work of a single generation to give completeness to the feudal system in this country. It was the work of many generations so far to displace it.

We have seen that the Saxon and Danish periods in English history were in many respects unfavourable to the progress of industrial art; and the same may be said of the times which followed, until something more than a century has passed. But we have now reached the point when two probabilities concerning the future of this country become perceptible. England now promises to be a great industrial power, and a power of much influence in Continental affairs. The nation has become one, is comparatively free, and the land is covered with myriads of men busy in constructing ships, in creating towns, in rearing castles and cathedrals, in adorning palaces, and bent on competing in artistic skill with the most favoured states. The ships of all countries float in the seaports of England; and the English merchant, visited by traders from all lands in his own mart, is greeted in his turn in the marts of distant nations. The influence of this industrial power on the intelligence, the liberty and the religion of the nation remains to be considered; while, in regard to foreign politics, the relations which subsisted between our Norman kings and France, continued long enough to raise the growing unity and wealth of England into the place of a new power in the affairs of Europe.

In this land of free men the first and most important of the successful struggles between king and people was fought. There was something in the spirit of the English people which made them take the lead in the realizing and the claiming of both personal and political liberties—a realizing and claiming on the part of the lower orders often paralleled by an acknowledging on the part of the higher orders. And it was the parliamentary system, as consolidated in the seventeenth century, which Britain exported to all its dominions overseas, and which was copied in many European countries.

The last two lectures have filled in the background against which the long struggle for political liberty in the seventeenth century stands out. Magna Carta may have put one king in his place below the law, but others needed to be reminded of this place, and to be persuaded or forced to occupy it. The first two Stuart kings refused to accept the position, or rather they refused to accept the interpretation of the law and of old precedents which satisfied the Commons. It is important to remember that all through the struggle between Charles I and the Parliamentarians, both sides claimed that they were acting in accordance with the law. The real strength of the case presented by Eliot, Pym, and Hampden, was that they looked beyond the mere letter of the law to the eternal spirit of justice which animates it.

James I, cautious in his obstinate adherence to his theory that a divinely appointed king can do no wrong, as well befitted " the wisest fool in Christendom ", managed to prevent his bickering with Parliament from developing into open hostilities, although he did, with his own hands, tear out of their records the pages containing their protestation " that the liberties, franchises, privileges and jurisdictions of parliament are the ancient and undoubted birthright and inheritance of the subjects of England ". His son, Charles I, immensely popular at his accession, produced a quicker change of feeling among his subjects than any other king of England has ever done. He came to the throne in 1625 ; his first Parliament met him, in Green's words, " in a passion of loyalty ". But let us ask Green to take over for this occasion the duty of introducing one of the most important of the speeches which were made in this historic struggle. The extracts are taken from his colourful *Short History of the English People*.

J. R. GREEN

THE KING AND THE PEOPLE

IF Hampden and Pym are the great figures which embody the later national resistance, the earlier struggle for parliamentary liberty centres in the figure of Sir John Eliot.

Of an old family—ennobled since his time—which had

settled under Elizabeth near the fishing hamlet of St. Germains, and whose stately mansion gives its name of Port Eliot to a little town on the Tamar, he had risen to the post of Vice-Admiral of Devonshire under the patronage of Buckingham, and had seen his activity in the suppression of piracy in the Channel rewarded by an unjust imprisonment. He was now in the first vigour of manhood, with a mind exquisitely cultivated and familiar with the poetry and learning of his day, a nature singularly lofty and devout, a fearless and vehement temper. There was a hot impulsive element in his nature which showed itself in youth in his drawing sword on a neighbour who denounced him to his father, and which in later years gave its characteristic fire to his eloquence. But his intellect was as clear and cool as his temper was ardent. In the general enthusiasm which followed on the failure of the Spanish Marriage, he had stood almost alone in pressing for a recognition of the rights of Parliament, as a preliminary to any real reconciliation with the Crown.

He fixed, from the very outset of his career, on the responsibility of the royal ministers to Parliament, as the one critical point for English liberty. It was to enforce the demand of this that he availed himself of Buckingham's sacrifice of the Treasurer, Cranfield, to the resentment of the Commons. "The greater the delinquent" he urged "the greater the delict. They are a happy thing, great men and officers, if they be good, and one of the greatest blessings of the land: but power converted into evil is the greatest curse that can befall it."

But the new Parliament had hardly met when he came to the front to threaten a greater criminal than Cranfield. So menacing were his words, as he called for an inquiry into the failure before Cadiz, that Charles himself stooped to answer threat with threat. "I see" he wrote to the House "you especially aim at the Duke of Buckingham. I must let you know that I will not allow any of my servants to be questioned among you, much less such as are of eminent place and near to me."

A more direct attack on a right already acknowledged in the impeachment of Bacon and Cranfield could hardly be imagined, but Eliot refused to move from his constitutional ground. The King was by law irresponsible, he " could do no wrong ". If the country, therefore, was to be saved from a pure despotism, it must be by enforcing the responsibility of the ministers who counselled and executed his acts.

Eliot persisted in denouncing Buckingham's incompetence and corruption, and the Commons ordered the subsidy which the Crown had demanded to be brought in " when we shall have presented our grievances, and received his Majesty's answer thereto ". Charles summoned them to Whitehall, and commanded them to cancel the condition. He would grant them " liberty of counsel, but not of control " ; and he closed the interview with a significant threat. "Remember" he said " that Parliaments are altogether in my power for their calling, sitting, and dissolution : and therefore, as I find the fruits of them to be good or evil, they are to continue or not to be."

But the will of the Commons was as resolute as the will of the King. Buckingham's impeachment was voted and carried to the Lords. The favourite took his seat as a peer to listen to the charge with so insolent an air of contempt that one of the managers appointed by the Commons to conduct it turned sharply on him. " Do you jeer, my Lord ! " said Sir Dudley Digges. " I can show you when a greater man than your Lordship—as high as you in place and power, and as deep in the King's favour—has been hanged for as small a crime as these articles contain."

The " proud carriage " of the Duke provoked an invective from Eliot which marks a new era in Parliamentary speech. From the first the vehemence and passion of his words had contrasted with the grave, colourless reasoning of older speakers. His opponents complained that Eliot aimed to " stir up affections ". The quick emphatic sentences he substituted for the cumbrous periods of the day, his rapid arguments, his vivacious and caustic allusions, his passionate appeals, his fearless invective, struck a new note in English eloquence.

The frivolous ostentation of Buckingham, his very figure blazing with jewels and gold, gave point to the fierce attack. " He has broken those nerves and sinews of our land, the stores and treasures of the King. There needs no search for it. It is too visible. His profuse expenses, his superfluous feasts, his magnificent buildings, his riots, his excesses, what are they but the visible evidences of an express exhausting of the State, a chronicle of the immensity of his waste of the revenues of the Crown ? "

With the same terrible directness Eliot reviewed the Duke's greed and corruption, his insatiate ambition, his seizure of all public authority, his neglect of every public duty, his abuse for selfish ends of the powers he had accumulated. " The pleasure of his Majesty, his known directions, his public acts, his acts of council, the decrees of courts—all must be made inferior to this man's will. No right, no interest may withstand him. Through the power of state and justice he has dared ever to strike at his own ends. . . . My Lords," he ended, after a vivid parallel between Buckingham and Sejanus, " you see the man ! What have been his actions, what he is like, you know ! I leave him to your judgment. This only is conceived by us, the knights, citizens, and burgesses of the Commons House of Parliament, that by him came all our evils, in him we find the causes, and on him must be the remedies ! Pereat qui perdere cuncta festinat. Opprimatur ne omnes opprimat ! " (He must be destroyed who hastens to destroy. He must be suppressed lest he suppress us all.)

The reply of Charles was as fierce and sudden as the attack of Eliot. He hurried to the House of Peers to avow as his own the deeds with which Buckingham was charged. Eliot and Digges were called from their seats, and committed prisoners to the Tower. The Commons, however, refused to proceed with public business till their members were restored ; and after a ten days' struggle Eliot was released. But his release was only a prelude to the close of the Parliament. " Not one moment ", the King replied, to the prayer of his Council for delay ; and the final remonstrance in which the Commons begged him to dismiss Buckingham from his service for ever was met by their instant dissolution. The remonstrance was burnt by Royal order, Eliot was deprived of his Vice-Admiralty and the subsidies which the Parliament had refused to grant till their grievances were redressed were levied in the arbitrary form of benevolences.

But the tide of public resistance was slowly rising. Refusals to give anything, " save by way of Parliament ", came in from county after county. The arguments of the judges, who summoned the subsidy-men of Middlesex and Westminster to persuade them to comply, were met by the crowd with a tumultuous shout of " a Parliament ! a Parliament ! else no subsidies ! " Kent stood out to a man. In Bucks the very justices neglected to ask for the " free gift ". The freeholders of Cornwall only answered that, " if they had but two kine, they would sell one of them for supply to his Majesty—in a parliamentary way ".

The failure of the voluntary benevolence was met by the levy of a forced loan. Commissioners were named to assess the amount which every landowner was bound to lend, and to examine on oath all who refused. Every means of persuasion, as of force, was resorted to. The High Church pulpits resounded with the cry of " passive obedience ". Dr. Mainwaring preached before Charles himself that the King needed no parliamentary warrant for taxation, and that to resist his will was to incur eternal damnation. Soldiers were quartered on recalcitrant boroughs. Poor men who refused to lend were pressed into the army or navy. Stubborn tradesmen were flung into prison. Buckingham himself undertook the task of overawing the nobles and the gentry. Among the bishops, the Primate and Bishop Williams of Lincoln alone resisted the King's will. The first was suspended on a frivolous pretext, and the second was disgraced.

But in the country at large resistance was universal. The

northern counties in a mass set the Crown at defiance. The Lincolnshire farmers drove the Commissioners from the town. Shropshire, Devon, and Warwickshire " refused utterly ". Eight peers, with Lord Essex and Lord Warwick at their head, declined to comply with the exaction as illegal. Two hundred country gentlemen, whose obstinacy had not been subdued by their transfer from prison to prison, were summoned before the Council. John Hampden, as yet only a young Buckinghamshire squire, appeared at the board to begin that career of patriotism which has made his name dear to Englishmen. " I could be content to lend " he said " but fear to draw on myself that curse in Magna Carta, which should be read twice a year against those who infringe it." So close an imprisonment in the Gate House rewarded his protest, " that he never afterwards did look like the same man he was before ".

With gathering discontent as well as bankruptcy before him, nothing could save the Duke but a great military success ; and he equipped a force of seven thousand men for the maddest and most profligate of all his enterprises. In the great struggle with Catholicism the hopes of every Protestant rested on the union of England with France against the House of Austria. From causes never fully explained, but in which a personal pique against the French minister, Cardinal Richelieu, mingled with the desire to win an easy popularity at home by supporting the French Huguenots, Buckingham at this juncture broke suddenly with France, sailed in person to the Isle of Rhé, and roused the great Huguenot city of Rochelle to revolt. The expedition was as disastrous as it was impolitic. After a useless siege of the castle of St. Martin, the English troops were forced to fall back along a narrow causeway to their ships ; and in the retreat two thousand fell, without the loss of a single man to their enemies.

The first result of Buckingham's folly was the fall of Rochelle and the ruin of the Huguenot cause in France. Indirectly, as we have seen, it helped on the ruin of the cause of Protestantism in Germany. But in England it forced on Charles, overwhelmed as he was with debt and shame, the summoning of a new Parliament ; a Parliament which met in a mood even more resolute than the last. The Court candidates were everywhere rejected. The patriot leaders were triumphantly returned. To have suffered in the recent resistance to arbitrary taxation was the sure road to a seat.

In spite of Eliot's counsel, all other grievances, even that of Buckingham himself, gave place to the craving for redress of wrongs done to personal liberty. " We must vindicate our ancient liberties " said Sir Thomas Wentworth, in words soon to be remembered against himself : " we must reinforce the laws made by our ancestors. We must set such a stamp upon them, as no licentious spirit shall dare hereafter to invade them." Heedless of sharp and menacing messages from the King, of demands that they should take his " Royal word " for their liberties, the House bent itself to one great work, the drawing up of a Petition of Right.

The statutes that protected the subject against arbitrary taxation, against loans and benevolences, against punishment, outlawry, or deprivation of goods, otherwise than by lawful judgment of his peers, against arbitrary imprisonment without stated charge, against billeting of soldiery on the people or enactment of martial law in time of peace, were formally recited. The breaches of them under the last Parliament, were recited as formally. At the close of this significant list, the Commons prayed " that no man hereafter be compelled to make or yield any gift, loan, benevolence, tax, or such like charge, without common consent by Act of Parliament. And that none be called to make answer, or to take such oaths, or to be confined or otherwise molested or disputed concerning the same, or for refusal thereof. And that no freeman may in such manner as is before mentioned be imprisoned or detained. And that your Majesty would be pleased to remove the said soldiers and mariners, and that your people may not be so burthened in time to come. And that the commissions for proceeding by martial law may be revoked and annulled, and that hereafter no commissions of like nature may issue forth to any person or persons whatsoever to be executed as aforesaid, lest by colour of them any of your Majesty's subjects be destroyed and put to death, contrary to the laws and franchises of the land."

It was in vain that the Lords desired to conciliate Charles by a reservation of his " sovereign power ". " Our petition " Pym quietly replied " is for the laws of England, and this power seems to be another power distinct from the power of the law." The Lords yielded, but Charles gave an evasive reply ; and the failure of the more moderate counsels for which his own had been set aside, called Eliot again to the front. In a speech of unprecedented boldness he moved the presentation to the King of a Remonstrance on the state of the realm.

And here is the speech which Eliot made. He does not mention Buckingham by name, but everyone knew who it was that he was blaming for the set-backs to English prestige, and the disasters which had befallen the cause of Protestantism on the Continent. He refrained from any personal attack partly because he could see, possibly more clearly than anyone else, the importance of the principle involved, and partly because he did not want to precipitate another dissolution, as had happened when Buckingham was criticized in Charles's first parliament. *Who first insisted on the King's ministers being responsible to Parliament for their actions ?*

SIR JOHN ELIOT

ON THE RESPONSIBILITY OF MINISTERS TO PARLIAMENT

WE sit here as the great Council of the King, and in that company it is our duty to take into consideration the state and affairs of the kingdom, and when there is occasion to give a true representation of them by way of counsel and advice, with what we conceive necessary or expedient to be done.

In this consideration I confess many a sad thought hath affrighted me, and that not only in respect of our dangers from abroad (which yet I know are great, as they have been often pressed and dilated to us), but in respect of our disorders here at home, which do enforce those dangers and by which they are occasioned. For I believe I shall make it clear to you that both at first the cause of these dangers were our disorders, and our disorders now are yet our greatest dangers ; that not so much the potency of our enemies as the weakness of ourselves doth threaten us ; so that the saying of one of the Fathers may be presumed by us, "Non tam potentia sua quam negligentia nostra" (Not so much by their power as by our neglect). Our want of true devotion to Heaven ; our insincerity and doubting in religion ; our want of counsels ; our precipitate actions ; the insufficiency or unfaithfulness of our generals abroad ; the ignorance or corruption of our ministers at home ; the impoverishing of the sovereign ; the oppression and depression of the subject ; the exhausting of our treasures ; the waste of our provisions ; consumption of our ships ; destruction of our men ;—these make the advantage to our enemies, not the reputation of their arms ; and if in these there be not reformation, we need no foes abroad ; time itself will ruin us.

To show this more fully, I believe you will all hold it necessary that what I say should not seem an aspersion on the State or imputation on the Government, as I have known such motions misinterpreted. But far is this from me to propose, who have none but clear thoughts of the excellency of the King ; nor can I have other ends but the advancement of his Majesty's glory. I shall desire a little of your patience extraordinary, as I lay open the particulars, which I shall do with what brevity I may, answerable to the importance of the cause and the necessity now upon us ; yet with such respect and observation to the time, as I hope it shall not be thought troublesome.

1. For the first, then, our insincerity and doubting in religion is the greatest and most dangerous disorder of all others. This hath never been unpunished ; and of this we have many strong examples of all states and in all times to awe us. . . .

2. For the second, our want of counsels, that great disorder in a State under which there cannot be stability. If effects may show their causes (as they are often a perfect demonstration of them), our misfortunes, our disasters, serve to prove our deficiencies in counsel, and the consequences they draw with them. If reason be allowed in this dark age, the judgment of dependencies and foresight of contingencies in affairs do confirm my position. For, if we view ourselves at home, are we in strength, are we in reputation, equal to our ancestors ? If we view ourselves abroad, are our friends as many ? Are our enemies no more ? Do our friends retain their safety and possessions ? Do not our enemies enlarge themselves, and gain from them and us ? To what counsel owe we the loss of the Palatinate, where we sacrificed both our honour and our men sent thither, stopping those great powers appointed for the service, by which it might have been defended ? What counsel gave direction to the late action, whose wounds are yet bleeding ? I mean the expedition to Rhé, of which there is yet so sad a memory in all men. What design for us or advantage to our State could that impart ?

You know the wisdom of your ancestors, and the practice of their times, how they preserved their safeties. We all know, and have as much cause to doubt [i.e. distrust or guard against] as they had, the greatness and ambition of that kingdom, which the Old World could not satisfy. Against this greatness and ambition we likewise know the proceedings of that princess, that never-to-be-forgotten, excellent Queen Elizabeth, whose name, without admiration, falls not into mention even with her enemies. You know how she advanced herself, and how she advanced the nation in glory and in state ; how she depressed her enemies, and how she upheld her

L

friends ; how she enjoyed a full security, and made those our scorn who now are made our terror.

Some of the principles she built on were these, and if I mistake, let reason and our statesmen contradict me :

First, to maintain, in what she might, a unity in France, that the kingdom, being at peace within itself, might be a bulwark to keep back the power of Spain by land.

Next, to preserve an amity and league between that State and us, that so we might come in aid of the Low Countries [Holland], and by that means receive their ships, and help them by sea.

This triple cord, so working between France, the States [Holland], and England, might enable us, as occasion should require, to give assistance unto others. And by this means, as the experience of that time doth tell us, we were not only free from those fears that now possess and trouble us, but then our names were fearful to our enemies. See now what correspondency our action had with this. Try our conduct by these rules. It did induce, as a necessary consequence, a division in France between Protestants and their King, of which there is too woeful and lamentable experience. It hath made an absolute breach between that State and us, and so entertains us against France, and France in preparation against us, that we have nothing to promise to our neighbours, nay, hardly to ourselves. Next, observe the time in which it was attempted, and you shall find it not only varying from those principles, but directly contrary and opposite to those ends ; and such, as from the issue and success, rather might be thought a conception of Spain than begotten here with us.

You know the dangers of Denmark, and how much they concern us ; what in respect of our alliance and the country ; what in the importance of the Sound ; what an advantage to our enemies the gain thereof would be ! What loss, what prejudice, to us by this disunion ; we breaking in upon

France, France enraged by us, and the Netherlands at amazement between both! Neither could we intend to aid that luckless King [Christian IV of Denmark], whose loss is our disaster.

Can those [the King's ministers] that express their trouble at the hearing of these things, and have so often told us in this place of their knowledge in the conjunctures and disjunctures of affairs—can they say they advised in this? Was this an act of counsel, Mr. Speaker? I have more charity than to think it; and, unless they make confession of it themselves, I cannot believe it.

3. For the next, the insufficiency and unfaithfulness of our generals (that great disorder abroad), what shall I say? I wish there were not cause to mention it; and but for the apprehension of the danger that is to come, if the like choice hereafter be not prevented, I could willingly be silent. But my duty to my sovereign, my service to this House, and the safety and honour of my country, are above all respects; and what so nearly trenches to the prejudice of these must not, shall not, be forborne.

At Cadiz, when in that first expedition we made, when we arrived and found a conquest ready—the Spanish ships, I mean—fit for the satisfaction of a voyage, and of which some of the chiefest then there themselves have since assured me that the satisfaction would have been sufficient, either in point of honour or in point of profit—why was it neglected? Why was it not achieved, it being granted on all hands how feasible it was?

Afterwards when, with the destruction of some of our men and the exposure of others, who (though their fortune since has not been such), by chance, came off safe—when, I say, with the loss of our serviceable men, that unserviceable fort was gained, and the whole army landed, why was there nothing done? Why was there nothing attempted? If nothing was intended, wherefore did they land? If there was a service, wherefore were they shipped again? Mr. Speaker, it satisfies me too much [*i.e.* I am over-satisfied] in this case—when I think of their dry and hungry march into that drunken quarter (for so the soldiers termed it) which was the period of their journey—that divers of our men being left as a sacrifice to the enemy, that labour was at end.

For the next understanding at Rhé, I will not trouble you with much, only this in short. Was not that whole action carried against the judgment and opinion of those officers that were of the council ? Was not the first, was not the last, was not all in the landing, in the entrenching, in the continuance there, in the assault, in the retreat, without their assent ? Did any advice take place of such as were of the council ? If there should be made a particular inquisition thereof, these things will be manifest and more. I will not instance the manifest that was made, giving the reason of these arms ; nor by whom, nor in what manner nor on what grounds it was published, nor what effects it hath wrought, drawing, as it were, almost the whole world into league against us. Nor will I mention the leaving of the wines, the leaving of the salt, which were in our possession, and of a value, as it is said, to answer much of our expense. Nor will I dwell on that great wonder (which no Alexander or Cæsar ever did), the enriching of the enemy by courtesies when our soldiers wanted help ; nor the private intercourse and parleys with the fort, which were continually held. What they intended may be read in the success ; and upon due examination thereof, they would not want their proofs.

For the last voyage to Rochelle there need be no observations ; it is so fresh in memory ; nor will I make an inference or corollary on all. Your own knowledge shall judge what truth or what sufficiency they express.

4. For the next, the ignorance and corruption of our ministers, where can you miss of instances ? If you survey the court, if you survey the country ; if the Church, if the city be examined ; if you observe the Bar, if the Bench, if the ports, if the shipping, if the land, if the seas,—all these will render

you variety of proofs, and that in such measure and proportion as shows the greatness of our disease to be such that if there be not some speedy application for remedy, our case is almost desperate.

5. Mr. Speaker, I fear I have been too long in these particulars that are past, and am unwilling to offend you; therefore in the rest I shall be shorter; and as to that which concerns the impoverishing of the King, no other arguments will I use than such as all men grant.

The exchequer, you know, is empty, and the reputation thereof gone; the ancient lands are sold; the jewels pawned; the plate engaged; the debt still great; almost all charges, both ordinary and extraordinary, borne up by projects! What poverty can be greater? What necessity so great? What perfect English heart is not almost dissolved into sorrow for this truth?

6. For the oppression of the subject, which, as I remember, is the next particular I proposed, it needs no demonstration. The whole kingdom is proof; and, for the exhausting of our treasures, that very oppression speaks it. What waste of our provisions, what consumption of our ships, what destruction of our men there hath been! Witness that expedition to Algiers; witness that with Mansfeldt; witness that to Cadiz; witness the next—witness that to Rhé; witness the last (I pray God we may never have more such witnesses!)—witness, likewise, the Palatinate; witness Denmark, witness the Turks, witness the Dunkirkers, witness all! What losses we have sustained! How we are impaired in munitions, in ships, in men!

It is beyond contradiction that we were never so weakened, not ever had less hope how to be restored.

These, Mr. Speaker, are our dangers, these are they who do threaten us, and these are, like the Trojan horse, brought in cunningly to surprise us. In these do lurk the strongest of our enemies, ready to issue on us, and if we do not speedily expel them, these are the signs, these are the invitations to others!

These are the things, sir, I shall desire to have taken into consideration ; that as we are the great council of the kingdom, and have the apprehension of these dangers, we may truly represent them unto the King, which I conceive we are bound to do by a triple obligation—of duty to God, of duty to his Majesty, and of duty to our country.

And therefore I wish it may so stand with the wisdom and judgment of the House that these things may be drawn into the body of Remonstrance, and in all humility expressed, with a prayer to his Majesty that, for the safety of himself, for the safety of the kingdom, for the safety of religion, he will be pleased to give us time to make perfect inquisition thereof, or to take them into his own wisdom, and there give them such timely reformation as the necessity and justice of the case doth import.

And thus, sir, with a large affection and loyalty to his Majesty, and with a firm duty and service to my country, I have suddenly (and it may be with some disorder) expressed the weak apprehensions I have ; wherein, if I have erred, I humbly crave your pardon, and so submit myself to the censure of the House.

Charles was not likely to allow any such inquisition into the conduct of his favourite. He sent a message to Parliament forbidding them to " lay any scandal or aspersion upon the State, Government, or ministers thereof ". At this defiance of their right of free speech there was a moment's dead silence, and then such an uproar as the House had never before seen—" some weeping, some expostulating, some prophesying of the fatal ruin of our kingdom " as one of the Members wrote. Charles had linked himself indissolubly with Buckingham ; a further attack on the Minister was an attack on the King, and many of the rank and file drew back from any such thought. But the Puritans pressed on, strong in their Calvinistic belief in the equality of all men before God. They alone could see the struggle clearly as one between tyranny and liberty. They insisted on placing the Duke's name in the Remonstrance. Charles gave in, and signed the Petition of Right, which thus became law. There was no need now to look for ancient precedents when the rights of the individual were in dispute. Charles, however, though he had signed the Petition, was as determined as ever to insist on " the right divine of kings to govern wrong ". *How did Charles I rule without a Parliament ?* The story is told, again by Green.

J. R. GREEN

THE TYRANNY

THE Commons, who had deferred all grant of customs till the wrong done in the illegal levy of them was redressed, had summoned the farmers of those dues to the bar ; but though they appeared, they pleaded the King's command as a ground for their refusal to answer. The House was proceeding to protest, when the Speaker signified that he had received a Royal order to adjourn. Dissolution was clearly at hand, and the long-suppressed indignation broke out in a scene of strange disorder. The Speaker was held down in the chair, while Eliot, still clinging to his great principle of ministerial responsibility, denounced the new Treasurer as the adviser of the measure. " None have gone about to break Parliaments " he added in words to which after events gave a terrible significance " but in the end Parliaments have broken them." The doors were locked, and in spite of the Speaker's protests, of the repeated knocking of the usher sent by Charles to summon the Commons to his presence in the Lords' chamber, and of the gathering tumult within the House itself, the loud " Aye, Aye " of the bulk of the members supported Eliot in his last vindication of English liberty. By successive resolutions the Commons declared whosoever should bring in innovations in religion, or whatsoever minister advised the levy of subsidies not granted in Parliament, " a capital enemy to the Kingdom and Commonwealth ", and every subject voluntarily complying with illegal acts and demands " a betrayer of the liberty of England, and an enemy of the same ".

At the opening of his Third Parliament Charles had hinted in ominous words that the continuance of Parliament at all depended on its compliance with his will. " If you do not your duty " said the King " mine would then order me to use those other means which God has put into my hand." The threat, however, failed to break the resistance of the Commons, and the ominous words passed into a settled policy. " We have showed " said a Royal Proclamation which followed on the dissolution of the Houses " by our frequent meeting our people, our love to the use of Parliament ; yet, the late abuse having for the present driven us unwillingly out of that course, we shall account it presumption for any to prescribe any time unto us for Parliament."

No Parliament, in fact, met for eleven years. But it would be unjust to charge the King at the outset of this period with any definite scheme of establishing a tyranny, or of changing what he conceived to be the older constitution of the realm. He " hated the very name of Parliaments ", but in spite of his hate he had no settled purpose in abolishing them. His belief was that England would in time recover its senses, and that then Parliament might reassemble without inconvenience to the Crown.

In the interval, however long it might be, he proposed to govern single-handed by the use of " those means which God had put into his hands ". Resistance, indeed, he was resolved to put down. The leaders of the country party in the last Parliament were thrown into prison ; and Eliot died, the first martyr of English liberty, in the Tower. Men were forbidden to speak of the reassembling of a Parliament. Laud was encouraged to break the obstinate opposition of the Puritans by the enforcement of religious uniformity.

But here the King stopped. The opportunity which might have suggested dreams of organized despotism to a Richelieu, suggested only means of filling the Exchequer to Charles. He had in truth neither the grander nor the meaner instincts of the born tyrant. He did not seek to gain an absolute power over his people, because he believed that his absolute power was already a part of the constitution of the country. He set up no standing army to secure it, partly because he was poor, but yet more because his faith in his position was such that he never dreamt of any effectual resistance.

His expedients for freeing the Crown from that dependence on Parliaments against which his pride as a sovereign revolted were simply peace and economy. To secure the first he sacrificed an opportunity greater than ever his father had trodden under foot. The fortunes of the great struggle in Germany were suddenly reversed at this juncture by the appearance of Gustavus Adolphus, with a Swedish army, in the heart of Germany. Tilly was defeated and slain ; the Catholic League humbled in the dust ; Munich, the capital of its Bavarian leader, occupied by the Swedish army, and the Lutheran princes of North Germany freed from the pressure of the Imperial soldiery ; while the Emperor himself, trembling within the walls of Vienna, was driven to call for aid from Wallenstein, an adventurer whose ambition he dreaded, but whose army could alone arrest the progress of the Protestant conqueror. The ruin that James had wrought was suddenly averted ; but the victories of Protestantism had no more power to draw Charles out of the petty circle of his politics at home than its defeats had had power to draw James out of the circle of his imbecile diplomacy. To support Gustavus by arms, or even by an imposing neutrality, meant a charge on the Royal Treasury which necessitated a fresh appeal to the Commons ; and this appeal Charles was resolved never to make. At the very crisis of the struggle, therefore, he patched up a hasty peace with both the two great Catholic powers of France and Spain, and fell back from any interference with the affairs of the Continent.

His whole attention was absorbed by the pressing question of revenue. The debt was a large one ; and the ordinary income of the Crown, unaided by parliamentary supplies, was utterly inadequate to meet its ordinary expenditure. Charles was himself frugal and laborious ; and the administration of Weston, the new Lord Treasurer, whom he created Earl of Portland, contrasted advantageously with the waste and extravagance of the government under Buckingham. But economy failed to close the yawning gulf of the Treasury, and the course into which Charles was driven by the financial pressure showed with how wise a prescience the Commons had fixed on the point of arbitrary taxation as the chief danger to constitutional freedom.

It is curious to see to what shifts the Royal pride was driven in its effort at once to fill the Exchequer, and yet to avoid, as far as it could, any direct breach of constitutional law in the imposition of taxes by the sole authority of the Crown. The dormant powers of the prerogative were strained to their utmost. The right of the Crown to force knighthood on the landed gentry was revived, in order to squeeze them into composition for the refusal of it. Fines were levied on them for the redress of defects in their title-deeds. A Commission of the Forests exacted large sums from the neighbouring landowners for their encroachments on Crown lands. London, the special object of courtly dislike, on account of its stubborn Puritanism, was brought within the sweep of Royal extortion by the enforcement of an illegal proclamation which James had issued, prohibiting its extension. Every house throughout the large suburban districts in which the prohibition had been disregarded was only saved from demolition by the payment of three years' rental to the Crown. The Treasury gained a hundred thousand pounds by this clever stroke, and Charles gained the bitter enmity of the great city whose strength and resources were fatal to him in the coming war.

Shifts of this kind, however, did little to fill the Treasury, great as was the annoyance they caused. Charles was driven from courses of doubtful legality to a more open defiance of law. Monopolies, abandoned by Elizabeth, extinguished by Act of Parliament under James, and denounced with his own assent in the Petition of Right, were revived on a scale far more gigantic than had been seen before, the companies who undertook them paying a fixed duty on their profits as well as a large sum for the original concession of the monopoly. Wine, soap, salt, and almost every article of domestic consumption fell into the hands of monopolists, and rose in price out of all proportion to the profit gained by the Crown. " They sup in our cup " Colepepper said afterwards in the Long Parliament " they dip in our dish, they sit by our fire ; we find them in the dye-vat, the wash-bowls, and the powdering tub. They share with the cutler in his box. They have marked and sealed us from head to foot."

Nothing, indeed, better marks the character of Charles than his conduct as to the Petition of Right. He had given his assent to it, he was fond of bidding Parliament rely on his " Royal word ", but the thought of his pledge seems never to have troubled him for an instant. From the moment he began his career of government without a Parliament every one of the abuses he had promised to abolish, such as illegal imprisonment, or tampering with the judges, was resorted to as a matter of course.

His penury, in spite of the financial expedients we have described, drove him inevitably on to the fatal rock of illegal taxation. The exaction of Customs duties went on as of old at the ports. Writs were issued for the levy of " benevolences " from the shires. The resistance of the London merchants was roughly put down by the Star Chamber. Chambers, an alderman of London, who complained bitterly that men were worse off in England than in Turkey, was ruined by a fine of two thousand pounds, and died broken-hearted in prison.

The freeholders of the counties were more difficult to deal with. When those of Cornwall were called together at Bodmin to contribute to a voluntary loan, half the hundreds refused, and the yield of the rest came to little more than two thousand pounds. One of the Cornishmen has left an amusing record

of the scene before the Commissioners appointed for assess-
ment of the loan. " Some with great words and threatenings,
some with persuasions " he says " were drawn to it. I was like
to have been complimented out of my money ; but knowing
with whom I had to deal, I held, when I talked with them,
my hands fast in my pockets."

Vexatious, indeed, and illegal as were the proceedings of
the Crown, there seems to have been little apprehension of
any permanent danger to freedom in the country at large.
To those who read the letters of the time there is something
inexpressibly touching in the general faith of their writers in
the ultimate victory of the Law. Charles was obstinate, but
obstinacy was too common a foible amongst Englishmen to
rouse any vehement resentment. The people were as stubborn
as their King, and their political sense told them that the
slightest disturbance of affairs must shake down the financial
fabric which Charles was slowly building up, and force him
back on subsidies and a Parliament. Meanwhile they would
wait for better days, and their patience was aided by the
general prosperity of the country. The long peace was pro-
ducing its inevitable results in a vast extension of commerce
and a rise of manufactures in the towns of the West Riding of
Yorkshire. Fresh land was being brought into cultivation,
and a great scheme was set on foot for reclaiming the Fens.
The new wealth of the country gentry, through the increase of
rent, was seen in the splendour of the houses which they were
raising.

The contrast of this peace and prosperity with the ruin
and bloodshed of the Continent afforded a ready argument
to the friends of the King's system. So tranquil was the outer
appearance of the country that in Court circles all sense of
danger had disappeared. " Some of the greatest statesmen
and privy councillors " says May " would ordinarily laugh
when the word, ' liberty of the subject ', was named." There
were courtiers bold enough to express their hope that " the
King would never need any more Parliaments ". But beneath

this outer calm " the country " Clarendon honestly tells us while eulogizing the Peace " was full of pride and mutiny and discontent ".

[Charles had the services of two vigorous and unscrupulous ministers : Thomas Wentworth, later Earl of Strafford, who became Lord Lieutenant of Ireland ; and Archbishop Laud, of the High Church party, whose chief aim was to enforce the use of the Prayer Book throughout the whole of Britain.]

In spite of the severe economy of Charles and his ministers, new exactions were necessary, at a time when the rising discontent made every new exaction a challenge to revolt. But danger and difficulty were lost on the temper of the two men who really governed England. To Laud and Strafford, indeed, the King seemed over-cautious, the Star Chamber feeble, the judges over-scrupulous. " I am for Thorough ", the one writes to the other in alternate fits of impatience at the slow progress they are making. Strafford was anxious that his good work might not " be spoiled on that side ". Laud echoed the wish, while he envied the free course of the Lord Lieutenant. " You have a good deal of humour here " he writes " for your proceeding. Go on a' God's name. I have done with expecting of Thorough on this side." The financial pressure was seized by both to force the King on to a bolder course.

" The debt of the Crown being taken off " Strafford urged " you may govern at your will." All pretence of precedents was thrown aside, and Laud resolved to find a permanent revenue in the conversion of the " ship-money " levied on ports and the maritime counties into a general tax imposed by the Royal will upon the whole country. The sum expected from the tax was no less than a quarter of a million a year. " I know no reason " Strafford had written significantly " but you may as well rule the common lawyers in England as I, poor beagle, do here " ; and a bench of judges, remodelled on his hint for the occasion, no sooner declared the new impost to be legal than he drew the logical deduction from their decision.

" Since it is lawful for the King to impose a tax for the equipment of the navy, it must be equally so for the levy of an army : and the same reason which authorizes him to levy an army to resist, will authorize him to carry that army abroad that he may prevent invasion. Moreover, what is law in England is law also in Scotland and Ireland. The decision of the judges will therefore make the King absolute at home and formidable abroad. Let him only abstain from war for a few years that he may habituate his subjects to the payment of that tax, and in the end he will find himself more powerful and respected than any of his predecessors."

But there were men who saw the danger to freedom in this levy of ship-money as clearly as Strafford himself. John Hampden, a friend of Eliot, a man of consummate ability, of unequalled power of persuasion, of a keen intelligence, ripe learning, and a character singularly pure and lovable, had already shown the firmness of his temper in his refusal to contribute to the forced loan of 1626. He now repeated his refusal, declared ship-money an illegal impost, and resolved to rouse the spirit of the country by an appeal for protection to the law.

The news of Hampden's resistance thrilled through England at the very moment when men were roused by the news of resistance in the north. The submission with which Scotland had bent to aggression after aggression found an end at last. The Dean of Edinburgh had no sooner opened the new Prayer Book than a murmur ran through the congregation, and the murmur soon grew into a formidable riot. The Church was cleared, the service read, but the rising discontent frightened the judges into a decision that the Royal writ enjoined the purchase, and not the use, of the Prayer Book. Its use was at once discontinued, and the angry orders which came from England for its restoration were met by a shower of protests from every part of Scotland. The Duke of Lennox alone took sixty-eight petitions with him to the Court; while ministers, nobles, and gentry poured into Edinburgh to organize the national resistance.

The effect of these events in Scotland was at once seen in the open demonstration of discontent south of the border. Prynne and his fellow pamphleteers, when Laud dragged them before the Star Chamber as " trumpets of sedition ", listened with defiance to their sentence of exposure in the pillory and imprisonment for life; and the crowd who filled Palace Yard to witness their punishment groaned at the cutting off of their ears, and " gave a great shout " when Prynne urged that the sentence on him was contrary to the law. A hundred thousand Londoners lined the road as they passed on the way to prison; and the journey of these " Martyrs ", as the spectators called them, was like a triumphal progress. Startled as he was at the sudden burst of popular feeling, Laud was dauntless as ever; and Prynne's entertainers, as he passed through the country, were summoned before the Star Chamber, while the censorship struck fiercer blows at the Puritan press.

But the real danger lay not in the libels of silly zealots but in the attitude of Scotland, and in the effect which was being produced in England at large by the trial of Hampden. For twelve days the cause of ship-money was solemnly argued before the full bench of judges. It was proved that the tax in past times had been levied only in cases of sudden emergency, and confined to the coast and port towns alone, and that even the show of legality had been taken from it by formal Statute and by the Petition of Right.

The case was adjourned, but the discussion told not merely on England but on the temper of the Scots. Charles had replied to their petitions by a simple order to all strangers to leave the capital. But the Council was unable to enforce his order; and the nobles and gentry before dispersing to their homes named a body of delegates, under the odd title of " the Tables ", who carried on through the winter a series of negotiations with the Crown.

The negotiations were interrupted in the following spring by a renewed order for their dispersion, and for the acceptance of a Prayer Book; while the judges in England delivered at last their long-delayed decision on Hampden's case. All save two laid down the broad principle that no statute prohibiting arbitrary taxation could be pleaded against the King's will. " I never read or heard " said Judge Berkley " that lex was rex, but it is common and most true that rex is lex." Finch, the Chief-Justice, summed up the opinions of his fellow judges. " Acts of Parliament to take away the King's Royal power in the defence of his kingdom are void", he said: " they are void Acts of Parliament to bind the King not to command the subjects, their persons, and goods, and I say their money too, for no Acts of Parliament made any difference."

" I wish Mr. Hampden and others to his likeness " the Lord Lieutenant wrote bitterly from Ireland " were well whipt into their right senses." Amidst the exultation of the Court over the decision of the judges, Wentworth saw clearly that Hampden's work had been done. His resistance had roused England to a sense of the danger to her freedom, and forced into light the real character of the Royal claims.

How stern and bitter the temper even of the noblest Puritans had become at last we see in the poem which Milton produced at this time, his elegy of " Lycidas ". Its grave and tender lament is broken by a sudden flash of indignation at the dangers around the Church, at the " blind mouths that scarce themselves know how to hold a sheep-hook ", and to whom " the hungry sheep look up, and are not fed ", while " the grim wolf " of Rome " with privy paw daily devours apace, and nothing said ! " The stern resolve of the people to demand justice on their tyrants spoke in his threat of the axe. Strafford and Laud, and Charles himself, had yet to reckon with " that two-handed engine at the door " which stood " ready to smite once, and smite no more ".

But stern as was the general resolve, there was no need for immediate action, for the difficulties which were gathering in the north were certain to bring a strain on the Government which would force it to seek support from the people. The King's demand for immediate submission, which reached Edinburgh with the significant comment of the Hampden judgment, at once gathered the whole body of remonstrants together round " the Tables " at Stirling ; and a protestation, read at Edinburgh, was followed, on Archibald Johnston of Warrington's suggestion, by the renewal of the Covenant with God which had been drawn up and sworn to in a previous hour of peril, when Mary was still plotting against Protestantism, and Spain was preparing its Armada.

[The Scots quickly raised an army to defend their religious freedom. Charles sent the royal fleet into the Forth and tried to raise a force sufficient to subdue them.]

Charles, however, was not strong enough to fight, and the two armies returned home—on his consent to the gathering of a free Assembly and Parliament. But the pacification at Berwick was a mere suspension of arms ; the King's summons of Wentworth—now created Earl of Strafford—from Ireland was a proof that violent measures were in preparation, and the Scots met the challenge by demands for the convocation of triennial Parliaments, for freedom of elections and of debate. Strafford counselled that they should be whipped back into their senses ; and the discovery of a correspondence which was being carried on between some of the Covenanter leaders and the French Court raised hopes in the King that an appeal to the country for aid against " Scotch treason " would still find an answer in English loyalty.

While Strafford hurried to Ireland to levy forces, Charles summoned what, from its brief duration, is known as the Short Parliament. The Houses met in a mood which gave hopes of an accommodation with the Crown, but all hope of bringing them into an attack on Scotland proved fruitless. The intercepted letters were quietly set aside, and the Commons declared as of old that redress of grievances must precede the

M

grant of supplies. Even an offer to relinquish ship-money failed to draw Parliament from its resolve, and after three weeks' sitting it was roughly dissolved. " Things must go worse before they go better " was the cool comment of St. John, one of the patriot leaders. But the country was strangely moved. " So great a defection in the kingdom " wrote Lord Northumberland " hath not been known in the memory of man." Strafford alone stood undaunted. He had returned from Ireland, where he had easily obtained money and men from his servile Parliament, to pour fresh vigour into the Royal counsels, and to urge that, by the refusal of the Parliament to supply the King's wants, Charles was freed from all rule of government, and entitled to supply himself at his will. The Earl was bent upon war, and took command of the Royal army, which again advanced to the north.

But the Scots were already across the Border ; forcing the passage of the Tyne in the face of an English detachment, they occupied Newcastle, and despatched from that town their proposals of peace. They prayed the King to consider their grievances and " with the advice and consent of the Estates of England convened in Parliament, to settle a firm and desirable peace ". The prayer was backed by preparations for a march upon York, where Charles had already abandoned himself to despair.

Behind him, in fact, England was all but in revolt. The London apprentices mobbed Laud at Lambeth, and broke up the sittings of the High Commission at St. Paul's. The war was denounced everywhere as " the Bishops' war ", and the new levies murdered officers whom they suspected of Papistry, broke down altar-rails in every church they passed, and deserted to their homes. Even in the camp itself neither the threats nor prayers of Strafford could recall the troops to their duty, and he was forced to own that two months were required before they could be fit for the field. The success of the Scots emboldened two peers, Lord Wharton and Lord Howard, to present a petition for peace to the King himself ;

and though Strafford arrested and proposed to shoot them, the Council shrank from desperate courses. The threat of a Scotch advance forced Charles at last to give way, and after endeavouring to evade the necessity of convoking a Parliament by summoning a " Great Council of the Peers " at York, the general repudiation of his project drove him to summon the Houses once more to Westminster.

When the Long Parliament met in 1640 the mantle of leadership fell without debate on the shoulders of John Pym. He had been fighting for constitutional liberty ever since he first entered Parliament in 1614, and now that finance seemed likely to be replaced by force as the chief weapon in the struggle, this man of the clear intellect, the long views, and the patient but implacable purpose, came as of right to occupy the place of leader in the Commons. As guardian of the State and of the liberties of the people he placed Parliament far above the monarchy, while in Parliament itself the real power, he considered, lay with the Commons. He anticipated the Revolution of 1688 which removed James II and placed William III on the throne ; and also the Reform Act of 1832, when the supremacy of the Commons was determined once for all.

Pym's first speech to the Long Parliament was a lengthy affair, but every word was listened to with deep attention. We have room only for his summing up in which he fixed the minds of the Members on their main grievances, and chiefly on the wrongdoings of the King's favourites and of those ministers who had consistently refused to accept any responsibility to Parliament for their actions.

JOHN PYM

GRIEVANCES AGAINST CHARLES I

THE distempers of this kingdom are well known ; they need not repetition ; for though we have good laws, yet they want their execution : or if they were executed, it is in a wrong sense. I shall endeavour to apply a remedy to the breaches that are made. . . .

Firstly, the political interpretation of the law to serve their terms, and thus to impose taxes with a colour of law ; a judge said it when a *habeas corpus* was paid for.

Secondly, by keeping the King in continual want, that he may seek to their counsel for relief : to this purpose, to keep the Parliaments in distaste, that their counsels may be taken. The King by them is brought to this, as a woman that used herself to poison could not live with good meat. Search the chronicles, and we see no king that ever used Parliaments was brought to this want.

Thirdly, arbitrary proceedings in courts of justice ; we have all law left to the conscience of a single man. All courts are now courts of conscience, without conscience.

Fourthly, plotters to enforce a war between Scotland and us, that when we had well wearied one another, we might be both brought to what scorn they pleased.

Fifthly, the sudden dissolving of Parliaments, and punishing of Parliament men, all to affright us from speaking what we think. One was committed for not delivering up the petitions of the House ; then a declaration which slandered our proceedings, as full of lies as leaves, who would have the first ground to be our example. And Papists are under appearance to the King his best subjects, for they contribute money to the war, which the Protestants will not do.

Sixthly, another is military, by getting places of importance into the Papists' hands, as who are commanders in the last army but they ? none more strong in arms than they, to whom their armour is delivered contrary to the statute. Their endeavour is to bring in strangers to be billeted upon us ; we have had no accompt of the Spanish navy, and now our fear is from Ireland.

" And now our fear is from Ireland." In these words Pym renewed his attack on Wentworth, now Earl of Strafford, who had come over from Ireland to advise the King in the struggle which was impending.

When Strafford had transferred his allegiance to the King, after Buckingham's death, Pym had said to him, " Remember what I tell you—that though you leave us now, I will never leave you while your head is upon your shoulders ". The threat was soon to be implemented. Having impeached the judges who had declared ship-money legal, the Long Parliament turned to the impeachment of Strafford. Pym's speech on this occasion is memorable for the eloquence and fervour with which, in words of lasting importance, he stated the case for Law as the safeguard of liberty. Strafford tried to justify himself in a long and subtle speech, but to this Pym made the stern reply that he had separated the King from his people. " The king and his people " said Pym " are obliged to one another in the nearest relations; they have the same interest; they are inseparable in their condition, be it good or evil. He is their head; they are the body. There is such an incorporation as cannot be destroyed without the destruction of both." Charles resented this speech very strongly, and he so exasperated the Commons that they dropped the impeachment and brought in a Bill of Attainder against Strafford. This needed no judicial evidence as with an impeachment, and it was quickly passed by the Commons. But it did need the King's signature. Charles wrote to Strafford that " on the word of a king " (his usual guarantee) " you shall not suffer in life, honour or fortune ". A few days later the London mob quickly induced Charles to find good reason for breaking his word, and Strafford was executed on May 12.

And now events moved rapidly towards that trial of strength by arms which Hampden and Pym had probably foreseen as a sort of bad dream which might come true. The time for argument, for speeches, for appeals to law and tradition was past. The public safety had become, in Falkland's words, the supreme and only law. There is no room here for an account of the Civil War. Essex, the first Parliamentary leader was hesitant and inefficient. Under Cromwell the end soon came, although the country did but exchange one tyranny for another. Let us ask John Milton, Cromwell's foreign secretary, to sum up the Parliamentary case. *What are the true relations between King, Parliament, and People ?* The answer is given in extracts from Milton's pamphlet, *Defence of the English People.*

JOHN MILTON

THE KING, PARLIAMENT, AND PEOPLE

WHEN the king summons or calls together a parliament, he does it by virtue and in discharge of that office, which he has received from the people, that he may advise with them about the weighty affairs of the kingdom, not his own particular affairs. Or when, at any time, the parliament debated of the king's own affairs, if any could properly be called his own, they were always the last things they did ; and it was in their choice when to debate of them, and whether at all or no, and depended not upon the king's pleasure. And they whom it concerns to know this, know very well, that parliaments anciently, whether summoned or not, might by law meet twice a year.

But the laws are called too, " the king's laws ". These are flattering ascriptions ; a king of England can of himself make no law ; for he was not constituted to make laws, but to see those laws kept, which the people made . . . wherefore the law is also called the law of the land, and the people's law. Whence King Ethelstane in the preface to his laws, speaking to all the people, " I have granted you everything " says he " by your own law ".

And in the form of the oath, which the kings of England used to take before they were made kings, the people stipulate with them thus : " Will you grant those just laws, which the people shall choose ? " The king answers, " I will ".

And you are infinitely mistaken in saying, that " when there is no parliament sitting, the king governs the whole state of the kingdom, to all intents and purposes, by a regal power ". For he can determine nothing of any moment, with respect to either peace or war : nor can he put any stop to the proceedings of the courts of justice. And the judges therefore swear, that they will do nothing judicially, but according to law, though the king by word, or mandate, or letters under his own seal, should command the contrary.

Hence it is that the king is often said in our law to be an infant; and to possess his rights and dignities as a child or a ward does his; see the *Mirror*, cap. 4, sect. 22. And hence is that common saying amongst us, that "the king can do no wrong": which you, like a rascal, interpret thus, "Whatever the king does, is no injury, because he is not liable to be punished for it". By this very comment, if there were nothing else, the wonderful impudence and villainy of this fellow discovers itself sufficiently. "It belongs to the head" you say "to command, and not to the members: the king is the head of the parliament." You would not trifle thus, if you had any guts in your brains.

You are mistaken again (but there is no end to your mistakes) in not distinguishing the king's counsellors from the states of the realm: for neither ought he to make choice of all of them, nor of any of them, which the rest do not approve of; but for electing any member of the House of Commons, he never so much as pretended to it. Whom the people appointed to that service, they were severally chosen by the votes of all the people in their respective cities, towns, and counties. . . .

"But the power of judicature" you say "never was invested in the House of Commons." Nor was the king ever possessed of it: remember though, that originally all power proceeded, and yet does proceed, from the people. Which Marcus Tullius excellently well shows in his oration, *De lege Agraria*, of the Agrarian law: "As all powers, authorities, and public administrations ought to be derived from the whole body of the people; so those of them ought in an especial manner so to be derived, which are ordained and appointed for the common benefit and interest of all, to which employments every particular person may both give his vote for the choosing such persons as he thinks will take most care of the public, and withal by voting and making interest for them, lay such obligations upon them as may entitle them to their friendship and good offices in time to come."

Here you see the true rise and original of parliaments, and that it was much ancienter than the Saxon chronicles. Whilst we may dwell in such a light of truth and wisdom, as Cicero's age afforded, you labour in vain to blind us with the darkness of obscurer times. By the saying whereof I would not be understood to derogate in the least from the authority and prudence of our ancestors, who most certainly went further in the enacting of good laws, than either the ages they lived in, or their own learning or education seem to have been capable of; and though sometimes they made laws that were none of the best, yet as being conscious to themselves of the ignorance and infirmity of human nature, they have conveyed this doctrine down to posterity, as the foundation of all laws which likewise all our lawyers admit, that if any law or custom be contrary to the law of God, of nature, or of reason, it ought to be looked upon as null and void.

Whence it follows, that though it were possible for you to discover any statute, or other public sanction, which ascribed to the king a tyrannical power, since that would be repugnant to the will of God, to nature and to right reason, you may learn from that general and primary law of ours, which I have just now quoted, that it will be null and void. But you will never be able to find, that any such right of kings has the least foundation in our law. It is plain, therefore, that the power of judicature was originally in the people themselves, and that the people never did by any royal law part with it to the king. . . .

Under the religious and political oppression of the early Stuarts, many people preferred to leave the country rather than submit to the authority of king and bishop. As early as 1608 some of these exiles for conscience's sake left England for Holland. In 1620 they sailed for America in the *Mayflower*, picking up more men of like spirit at Southampton on the way. Other ships followed in later years, and so great was the exodus under Charles I that he gave orders for it to be

stopped for a time. It is said—and here we have one of the great
" might-have-beens " of history—that among the men already on a
boat in the Thames and bound for America when that order was given,
were John Hampden and Oliver Cromwell.

*Why do the Americans prefer to regard the Pilgrim Fathers as the
founders of their country rather than earlier settlers ?* An answer to this
question, together with some interesting details of the ideals which
inspired the Pilgrims, is given below. The speech was given in 1802
at one of the annual meetings in commemoration of the landing at
Plymouth, Massachusetts. The ornate style obviously belongs to a
more leisured age, but the speech clearly portrays the higher principles
which animated the early settlers in New England. Adams was
President of the United States from 1825 to 1829.

JOHN QUINCY ADAMS

THE PILGRIM FATHERS

OF the various European settlements upon this continent,
which have finally merged in one independent nation,
the first establishments were made at various times, by
several nations, and under the influence of different motives.
In many instances, the conviction of religious obligation
formed one, and a powerful inducement of the adventures;
but in none, excepting the settlement at Plymouth, did they
constitute the sole and exclusive actuating cause. Worldly
interest and commercial speculation entered largely into the
views of other settlers, but the commands of conscience were
the only stimulus to the emigrants from Leyden. Previous
to their expedition hither, they had endured a long banishment from their native country. Under every species of dis-
couragement, they undertook the voyage ; they performed it
in spite of numerous and almost insuperable obstacles ; they
arrived upon a wilderness bound with frost and hoary with
snow, without the boundaries of their charter, outcasts from
all human society, and coasted five weeks together, in the
dead of winter, on this tempestuous shore, exposed at once

to the fury of the elements, to the arrows of the native savage, and to the impending horrors of famine.

Courage and perseverance have a magical talisman, before which difficulties disappear and obstacles vanish into air. These qualities have ever been displayed in their mightiest perfection, as attendants in the retinue of strong passions. From the first discovery of the Western Hemisphere by Columbus until the settlement of Virginia which immediately preceded that of Plymouth, the various adventurers from the ancient world had exhibited upon innumerable occasions that ardour of enterprise and that stubbornness of pursuit which set all danger at defiance, and chained the violence of nature at their feet. But they were all instigated by personal interests. Avarice and ambition had tuned their souls to that pitch of exaltation. Selfish passions were the parents of their heroism. It was reserved for the first settlers of New England to perform achievements equally arduous, to trample down obstructions equally formidable, to dispel dangers equally terrific, under the single inspiration of conscience. To them even liberty herself was but a subordinate and secondary consideration. They claimed exemption from the mandates of human authority, as militating with their subjection to a superior power. Before the voice of heaven they silenced even the calls of their country.

It were an occupation peculiarly pleasing to cull from our early historians, and exhibit before you every detail of this transaction; to carry you in imagination on board their bark at the first moment of her arrival in the bay; to accompany Carver, Winslow, Bradford, and Standish, in all their excursions upon the desolate coast; to follow them into every rivulet and creek where they endeavoured to find a firm footing, and to fix, with a pause of delight and exultation, the instant when the first of these heroic adventurers alighted on the spot where you, their descendants, now enjoy the glorious and happy reward of their labours. But in this grateful task, your former orators, on this anniversary, have anticipated all that the most ardent industry could collect, and gratified all that the most inquisitive curiosity could desire. To you, my friends, every occurrence of that momentous period is already familiar. A transient allusion to a few characteristic instances, which mark the peculiar history of the Plymouth settlers, may properly supply the place of a narrative which, to this auditory, must be superfluous.

One of these remarkable incidents is the execution of that instrument of government by which they formed themselves into a body politic, the day after their arrival upon the coast, and previous to their first landing. This is, perhaps, the only instance in human history of that positive, original social compact, which speculative philosophers have imagined as the only legitimate source of government. Here was a unanimous and personal assent, by all the individuals of the community, to the association by which they became a nation. It was the result of circumstances and discussions which had occurred during their passage from Europe, and is a full demonstration that the nature of civil government, abstracted from the political institutions of their native country, had been an object of their serious meditation.

The settlers of all the former European colonies had contented themselves with the powers conferred upon them by their respective charters, without looking beyond the scal of the royal parchment for the measure of their rights and the rule of their duties. The founders of Plymouth had been impelled by the peculiarities of their situation to examine the subject with deeper and more comprehensive research. After twelve years of banishment from the land of their first allegiance, during which they had been under an adoptive and temporary subjection to another sovereign, they must naturally have been led to reflect upon the relative rights and duties of allegiance and subjection. They had resided in a city, the seat of a university, where the polemical and political controversies of the time were pursued with uncommon fervour. In this period they had witnessed the deadly struggle between the two parties, into which the people of the United Provinces, after their separation from the crown of Spain, had divided themselves. The contest embraced within its compass not only theological doctrines, but political principles, and Maurice and Barnevelt were the temporal leaders of the same rival factions, of which Episcopius and Polyander were the ecclesiastical champions.

That the investigation of the fundamental principles of government was deeply implicated in these dissensions is evident from the immortal work of Grotius, upon the rights of war and peace, which undoubtedly originated from them. Grotius himself had been a most distinguished actor and sufferer in those important scenes of internal convulsion, and his work was first published very shortly after the departure of our forefathers from Leyden.

Another incident, from which we may derive occasion for important reflections, was the attempt of these original settlers to establish among them that community of goods and of labour, which fanciful politicians, from the days of Plato to those of Rousseau, have recommended as the fundamental law of a perfect republic. This theory results, it must be acknowledged, from principles of reasoning most flattering to the human character. If industry, frugality, and disinterested integrity were alike the virtues of all, there would, apparently, be more of the social spirit, in making all property a common stock, and giving to each individual a proportional title to the wealth of the whole. Such is the basis upon which Plato forbids, in his Republic, the division of property. Such is the system upon which Rousseau pronounces the first man who enclosed a field with a fence, and said " This is mine ", a traitor to the human species. A wiser and more useful philosophy, however, directs us to consider man according to the nature in which he was formed; subject to infirmities, which no wisdom can remedy; to weaknesses, which no institution can strengthen; to vices, which no legislation can correct.

Hence, it becomes obvious that separate property is the natural and indisputable right of separate exertion; that community of goods without community of toil is oppressive and unjust; that it counteracts the laws of nature, which prescribe that he only who sows the seed shall reap the harvest; that it discourages all energy, by destroying its rewards; and makes the most virtuous and active members of society the slaves and drudges of the worst. Such was the issue of this experiment among our forefathers, and the same event demonstrated the error of the system in the elder settlement of Virginia. Let us cherish that spirit of harmony which prompted our forefathers to make the attempt, under circumstances more favourable to its success than, perhaps, ever occurred upon earth. Let us no less admire the candour with which they relinquished it, upon discovering its irremediable inefficacy.

To found principles of government upon too advantageous an estimate of the human character is an error of inexperience, the source of which is so amiable that it is impossible to censure it with severity. We have seen the same mistake, committed in our own age, and upon a larger theatre. Happily for our ancestors, their situation allowed them to repair it before its effects had proved destructive. They had no pride of vain philosophy to support, no perfidious rage of faction to glut, by persevering in their mistakes until they should be extinguished in torrents of blood.

As the attempt to establish among themselves the community of goods was a seal of that sacred bond which knit them so closely together, so the conduct they observed towards the natives of the country displays their steadfast adherence to the rules of justice and their faithful attachment to those of benevolence and charity.

No European settlement ever formed upon this continent has been more distinguished for undeviating kindness and equity towards the savages. There are, indeed, moralists who have questioned the right of the Europeans to intrude upon the possessions of the aboriginals in any case, and under any limitations whatsoever. But have they maturely considered the whole subject? The Indian right of possession itself stands, with regard to the greatest part of the country, upon a questionable foundation. Their cultivated fields ; their constructed habitations ; a space of ample sufficiency for their subsistence, and whatever they had annexed to themselves by personal labour, was undoubtedly, by the laws of nature, theirs. But what is the right of a huntsman to the forest of a thousand miles over which he has accidentally ranged in quest of prey ?

Shall the liberal bounties of Providence to the race of man be monopolized by one of ten thousand for whom they were created ? Shall the exuberant bosom of the common mother, amply adequate to the nourishment of millions, be claimed exclusively by a few hundreds of her offspring ? Shall the lordly savage not only disdain the virtues and enjoyments of civilization himself, but shall he control the civilization of a world ? Shall he forbid the wilderness to blossom like a rose ? Shall he forbid the oaks of the forest to fall before the axe of industry, and to rise again, transformed into the habitations of ease and elegance ? Shall he doom an immense region of the globe to perpetual desolation, and to hear the howlings of the tiger and the wolf silence for ever the voice of human gladness ? Shall the fields and the valleys, which a beneficent God has formed to teem with the life of innumerable multitudes, be condemned to everlasting barrenness ? Shall the mighty rivers, poured out by the hand of nature as channels of communication between numerous nations, roll their waters in sullen silence and eternal solitude to the deep ? Have hundreds of commodious harbours, a thousand leagues of coast, and a boundless ocean, been spread in the front of this land, and shall every purpose of utility to which they could apply be prohibited by the tenant of the woods ?

No, generous philanthropists ! Heaven has not been thus inconsistent in the works of its hands. Heaven has not thus placed at irreconcilable strife its moral laws with its physical creation. The Pilgrims of Plymouth obtained their right of possession to the territory on which they settled, by titles as fair and unequivocal as any human property can be held. By their voluntary association they recognized their allegiance to the government of Britain, and in process of time received whatever powers and authorities could be conferred upon them by a charter from their sovereign. The spot on which they fixed had belonged to an Indian tribe, totally extirpated by that devouring pestilence which had swept the country shortly before their arrival. The territory, thus free from all exclusive possession, they might have taken by the natural right of occupancy. Desirous, however, of giving ample satisfaction to every pretence of prior right, by formal and solemn conventions with the chiefs of the neighbouring tribes, they acquired the further security of a purchase. At their hands the children of the desert had no cause of complaint. . . .

The changes in the forms and principles of religious worship were introduced and regulated in England by the hand of public authority. But that hand had not been uniform or steady in its operations. During the persecutions inflicted, in the interval of Popish restoration under the reign of Mary, upon all who favoured the reformation, many of the most zealous reformers had been compelled to fly their country. While residing on the continent of Europe, they had adopted the principles of the most complete and rigorous reformation, as taught and established by Calvin. On returning afterwards to their native country, they were dissatisfied with the partial reformation, at which, as they conceived, the English establishment had rested; and claiming the privilege of private conscience, upon which alone any departure from the Church of Rome could be justified, they insisted upon the right of adhering to the system of their own preference, and, of course, upon that of nonconformity to the establishment prescribed by the royal authority.

The only means used to convince them of error and reclaim them from dissent was force, and force served but to confirm the opposition it was meant to suppress. By driving the founders of the Plymouth Colony into exile, it constrained them to absolute separation from the Church of England ; and by the refusal afterwards to allow them a positive toleration, even in this American wilderness, the council of James I rendered that separation irreconcilable.

Two centuries have not yet elapsed since the first European foot touched the soil which now constitutes the American Union. Two centuries more and our numbers must exceed those of Europe itself. The destinies of this empire, as they appear in prospect before us, disdain the powers of human calculation. Yet, as the original founder of the Roman state is said once to have lifted upon his shoulders the fame and fortunes of all his posterity, so let us never forget that the glory and greatness of all our descendants is in our hands.

After Cromwell's death the country soon welcomed the return of another Stuart king. The Commonwealth had not proved a satisfactory answer to that problem of government about which so much blood had been shed in the Civil War. But the later Stuarts, fortunately, no doubt, for the ultimate welfare of the country, were almost as unsatisfactory as the earlier ones had been, and in 1688 came the bloodless Revolution which dethroned James II, king by heredity and "divine right", and installed William III, king by virtue of the will of the people.

The man who interpreted and justified this Revolution, not only for those who had taken part in it, but for other ages and other countries to ponder over, was John Locke. A hundred years earlier Richard Hooker had shown that laws were the product of man's reason, and that government is founded upon a social compact entered into by free men. If a government failed in its duty, said Hooker, those who established it could undo it and set up another. Thomas Hobbes, in the time of Charles I, said that government authority once established became absolute. The State, for Hobbes, was Leviathan, a great body politic which could have only one head. It remained for Locke to justify the history of the seventeenth century, and the example of Britain in dethroning two of the Stuart kings in her determination to work out a practical form of limited monarchy. For Locke, the safety and the welfare of the State depended on three things : the rule of law, freedom of speech and toleration for all opinions, and government by the majority opinion among the propertied class. Locke's writings were very popular and very influential, not only in Britain but also in the American colonies and on the Continent, mainly, no doubt, because he always kept in mind the practical application of his political theory. The following extracts are taken from his second *Treatise on Civil Government*.

JOHN LOCKE

POLITICAL POWER

TO understand political power aright, and derive it from its original, we must consider what estate all men are naturally in, and that is, a state of perfect freedom to order their actions, and dispose of their possessions and persons as they think fit, within the law of Nature, without asking leave or depending upon the will of any other man.

A state also of equality, wherein all the power and jurisdiction is reciprocal, no one having more than another, there being nothing more evident than that creatures of the same species and rank, promiscuously born to all the same advantages of Nature, and the use of the same faculties, should also be equal one amongst another, without subordination or subjection, unless the lord and master of them should, by any manifest declaration of his will, set one above another, and confer on him, by an evident and clear appointment, an undoubted right to dominion and sovereignty.

This equality of men by Nature, the judicious Hooker looks upon as so evident in itself, and beyond all question, that he makes it the foundation of that obligation to mutual love amongst men on which he builds the duties they owe one another, and from whence he derives the great maxims of justice and charity. . . .

The natural liberty of man is to be free from any superior

N

power on earth, and not to be under the will or legislative authority of man, but to have only the law of Nature for his rule. The liberty of man in society is to be under no other legislative power but that established by consent in the commonwealth, nor under the dominion of any will, or restraint of any law, but what that legislative shall enact according to the trust put in it.

If man in the state of Nature be so free as has been said, if he be absolute lord of his own person and possessions, equal to the greatest and subject to nobody, why will he part with this freedom, this empire, and subject himself to the dominion and control of any other power? To which it is obvious to answer, that though in the state of Nature he hath such a right, yet the enjoyment of it is very uncertain and constantly exposed to the invasion of others; for all being kings as much as he, every man his equal, and the greater part no strict observers of equity and justice, the enjoyment of the property he has in this state is very unsafe, very insecure. This makes him willing to quit this condition which, however free, is full of fears and continual dangers; and it is not without reason that he seeks out and is willing to join in society with others who are already united, or have a mind to unite for the mutual preservation of their lives, liberties, and estates, which I call by the general name—property.

The great and chief end, therefore, of men uniting into commonwealths, and putting themselves under government, is the preservation of their property; to which in the state of Nature there are many things wanting.

Firstly: There wants an established, settled, known law, received and allowed by common consent to be the standard of right and wrong, and the common measure to decide all controversies between them. For though the law of Nature be plain and intelligible to all rational creatures, yet men, being biased by their interest, as well as ignorant for want of study of it, are not apt to allow of it as a law binding to them in the application of it to their particular cases.

Secondly : in the state of Nature there wants a known and indifferent judge, with authority to determine all differences according to the established law. For every one in that state being both judge and executioner of the law of Nature, men being partial to themselves, passion and revenge is very apt to carry them too far, and with too much heat in their own cases, as well as negligence and unconcernedness, make them too remiss in other men's.

Thirdly : in the state of Nature there often wants power to back and support the sentence when right, and to give it due execution. They who by any injustice are offended will seldom fail where they are able by force to make good their injustice. Such resistance many times makes the punishment dangerous, and frequently destructive to those who attempt it.

Thus mankind, notwithstanding all the privileges of the state of Nature, being but in an ill condition while they remain in it are quickly driven into society. Hence it comes to pass, that we seldom find any number of men live any time together in this state. The inconveniences that they are therein exposed to by the irregular and uncertain exercise of the power every man has of punishing the transgressions of others, make them take sanctuary under the established laws of government, and therein seek the preservation of their property. It is this makes them so willingly give up every one his single power of punishing to be exercised by such alone as shall be appointed to it amongst them, and by such rules as the community, or those authorized by them to that purpose, shall agree on. And in this we have the original right and rise of both the legislative and executive power as well as of the governments and societies themselves. . . .

But though men, when they enter into society, give up the equality, liberty, and executive power they had in the state of Nature into the hands of the society, to be so far disposed of by the legislative as the good of the society shall require, yet it being only with an intention in every one the better to preserve himself, his liberty and property (for no rational creature can be supposed to change his condition with an intention to be worse), the power of the society or legislative constituted by them can never be supposed to extend farther than the common good, but is obliged to secure every one's property by providing against those three defects above mentioned that made the state of Nature so unsafe and uneasy. And so, whoever has the legislative or supreme power of any commonwealth, is bound to govern by established standing laws, promulgated and known to the people, and not by extemporary decrees, by indifferent and upright judges, who are to decide controversies by those laws ; and to employ the force of the community at home only in the execution of such laws, or abroad to prevent or redress foreign injuries and secure the community from inroads and invasion. And all this to be directed to no other end but the peace, safety, and public good of the people.

The great end of men's entering into society being the enjoyment of their properties in peace and safety, and the great instrument and means of that being the laws established in that society, the first and fundamental positive law of all commonwealths is the establishing of the legislative power ; as the first and fundamental natural law, which is to govern even the legislative itself, is the preservation of the society and (as far as will consist with the public good) of every person in it. This legislative is not only the supreme power of the commonwealth, but sacred and unalterable in the hands where the community have once placed it. Nor can any edict of anybody else, in what form soever conceived, or by what power soever backed, have the force and obligation of a law which has not its sanction from that legislative which the public has chosen and appointed ; for without this the law could not have that which is absolutely necessary to its being a law, the consent of the society. . . .

Though the legislative, whether placed in one or more, whether it be always in being or only by intervals, though it be the supreme power in every commonwealth ; yet, first, it is not, nor can possibly be, absolutely arbitrary over the lives and fortunes of the people. For it being but the joint power of every member of the society given up to that person or assembly which is legislator, it can be no more than those persons had in a state of Nature before they entered into society, and gave it up to the community. For nobody can transfer to another more power than he has in himself, and nobody has an absolute arbitrary power over himself, or over any other, to destroy his own life, or take away the life or property of another. A man, as has been proved, cannot subject himself to the arbitrary power of another ; and having, in the state of Nature, no arbitrary power over the life, liberty, or possession of another, but only so much as the law of Nature gave him for the preservation of himself and the rest of mankind, this is all he doth, or can give up to the commonwealth, and by it to the legislative power, so that the legislative can have no more than this. Their power in the utmost bounds of it is limited to the public good of the society. It is a power that hath no other end but preservation, and therefore can never have a right to destroy, enslave, or designedly to impoverish the subjects ; the obligations of the law of Nature cease not in society, but only in many cases are drawn closer, and have, by human laws, known penalties annexed to them to enforce their observation. Thus the law of Nature stands as an eternal rule to all men, legislators as well as others. The rules that they make for other men's actions must, as well as their own and other men's actions, be conformable to the law of Nature—*i.e.* to the will of God, of which that is a declaration, and the fundamental law of Nature being the preservation of mankind, no human sanction can be good or valid against it.

Secondly, the legislative or supreme authority cannot assume to itself a power to rule by extemporary arbitrary decrees, but is bound to dispense justice and decide the rights of the subject by promulgated standing laws, and known authorized judges. For the law of Nature being unwritten, and so nowhere to be found but in the minds of men, they who, through passion or interest, shall miscite or misapply it, cannot so easily be convinced of their mistake where there is no established judge ; and so it serves not as it ought, to determine the rights and fence the properties of those that live under it. . . .

Thirdly, the supreme power cannot take from any man any part of his property without his consent. For the preservation of property being the end of government, and that for which men enter into society, it necessarily supposes and requires that the people should have property, without which they must be supposed to lose that by entering into society, which was the end for which they entered into it ; too gross an absurdity for any man to own. Men, therefore, in society having property, they have such a right to the goods, which by the law of the community are theirs, that nobody hath a right to take them, or any part of them, from them without their own consent ; without this they have no property at all. For I have truly no property in that which another can by right take from me when he pleases against my consent. Hence it is a mistake to think that the supreme or legislative power of any commonwealth can do what it will, and dispose of the estates of the subject arbitrarily, or take any part of them at pleasure.

This is not much to be feared in governments where the legislative consists wholly or in part in assemblies which are variable, whose members upon the dissolution of the assembly are subjects under the common laws of their country, equally with the rest. But in governments where the legislative is in one lasting assembly, always in being or in one man as in absolute monarchies, there is danger still, that they will think themselves to have a distinct interest from the rest of the community, and so will be apt to increase their own riches and power by taking what they think fit from the people. For a man's property is not at all secure, though there be good and equitable laws to set the bounds of it between him and his fellow-subjects, if he who commands those subjects have power to take from any private man what part he pleases of his property, and use and dispose of it as he thinks good.

Fourthly. The legislative cannot transfer the power of making laws to any other hands, for it being but a delegated power from the people, they who have it cannot pass it over to others. The people alone can appoint the form of the commonwealth, which is by constituting the legislative, and appointing in whose hands that shall be. And when the people have said, " We will submit, and be governed by laws made by such men, and in such forms ", nobody else can say other men shall make laws for them ; nor can they be bound by any laws but such as are enacted by those whom they have chosen and authorized to make laws for them.

These are the bounds which the trust that is put in them by the society and the law of God and Nature have set to the legislative power of every commonwealth, in all forms of government. First : They are to govern by promulgated established laws, not to be varied in particular cases, but to have one rule for rich and poor, for the favourite at Court, and the countryman at plough. Secondly : These laws also ought to be designed for no other end ultimately but the good of the people. Thirdly : They must not raise taxes on the property of the people without the consent of the people given by themselves or their deputies. And this properly concerns only such governments where the legislative is always in being, or at least where the people have not reserved any part of the legislative to deputies, to be from time to time chosen by themselves. Fourthly : Legislative neither must nor can transfer the power of making laws to anybody else, or place it anywhere but where the people have.

Magna Carta had put the law above the King. Events in Britain in the seventeenth century had put Parliament above the King. And in the eighteenth century there were times when Parliament thought that it was above the law as well. *If the law is superior to the King, what is above the legislature*—or at least above any whims of the law-makers ? Most countries have a written constitution which puts limits on the power of the legislature. But the British constitution is largely unwritten precedent, so what happens then ? Listen to the Earl of Chatham, the " Great Commoner ", as he explains why the foundations of juris-prudence must be laid in reason. He is speaking in the House of Lords in the famous case of John Wilkes. Wilkes, a most vigorous and out-spoken enemy of the Tory government, had been expelled from the Commons in 1764 because of the attack on the King's Speech made in his paper the *North Briton*. He was elected again for Middlesex in 1768, only to be expelled once more, early in 1769. Elected again on February 16, again expelled, re-elected on March 16, once more expelled, and elected for a fourth time on April 13 by 1143 votes to Luttrell's 296, he was again rejected by the Commons, who declared Luttrell elected.

This action was the signal for a popular outburst of fury. The artisans and lower middle class were all on Wilkes's side, but none of them had votes, so what could they do ? " Start agitating for the vote " was the reply, and this they began to do. Democracy started to march forward again after the repose of the early half of the eighteenth century, and it moved not only in England but even more swiftly in America and in France.

EARL OF CHATHAM

THE CONSTITUTION AND THE LAW

MY lords, I am a plain man, and have been brought up in a religious reverence for the original simplicity of the laws of England. By what sophistry they have been perverted, by what artifices they have been involved in obscurity, is not for me to explain. The principles, however, of the English laws are still sufficiently clear ; they are founded in reason, and are the masterpieces of human understanding ; but it is in the text that I would look for a direction to my judgment, not in the commentaries of modern professors. The noble lord assures us that he knows not in what code the law of Parliament

is to be found ; that the House of Commons, when they act
as judges, have no law to direct them but their own wisdom ;
that their decision is law ; and if they determine wrong, the
subject has no appeal but to heaven. What then, my lords ?
Are all the generous efforts of our ancestors, are all those
glorious contentions by which they meant to secure to themselves, and to transmit to their posterity, a known law, a certain
rule of living, reduced to this conclusion, that, instead of the
arbitrary power of a King, we must submit to the arbitrary
power of a House of Commons ? If this be true, what benefit
do we derive from the exchange ? Tyranny, my lords, is
detestable in every shape, but in none so formidable as when
it is assumed and exercised by a number of tyrants. But, my
lords, this is not the fact ; this is not the Constitution. We
have a law of Parliament. We have a code in which every
honest man may find it. We have Magna Carta. We have
the Statute Book, and the Bill of Rights.

If a case should arise unknown to these great authorities,
we have still that plain English reason left, which is the
foundation of all our English jurisprudence. That reason
tells us that every judicial court and every political society
must be invested with those powers and privileges which are
necessary for performing the office to which they are appointed.
It tells us, also, that no court of justice can have a power
inconsistent with, or paramount to, the known laws of the
land ; that the people, when they choose their representatives,
never mean to convey to them a power of invading the rights,
or trampling on the liberties of those whom they represent.
What security would they have for their rights, if once they
admitted that a court of judicature might determine every
question that came before it, not by any known positive law,
but by the vague, indeterminate, arbitrary rule of what the
noble lord is pleased to call the wisdom of the court ?

With respect to the decision of the courts of justice, I am
far from denying them their due weight and authority ; yet,
placing them in the most respectable view, I still consider

them, not as law, but as an evidence of the law. And before they can arrive even at that degree of authority, it must appear that they are founded in and confined by reason ; that they are supported by precedents taken from good and moderate times ; that they do not contradict any positive law ; that they are submitted to without reluctance by the people ; that they are unquestioned by the Legislature (which is equivalent to a tacit confirmation) ; and what, in my judgment, is by far the most important, that they do not violate the spirit of the Constitution.

My lords, this is not a vague or loose expression. We all know what the Constitution is. We all know that the first principle of it is that the subject shall not be governed by the *arbitrium* of any one man or body of men (less than the whole Legislature), but by certain laws, to which he has virtually given his consent, which are open to him to examine, which are not beyond his ability to understand. Now, my lords, I affirm, and am ready to maintain, that the late decision of the House of Commons upon the Middlesex election is destitute of every one of those properties and conditions which I hold to be essential to the legality of such a decision. It is not founded in reason ; for it carries with it a contradiction, that the representative should perform the office of the constituent body. It is not supported by a single precedent ; for the case of Sir Robert Walpole is but a half precedent, and even that half is imperfect. Incapacity was indeed declared, but his crimes are stated as the ground of the resolution, and his opponent was declared to be not duly elected, even after his incapacity was established. It contradicts Magna Carta and the Bill of Rights, by which it is provided that no subject shall be deprived of his freehold, unless by the judgment of his peers or the law of the land ; and that elections of members to serve in Parliament shall be free. So far is this decision from being submitted to the people, that they have taken the strongest measures, and adopted the most positive language to express their discontent. Whether it will be questioned by the Legislature will depend upon your lordships' resolution ; but that it violates the spirit of the Constitution will, I think, be disputed by no man who has heard this day's debate, and who wishes well to the freedom of his country.

Yet, if we are to believe the noble lord, this great grievance, this manifest violation of the first principles of the Constitution, will not admit of a remedy. It is not even capable of redress, unless we appeal at once to heaven ! My lords, I have better hopes of the Constitution, and a firmer confidence in the wisdom and constitutional authority of this House. It is to your ancestors, my lords, it is to the English barons, that we are indebted for the laws and Constitution we possess. Their virtues were rude and uncultivated, but they were great and sincere. Their understandings were as little polished as their manners, but they had hearts to distinguish right from wrong ; they had heads to distinguish truth from falsehood ; they understood the rights of humanity, and they had the spirit to maintain them.

My lords, I think that history has not done justice to their conduct, when they obtained from their sovereign that great acknowledgment of national rights contained in Magna Carta ; they did not confine it to themselves alone, but delivered it as a common blessing to the whole people. They did not say, these are the rights of the great barons, or these are the rights of the great prelates. No, my lords, they said, in the simple Latin of the times, *nullus liber homo* (no free man), and provided as carefully for the meanest subject as for the greatest. These are uncouth words, and sound but poorly in the ears of scholars ; neither are they addressed to the criticism of scholars, but to the hearts of free men. These three words, *nullus liber homo*, have meaning which interests us all, they deserve to be remembered—they deserve to be inculcated in our minds— they are worth all the classics. Let us not, then, degenerate from the glorious example of our ancestors. Those iron barons (for so I may call them when compared with the silken barons of modern days) were the guardians of the people ; yet their virtues, my lords, were never engaged in a question of such importance as the present. A breach has been made in the Constitution—the battlements are dismantled—the citadel is open to the first invader—the walls totter—the Constitution is not tenable. What remains, then, but for us to stand foremost in the breach, and repair it, or perish in it ?

Great pains have been taken to alarm us with the consequences of a difference between the two Houses of Parliament ; that the House of Commons will resent our presuming to take notice of their proceedings ; that they will resent our daring to advise the Crown, and never forgive us for attempting to save the State. My lords, I am sensible of the importance and difficulty of this great crisis ; at a moment such as this, we are called upon to do our duty, without dreading the resentment of any man. But if apprehensions of this kind are to affect us, let us consider which we ought to respect the most, the representative or the collective body of the people. My lords, 500 gentlemen are not 10 millions ; and if we must have a contention, let us take care to have the English nation on our side. If this question be given up, the freeholders of England are reduced to a condition baser than the peasants of Poland. If they desert their own cause, they deserve to be slaves ! My lords, this is not merely the cold opinion of my understanding, but the glowing expression of what I feel. It is my heart that speaks. I know I speak warmly, my lords ; but this warmth shall neither betray my argument nor my temper. The kingdom is in a flame. As mediators between a King and people, is it not our duty to represent to him the true condition and temper of his subjects ? It is a duty which no particular respects should hinder us from performing ; and whenever his Majesty shall demand our advice, it will then be our duty to inquire more minutely into the cause of the present discontents. Whenever that inquiry shall come on, I pledge myself to the House to prove that, since the first institution of the House of Commons, not a single precedent can be produced to justify their late proceedings. My noble and learned friend [the Lord Chancellor Camden] has pledged himself to the House that he will support that assertion. . . .

It is not impossible, my lords, that the inquiry I speak of may lead us to advise his Majesty to dissolve the present Parliament ; nor have I any doubt of our right to give that advice, if we should think it necessary. His Majesty will then determine whether he will yield to the united petitions of the people of England, or maintain the House of Commons in the exercise of a legislative power which heretofore abolished the House of Lords and overturned the monarchy. I willingly acquit the present House of Commons of having actually formed so detestable a design ; but they cannot themselves foresee to what excesses they may be carried hereafter ; and, for my own part, I should be sorry to trust to their future moderation. Unlimited power is apt to corrupt the minds of those who possess it ; and this I know, my lords, that where law ends, tyranny begins !

Before we turn our attention to the rise of democratic ideals in other centres of Western Civilization, here is one of the famous letters of " Junius ", which deals with the Wilkes case. " Junius ", whoever he may have been, was one of the most influential of the political writers of the day. His letters appeared in the London *Public Advertiser* from 1769 to 1772, and they were distinguished from others of a similar nature by their vigorous style and the intense passion of their attacks on the Tory government. The word " Tory ", by the way, originally meaning one of the Irish outlaws who, in the sixteenth and seventeenth centuries used a cloak of royalism as an excuse and disguise for brigandage, had by now come into common use in Britain as a descriptive title (first applied by its opponents, of course) for the party which stood for the maintenance of the royal prerogative, and a determined opposition to any broadening of the basis of power, either in Church or State. The following letter appeared on March 19, 1770. The City of London had addressed a remonstrance to the King when Luttrell was allowed to take his seat in the Commons after Wilkes had been elected to it.

JUNIUS

THE KING AND THE CITY

SIR, I believe there is no man, however indifferent about the interests of this country, who will not readily confess that the situation to which we are now reduced, whether it has arisen from the violence of faction, or from an arbitrary system of government, justifies the most melancholy apprehensions, and calls for the exertion of whatever wisdom or vigour is left among us. The king's answer to the remonstrance of the city of London, and the measures since adopted by the ministry, amount to a plain declaration that the principle on which Mr. Luttrell was seated in the House of Commons, is to be supported in all its consequences, and carried to its utmost extent.

The same spirit which violated the freedom of election, now invades the Declaration and Bill of Rights ; and threatens to punish the subject for exercising a privilege hitherto undisputed, of petitioning the Crown. The grievances of the people are aggravated by insults ; their complaints not merely disregarded, but checked by authority ; and every one of those acts against which they remonstrated, confirmed by the king's decisive approbation. At such a moment, no honest man will remain silent or inactive. However distinguished by rank or property, in the rights of freedom we are all equal.

As we are Englishmen, the least considerable man among us has an interest equal to the proudest nobleman in the laws and constitution of his country, and is equally called upon to make a generous contribution in support of them ; whether it be the heart to conceive, the understanding to direct, or the hand to execute. It is a common cause ; in which we are all interested, in which we should all be engaged. The man who deserts it at this alarming crisis, is an enemy to his country and (what I think of infinitely less importance) a traitor to his sovereign. The subject who is truly loyal to the chief magistrate, will neither advise nor submit to arbitrary measures.

The city of London have given an example which, I doubt not, will be followed by the whole kingdom. The noble spirit of the metropolis is the lifeblood of the state, collected at the heart : from that point it circulates, with health and vigour, through every artery of the constitution. The time is come when the body of the English people must assert their own cause ; conscious of their strength, and animated by a sense of their duty, they will not surrender their birthright to ministers, parliaments, or kings.

The city of London have expressed their sentiments with freedom and firmness : they have spoken truth boldly ; and in whatever light their remonstrance may be represented by courtiers, I defy the most subtle lawyer in this country to point out a single instance in which they have exceeded the truth. Even that assertion which we are told is most offensive to parliament, in the theory of the English constitution is strictly true. " If any part of the representative body be not chosen by the people, that part vitiates and corrupts the whole." If there be a defect in the representation of the people, that power which alone is equal to the making of the laws in this country, is not complete ; and the acts of parliament under that circumstance, are not the acts of a pure and entire legislature. I speak of the theory of our constitution ; and whatever difficulties or inconveniences may attend the practice, I am ready to maintain, that as far as the fact deviates from the principle, so far the practice is vicious and corrupt.

I have not heard a question raised upon any other part of the remonstrance. That " the principle on which the Middlesex election was determined, is more pernicious in its effects than either the levying of ship-money by Charles the First, or the dispensing power assumed by his son ", will hardly be disputed by any man who understands or wishes well to the English constitution. It is not an act of open violence done by the king, or any direct or palpable breach of the laws attempted by his minister, that can ever endanger the liberties of this country ; against such a king or minister the people would immediately take the alarm, and all parties unite to oppose him. The laws may be grossly violated in particular instances, without any direct attack upon the whole system. Facts of that kind stand alone ; they are attributed to necessity, not defended by principle. We can never be really in danger, till the forms of parliament are made use of to destroy the substance of our civil and political liberties : till parliament itself betrays its trust, by contributing to establish new principles of government ; and employing the very weapons committed to it by the collective body, to stab the constitution. . . .

The city of London have not desired the king to assume a power placed in other hands ; if they had, I should hope to see the person who dared to present such a petition, immediately impeached. They solicit their sovereign to exert that constitutional authority which the laws have vested in him, for the benefit of his subjects. They call upon him to make use of his lawful prerogative in a case which our laws evidently supposed might happen, since they have provided for it by trusting the sovereign with a discretionary power to dissolve the parliament. This request will, I am confident, be supported by remonstrances from all parts of the kingdom. His majesty will find at last, that this is the sense of his people ; and that it is not his interest to support either ministry or parliament, at the hazard of a breach with the collective body of his subjects.

That he is the king of a free people, is indeed his greatest glory. That he may long continue the king of a free people, is the second wish that animates my heart. The first is, that the people may be free.

The tide of democratic liberty was rising fast, as we have said, and not only in Europe but in America as well. The Tory tyranny which was so unpopular at home was hated even more violently by the colonists in America, and their refusal to be taxed led to the War of Independence. Some of the finest speeches ever uttered in the English Parliament were made on behalf of the colonies. The occasion is naturally more important for the story of Commonwealth and American History, but one of the speeches, that made by Burke, breathes so much of the spirit of Western political thought that some extracts must be included here. This speech on Conciliation is among the greatest classics of English oratory. It was delivered in the House of Commons on March 22, 1775. *How did Burke show that " a great empire and little minds go ill together " ?*

EDMUND BURKE

CONCILIATION WITH AMERICA

AMERICA, gentlemen say, is a noble object. It is an object well worth fighting for. Certainly it is, if fighting a people be the best way of gaining them. Gentlemen in this respect will be led to their choice of means by their complexions and their habits. Those who understand the military art will, of course, have some predilection for it. Those who wield the thunder of the State may have more confidence in the efficacy of arms. But I confess, possibly for want of this knowledge, my opinion is much more in favour of prudent management than of force, considering force not as an odious, but a feeble instrument for preserving a people so numerous, so active, so growing, so spirited as this, in a profitable and subordinate connexion with us.

First, sir, permit me to observe that the use of force alone is but temporary. It may subdue for a moment, but it does not remove the necessity of subduing again ; and a nation is not governed which is perpetually to be conquered.

My next objection is its uncertainty. Terror is not always the effect of force ; and an armament is not a victory. If you do not succeed you are without resource, for conciliation failing, force remains, but force failing, no further hope of

o

reconciliation is left. Power and authority are sometimes bought by kindness, but they can never be begged as alms by an impoverished and defeated violence.

A further objection to force is that you impair the object by your very endeavours to preserve it. The thing you fought for is not the thing which you recover ; but depreciated, sunk, wasted, and consumed in the contest. Nothing less will content me than whole America. I do not choose to consume its strength along with our own, because in all parts it is the British strength that I consume. I do not choose to be caught by a foreign enemy at the end of this exhausting conflict, and still less in the midst of it. I may escape ; but I can make no insurance against such an event. Let me add that I do not choose wholly to break the American spirit, because it is the spirit that has made the country.

Lastly, we have no sort of experience in favour of force as an instrument in the rule of our colonies. Their growth and their utility have been owing to methods altogether different. Our ancient indulgence has been said to be pursued to a fault. It may be so ; but we know, if feeling is evidence, that our fault was more tolerable than our attempt to mend it, and our sin far more salutary than our penitence.

These, sir, are my reasons for not entertaining that high opinion of untried force by which many gentlemen, for whose sentiments in other particulars I have great respect, seem to be so greatly captivated.

But there is still behind a third consideration concerning this object, which serves to determine my opinion on the sort of policy which ought to be pursued in the management of America, even more than its population and its commerce— I mean its temper and character. In this character of the Americans a love of freedom is the predominating feature, which marks and distinguishes the whole ; and, as an ardent is always a jealous affection, your colonies become suspicious, restive, and untractable, whenever they see the least attempt to wrest from them by force, or shuffle from them by chicane, what they think the only advantage worth living for. This fierce spirit of liberty is stronger in the English colonies, probably, than in any other people of the earth, and this from a variety of powerful causes which, to understand the true temper of their minds and the direction which this spirit takes, it will not be amiss to lay open somewhat more largely.

First, the people of the colonies are descendants of Englishmen. England, sir, is a nation which still, I hope, respects, and formerly adored, her freedom. The colonists emigrated from you when this part of your character was most predominant ; and they took this bias and direction the moment they parted from your hands. They are, therefore, not only devoted to liberty, but to liberty according to English ideas and on English principles. Abstract liberty, like other mere abstractions, is not to be found. Liberty inheres in some sensible object, and every nation has formed to itself some favourite point which, by way of eminence, becomes the criterion of their happiness. It happened, you know, sir, that the great contests for freedom in this country were, from the earliest times, chiefly upon the question of taxing. Most of the contests in the ancient commonwealths turned primarily on the right of election of magistrates, or on the balance among the several orders of the State. The question of money was not with them so immediate.

But in England it was otherwise. On this point of taxes the ablest pens and most eloquent tongues have been exercised ; the greatest spirits have acted and suffered. In order to give the fullest satisfaction concerning the importance of this point, it was not only necessary for those who in argument defended the excellence of the English constitution to insist on this privilege of granting money as a dry point of fact and to prove that the right has been acknowledged in ancient parchments and blind usages to reside in a certain body called the House of Commons. They went much further : they attempted to prove—and they succeeded—that in theory it ought to be so, from the particular nature of a House of Commons, as an immediate representative of the people, whether the old records had delivered this oracle or not. They took infinite pains to inculcate, as a fundamental principle, that, in all monarchies, the people must, in effect, themselves, mediately or immediately, possess the power of granting their own money, or no shadow of liberty could subsist.

The colonies draw from you, as with their life-blood, those ideas and principles, their love of liberty, as with you, fixed and attached on this specific point of taxing. Liberty might be safe or might be endangered in twenty other particulars, without their being much pleased or alarmed. Here they felt its pulse ; and, as they found that beat, they thought themselves sick or sound. I do not say whether they were right or wrong in applying your general arguments to their own case. It is not easy, indeed, to make a monopoly of theorems and corollaries. The fact is that they did thus apply those general arguments ; and your mode of governing them, whether through lenity or indolence, through wisdom or mistake, confirmed them in the imagination that they, as well as you, had an interest in these common principles.

They were further confirmed in these pleasing errors by the form of their provincial legislative assemblies. Their Governments are popular in a high degree ; some are merely popular ; in all, the popular representative is the most weighty ; and this share of the people in their ordinary government never fails to inspire them with lofty sentiments and with a strong aversion from whatever tends to deprive them of their chief importance.

If anything were wanting to this necessary operation of the form of government, religion would have given it a complete effect. Religion, always a principle of energy, in this new people is in no way worn out or impaired ; and their mode of professing it is also one main cause of this free spirit. The people are Protestants, and of that kind which is most averse to all implicit submission of mind and opinion. This is a

persuasion not only favourable to liberty, but built upon it. I
do not think, sir, that the reason of this averseness in the dissenting Churches from all that looks like absolute government
is so much to be sought in their religious tenets as in their
history.

Everyone knows that the Roman Catholic religion is at least
coeval with most of the governments where it prevails, that it
has generally gone hand in hand with them, and received great
favour and every kind of support from authority. The Church
of England, too, was formed from her cradle under the nursing
care of regular government. But the dissenting interests have
sprung up in direct opposition to all the ordinary powers of
the world, and could justify that opposition only on a strong
claim to natural liberty. Their very existence depended on
the powerful and unremitted assertion of that claim. All
Protestantism, even the most cold and passive, is a kind of
dissent.

But the religion most prevalent in our northern colonies is a
refinement on the principle of resistance ; it is the dissidence of
dissent, and the protestantism of the Protestant religion. . . .

The last cause of this disobedient spirit in the colonies is
hardly less powerful than the rest, as it is not merely moral
but laid deep in the natural constitution of things. Three
thousand miles of ocean lie between you and them. No
contrivance can prevent the effect of this distance in weakening
government. Seas roll and months pass between the order
and the execution, and the want of a speedy explanation of a
single point is enough to defeat the whole system. You have,
indeed, " winged ministers " of vengeance, who carry your
bolts in their pouches to the remotest verge of the sea. But
there a power steps in that limits the arrogance of raging
passion and furious elements, and says : " So far shalt thou
go, and no farther ".

Who are you, that should fret and rage, and bite the chains
of Nature ? Nothing worse happens to you than does to all
nations who have extensive empire ; and it happens in all the

forms into which empire can be thrown. In large bodies the circulation of power must be less vigorous at the extremities. Nature has said it. The Turk cannot govern Egypt and Arabia and Kurdistan as he governs Thrace, nor has he the same dominion in Crimea and Algiers which he has at Brusa and Smyrna. Despotism itself is obliged to truck and huckster. The Sultan gets such obedience as he can. He governs with a loose rein, that he may govern at all, and the whole of the force and vigour of his authority in his centre is derived from a prudent relaxation in all his borders. Spain, in her provinces, is, perhaps, not so well obeyed as you are in yours. She complies too ; she submits ; she watches times. This is the immutable condition, the eternal law, of extensive and detached empire.

Then, sir, from these six capital sources ; of descent ; of form of government ; of religion in the northern provinces ; of manners in the southern ; of education ; of the remoteness of situation from the first mover of government ; from all these causes a fierce spirit of liberty has grown up. It has grown with the growth of the people in your colonies, and increased with the increase of their wealth ; a spirit, that unhappily meeting with an exercise of power in England, which, however lawful, is not reconcilable to any ideas of liberty, much less with theirs, has kindled this flame that is ready to consume us. . . .

Next we know, that parties must ever exist in a free country. We know too, that the emulations of such parties, their contradictions, their reciprocal necessities, their hopes, and their fears, must send them all in their turns to him that holds the balance of the State. The parties are the gamesters ; but government keeps the table, and is sure to be the winner in the end. When this game is played, I really think it is more to be feared that the people will be exhausted, than that government will not be supplied. Whereas, whatever is got by acts of absolute power, ill obeyed because odious, or by contracts ill kept, because constrained, will be narrow, feeble, uncertain, and precarious. *" Ease would retract vows made in pain, as violent and void."*

I, for one, protest against compounding our demands : I declare against compounding for a poor limited sum, the immense, overgrowing, eternal debt, which is due to generous government from protected freedom. And so may I speed in the great object I propose to you, as I think it would not only be an act of injustice, but would be the worst economy in the world, to compel the colonies to a sum certain, either in the way of ransom, or in the way of compulsory compact.

But to clear up my ideas on this subject—a revenue from America transmitted hither—do not delude yourselves—you never can receive it. No, not a shilling. We have experience that from remote countries it is not to be expected. If, when you attempted to extract revenue from Bengal, you were obliged to return in loan what you had taken in imposition ; what can you expect from North America ? For certainly, if ever there was a country qualified to produce wealth, it is India ; or an institution fit for the transmission, it is the East India Company. America has none of these aptitudes. If America gives you taxable objects, on which you lay your duties here, and gives you, at the same time, a surplus by a foreign sale of her commodities to pay the duties on these objects, which you tax at home, she has performed her part to the British revenue. But with regard to her own internal establishments ; she may, I doubt not she will, contribute in moderation. I say in moderation ; for she ought not to be permitted to exhaust herself. She ought to be reserved to a war ; the weight of which, with the enemies that we are most likely to have, must be considerable in her quarter of the globe. There she may serve you, and serve you essentially.

For that service, for all service, whether of revenue, trade, or empire, my trust is in her interest in the British constitution. My hold of the colonies is in the close affection which grows from common names, from kindred blood, from similar privileges, and equal protection. These are ties which, though light as air, are as strong as links of iron. Let the colonies always keep the idea of their civil rights associated with your government ;—they will cling and grapple to you ; and no force under heaven will be of power to tear them from their allegiance. But let it be once understood that your government may be one thing and their privileges another ; that these two things may exist without any mutual relation ; the cement is gone ; the cohesion is loosened ; and everything hastens to decay and dissolution.

As long as you have the wisdom to keep the sovereign authority of this country as the sanctuary of liberty, the sacred temple consecrated to our common faith, wherever the chosen race and sons of England worship freedom, they will turn their faces towards you. The more they multiply, the more friends you will have ; the more ardently they love liberty, the more perfect will be their obedience. Slavery they can have anywhere. It is a weed that grows in every soil. They may have it from Spain, they may have it from Prussia. But, until you become lost to all feeling of your true interest and your natural dignity, freedom they can have from none but you. This is the commodity of price, of which you have the monopoly. This is the true act of navigation, which binds to you the commerce of the colonies, and through them secures to you the wealth of the world. Deny them this participation of freedom, and you break that sole bond, which originally made, and must still preserve, the unity of the empire.

Do not entertain so weak an imagination, as that your registers and your bonds, your affidavits and your sufferances, your cockets and your clearances, are what form the great securities of your commerce. Do not dream that your letters of office, and your instructions, and your suspending clauses, are the things that hold together the great contexture of the mysterious whole. These things do not make your government. Dead instruments, passive tools as they are, it is the spirit of the English communion that gives all their life and efficacy to them. It is the spirit of the English constitution, which, infused through the mighty mass, pervades, feeds, unites, invigorates, vivifies every part of the empire, even down to the minutest member.

Is it not the same virtue which does everything for us here in England ? Do you imagine then, that it is the land tax act which raises your revenue ? that it is the annual vote in the committee of supply which gives you your army ? or that it is the mutiny bill which inspires it with bravery and discipline ? No ! surely no ! It is the love of the people ; it is their attachment to their government, from the sense of the deep stake they have in such a glorious institution, which gives you your army and your navy, and infuses into both that liberal obedience, without which your army would be a base rabble, and your navy nothing but rotten timber.

All this, I know well enough, will sound wild and chimerical to the profane herd of those vulgar and mechanical politicians, who have no place among us ; a sort of people who think that nothing exists but what is gross and material ; and who, therefore, far from being qualified to be directors of the great movement of empire, are not fit to turn a wheel in the machinery. But to men truly initiated and rightly taught, these ruling and master principles, which, in the opinion of such men as I have mentioned have no substantial existence, are in truth everything, and all in all. Magnanimity in politics is not seldom the truest wisdom ; and a great empire and little minds go ill together.

If we are conscious of our situation, and glow with zeal to fill our place as becomes our station and ourselves, we ought to auspicate all our public proceedings on America with the old warning of the church, *sursum corda !* We ought to elevate our minds to the greatness of that trust to which the order of Providence has called us. By adverting to the dignity of this high calling, our ancestors have turned a savage wilderness into a glorious empire ; and have made the most extensive, and the only honourable conquests, not by destroying, but by promoting the wealth, the number, the happiness of the human race. Let us get an American revenue as we have got an American empire. English privileges have made it all that it is ; English privileges alone will make it all it can be.

Meanwhile across the Channel a greater man than Junius had long been writing and pleading for elementary justice. We have to say " across the Channel " instead of " in France " because Voltaire was constantly having to dash from one country to another to escape the attentions of the authorities whom he lampooned and satirized. Voltaire found refuge in England from 1726 to 1729, and was greatly impressed by the atmosphere of toleration and personal liberty of thought and of manners (not always favourably impressed as regards the latter). In 1733 he published his *Philosophic Letters on the English People* in which praise of England served as a transparent blind for a scathing attack on both Church and State as established in France. Having made a great reputation as a writer of plays and satires, and a great fortune by beating business men at their own game, he turned all his powers to the attack on the ignoble nobility, the worldly church, and the unjust judges of France. Even his long life was not enough for him to see the fall of the *ancien régime*, but he did see it shaken to its foundations by his pen. *How did Voltaire attack persecuting Privilege ?* Victor Hugo provides an answer in one of his most eloquent orations, given in 1878 on the centenary of Voltaire's death.

VICTOR HUGO

VOLTAIRE'S SMILE

ONE hundred years ago to-day a man died ! He died immortal, laden with years, with labours, and with the most illustrious and formidable of responsibilities—the responsibility of the human conscience informed and corrected.

He departed amid the curses of the past and the blessings of the future—and these are the two superb forms of glory !—dying amid the acclamations of his contemporaries and of posterity, on the one hand, and on the other with the hootings and hatreds bestowed by the implacable past on those who combat it. He was more than a man—he was an epoch ! He had done his work ; he had fulfilled the mission evidently chosen for him by the Supreme Will, which manifests itself as visibly in the laws of destiny as in the laws of Nature. The eighty-four years he had lived bridge over the interval between the apogee of the Monarchy and the dawn of the Revolution. At his birth, Louis XIV still reigned ; at his death Louis XVI had already mounted the throne. So that his cradle saw the last rays of the great throne and his coffin the first gleams from the great abyss. . . .

The court was full of festivities ; Versailles was radiant ; Paris was ignorant ; and meanwhile, through religious ferocity, judges killed an old man on the wheel and tore out a child's tongue for a song. Confronted by this frivolous and dismal society, Voltaire alone, sensible of all the forces marshalled against him—court, nobility, finance ; that unconscious power, the blind multitude ; that terrible magistracy, so oppressive for the subject, so docile for the master, crushing and flattering, kneeling on the people before the king ; that clergy, a sinister medley of hypocrisy and fanaticism—Voltaire alone declared war against this coalition of all social iniquities—against that great and formidable world.

He accepted battle with it. What was his weapon ? That which has lightness of the wind and the force of a thunderbolt —a pen. With that weapon Voltaire fought, and with that he conquered. Let us salute that memory ! He conquered ! He waged a splendid warfare—the war of one alone against all —the grand war of mind against matter, of reason against prejudice ; a war for the just against the unjust, for the oppressed against the oppressor, the war of goodness, the war of kindness.

He had the tenderness of a woman and the anger of a hero. His was a great mind and an immense heart. He conquered the old code, the ancient dogma ! He conquered the feudal lord, the Gothic judge, the Roman priest. He bestowed on the populace the dignity of the people ! He taught, pacified, civilized ! He fought for Sirven and Mont-bailly as for Calas and Labarre. Regardless of menaces, insults, persecutions, calumny, exile, he was indefatigable and immovable. He overcame violence by a smile, despotism by sarcasm, infallibility by irony, obstinacy by perseverance, ignorance by truth !

I have just uttered the word " smile ", and I pause at it ! " To smile ! " That is Voltaire. Let us repeat it—pacification is the better part of philosophy. In Voltaire the equilibrium was speedily restored. Whatever his just anger, it passed off. The angry Voltaire always gives place to the Voltaire of calmness ; and then in that profound eye appears his smile. That smile is wisdom—that smile, I repeat, is Voltaire. It sometimes goes as far as a laugh, but philosophic sadness tempers it. It mocks the strong, it caresses the weak. Disquieting the oppressor, it reassures the oppressed. It becomes raillery against the great ; pity for the little ! Ah ! let that smile sway us, for it had in it the rays of the dawn. It was an illumination for truth, for justice, for goodness, for the worthiness of the useful. It illuminated the inner stronghold of superstition. The hideous things it is salutary to see, he showed. It was a smile, fruitful as well as luminous ! The new society, the desire for equality and concession ; that beginning of fraternity called tolerance, mutual goodwill, the just accord of men and right, the recognition of reason as the supreme law, the effacing of prejudices, serenity of soul, the spirit of indulgence and pardon, harmony and peace. Behold what has resulted from that grand smile ! On the day— undoubtedly close at hand—when the identity of wisdom and clemency will be recognized, when the amnesty is proclaimed, I say it !—yonder in the stars Voltaire will smile !

Between two servants of humanity who appeared at 1800 years' interval, there is a mysterious relation. To combat Pharisaism, unmask imposture, overturn tyrannies, usurpations, prejudices, falsehoods, superstitions—to demolish the temple in order to rebuild it—that is to say, to substitute the true for the false, attack the fierce magistracy, the sanguinary priest-hood ; to scourge the money-changers from the sanctuary ; to reclaim the heritage of the disinherited ; to protect the weak, poor, suffering, and crushed ; to combat for the per-secuted and oppressed—such was the war of Jesus Christ ! And what man carried on that war ? It was Voltaire ! The evangelical work had for its complement the philosophic work ; the spirit of mercy commenced, the spirit of toler-ance continued ; let us say it with a sentiment of pro-found respect : Jesus wept—Voltaire smiled. From that divine tear and that human smile sprang the mildness of existing civilization.

The contribution of another great Frenchman, Jean-Jacques Rousseau, to the ferment of democratic opinion was equally important in a different way. He made the " general will " the basis of the State and of all government ; and in his opinion the general will was always " right ". His ideals often inspired the furious rhetoric of Mirabeau, the man who, in Lord Brougham's words, " contributed by his courage and his eloquence to the destruction of the old monarchy more than any one individual. . . . His was the first eloquence that emancipated France ever experienced. Admitted at length to assist in popular assemblies, addressed as the arbiters of the country's fate, called to perform their part by debating and hearing debates, it was by Mirabeau that the people were first made to feel the force of the orator, first taught what it was to hear spoken reason and spoken passion." It must be admitted, however, that soon after Mirabeau had brought about the overthrow of the old institutions, he was bribed by the Court to change sides.

We give below some extracts from his more important speeches.

COMTE DE MIRABEAU

REVOLUTION SPEECHES

[1. Given on February 3, 1789. France had long been ruled by the King, who appointed and dismissed ministers at his own pleasure. Nobles and clergy were practically exempt from taxation. Other people had no personal rights. The country was bankrupt, and early in 1789 the King issued the writs calling together the States-General, an assembly of the three estates—nobles, clergy, and commons—which had not met for almost two centuries. Mirabeau was of aristocratic birth, but his sympathies were all with the commons—the third estate. Here is the equivalent of an election address, given in Provence.]

AGAINST ARISTOCRACY

IN all countries, in all ages, have aristocrats implacably pursued the friends of the people ; and when, by I know not what combination of fortune, such a friend has uprisen from the very bosom of the aristocracy, it has been at him pre-eminently that they have struck, eager to inspire wider terror by the elevation of their victims. So perished the last of the Gracchi by the hands of the Patricians. But, mortally smitten, he flung dust towards heaven, calling the avenging gods to witness : and from that dust sprang Marius—Marius, less illustrious for having exterminated the Cimbri than for having beaten down the despotism of the nobility in Rome.

But you, Commons, listen to one who, unseduced by your applause, yet cherishes it in his heart. Man is strong only by union ; happy, only by peace. Be firm, not obstinate ; courageous, not turbulent ; free, not undisciplined ; prompt, not precipitate. Stop not, except at difficulties of moment ; and be then wholly inflexible. But disdain the contentions of self-love, and never thrust into the balance the individual against the country. Above all hasten, as much as in you lies, the epoch of those States-General, from which you are charged with flinching—the more acrimoniously charged, the more your accusers dread the results ; of those States-General, through which so many pretensions will be scattered, so many rights re-established, so many evils reformed ; of those States-General, in short, through which the monarch himself desires that France should regenerate herself.

For myself, who, in my public career, have had no other fear but that of wrongdoing—who, girt with my conscience and armed with my principles, would brave the universe—whether it shall be my fortune to serve you with my voice and my exertions in the National Assembly, or whether I shall be enabled to aid you there with my prayers only, be sure that the vain clamours, the wrathful menaces, the injurious pro-testations—all the convulsions, in a word, of expiring prejudices—shall not intimidate me ! What ! shall he now pause in his civic course, who, first among all the men of France, em-phatically proclaimed his opinions on national affairs, at a time when circumstances were much less urgent than now and the task one of much greater peril ? Never ! No measure of outrages shall bear down my patience. I have been, I am, I shall be, even to the tomb, the man of the public liberty, the man of the constitution. If to be such be to become the man of the people rather than of the nobles, then woe to the privileged order ! For privileges shall have an end, but the people is eternal !

[2. Given on April 19, 1790. When the States-General met, the nobles and clergy wanted the voting to take place by estates, so that together they could always count two votes against the single vote of the equally numerous commons. But the third estate, led by Mirabeau, successfully resisted this claim. Feeling that they had the great mass of the nation behind them, they decided to form a national assembly and to proceed with the making of new laws. Their first action was to pass a resolution that no taxes should be levied without their consent. The King's reply to this was to close the room where they had been meeting, and to put an armed guard over its doors. The third estate promptly gathered in one of the tennis courts at Versailles and took an oath never to separate until they had given a new constitution to France. The self-constituted National Assembly continued to meet, in spite of the opposition of King and nobles and higher clergy, who refused to recognize its authority. In the following speech Mirabeau replies to these critics and describes the scene in the tennis court.]

JUSTIFYING REVOLUTION

It is with difficulty, gentlemen, that I can repress an emotion of indignation when I hear hostile rhetoricians continually oppose the nation to the National Assembly, and endeavour to excite a sort of rivalry between them. As if it were not through the National Assembly that the nation had recognized, recovered, reconquered its rights! As if it were not through the National Assembly that the French had, in truth, become a nation! As if, surrounded by the monuments of our labours, our dangers, our services, we could become suspected by the people—formidable to the liberties of the people! As if the regards of two worlds upon you fixed, as if the spectacle of your glory, as if the gratitude of so many millions, as if the very pride of a generous conscience, which would have to blush too deeply to belie itself—were not a sufficient guarantee of your fidelity, of your patriotism, of your virtue!

Commissioned to form a constitution for France, I will not ask whether, with that authority, we did not receive also the power to do all that was necessary to complete, establish, and confirm that constitution. I will not ask: Ought we to have lost in pusillanimous consultations the time of action, while nascent liberty would have received her death-blow? But if gentlemen insist on demanding when and how, from simple deputies of bailiwicks, we became all at once transformed into a national convention, I reply : It was on that day, when, finding the hall where we were to assemble closed, and bristling and polluted with bayonets, we resorted to the first place where we could reunite, to swear to perish rather than submit to such an order of things ! That day, if we were not a national convention, we became one ; became one for the destruction of arbitrary power and for the defence of the rights of the nation from all violence. The strivings of despotism which we have quelled, the perils which we have averted, the violence which we have repressed—these are our titles ! Our successes have consecrated them ; the adhesion, so often renewed, of all parts of the empire, has legitimized and sanctified them. Summoned to its task by the irresistible tocsin of necessity, our national convention is above all imitation, as it is above all authority. It is accountable only to itself, and can be judged only by posterity.

Gentlemen, you all remember the instance of that Roman who, to save his country from a dangerous conspiracy, had been constrained to overstep the powers conferred on him by the laws. A captious tribune exacted of him the oath that he had respected those laws ; hoping, by this insidious demand, to drive the consul to the alternative of perjury or of an embarrassing avowal. " Swear " said the tribune " that you have observed the laws." " I swear," replied the great man— " I swear that I have saved the Republic." Gentlemen, I swear that you have saved France !

[3. Given on January 9, 1790. The vested interests in the provincial law courts of France were among the bitterest opponents of the National Assembly, and those in Brittany were outstandingly so. The judges at Rennes flatly refused to obey the Decrees of the Assembly, and here is Mirabeau's reply, appealing once again to the principles on which law and government rest.]

P

REASON, IMMUTABLE AND SOVEREIGN

When, during our session yesterday, those words which you have taught Frenchmen to unlearn—orders, privileges—fell on my ears ; when a private corporation of one of the provinces of this Empire spoke to you of the impossibility of consenting to the execution of your decrees, sanctioned by the King ; when certain magistrates declared to you that their conscience and their honour forbade their obedience to your laws, I said to myself : Are these, then, dethroned sovereigns, who, in a transport of imprudent but generous pride are addressing successful usurpers ? No ; these are men whose arrogant pretensions have too long been an insult to all ideas of social order ; champions, even more interested than audacious, of a system which has cost France centuries of oppression, public and private, political and fiscal, feudal and judicial, and whose hope is to make us regret and revive that system.

The people of Brittany have sent among you sixty-six representatives, who assure you that the new constitution crowns all their wishes ; and here come eleven judges of the province, who cannot consent that you should be the bene-factors of their country. They have disobeyed your laws ; and they pride themselves on their disobedience, and believe it will make their names honoured by posterity. No, gentle-men, the remembrance of their folly will not pass to posterity. What avail their pygmy efforts to brace themselves against the progress of a revolution the grandest and most glorious in the world's history, and one that must infallibly change the face of the globe and the lot of humanity ? Strange pre-sumption that would arrest liberty in its course and roll back the destinies of a great nation !

It is not to antiquated transactions—it is not to musty treaties, wherein fraud combined with force to chain men to the car of certain haughty masters—that the National Assembly have resorted, in their investigations into popular rights. The titles we offer are more imposing by far ; ancient as

Time, sacred and imprescriptible as Nature ! What ! Must the terms of the marriage contract of one Anne of Brittany make the people of that province slaves to the nobles till the consummation of the ages ? These refractory magistrates speak of the statutes which " immutably fix our powers of legislation ". Immutably fix ! Oh, how that word tears the veil from their innermost thoughts ! How would they like to have abuses immutable upon earth, and evil eternal ! Indeed, what is lacking to their felicity but the perpetuity of that feudal scourge, which unhappily has lasted only six centuries ? But it is in vain that they rage. All now is changed or changing. There is nothing immutable save reason—save the sovereignty of the people—save the inviolability of its decrees !

The French Revolution in its earlier stages was naturally welcomed by the liberty-loving people of Great Britain. " Bliss was it in that dawn to be alive, but to be young was very heaven ", wrote Wordsworth. In much the same way was the Russian Revolution of 1917 welcomed by those who knew how harsh had been the tyranny of the Tsars. And in both instances the early enthusiasm quickly waned when it was seen how the new leaders of the country were abusing their power. Edmund Burke took a cool and objective view of the French Revolution right from the start, and as the years passed, more and more people saw the essential wisdom of his *Reflections on the Revolution in France. What was Burke's opinion of the French Revolution?* It may be gathered from the following extracts from his *Reflections,* and in them, too, is given his view of those " rights of man " about which so much was heard at that time.

EDMUND BURKE

REFLECTIONS ON THE REVOLUTION IN FRANCE

I FLATTER myself that I love a manly, moral, regulated liberty as well as any gentleman of that society [the Revolution Society] be he who he will ; and perhaps I have given as good proofs of my attachment to that cause, in the whole course of my public conduct. I think I envy liberty as little as they do, to any other nation. But I cannot stand forward, and give praise or blame to anything which relates to human actions, and human concerns, on a simple view of the object, as it stands stripped of every relation, in all the nakedness and solitude of metaphysical abstraction. Circumstances (which with some gentlemen pass for nothing) give in reality to every political principle its distinguishing colour and discriminating effect. The circumstances are what render every civil and political scheme beneficial or noxious to mankind. Abstractedly speaking, government, as well as liberty, is good; yet could I, in common sense, ten years ago, have felicitated France on her enjoyment of a government (for she then had a government) without inquiry what the nature of that government was, or how it was administered? Can I now congratulate the same nation upon its freedom? Is it because liberty in the abstract may be classed amongst the blessings of mankind that I am seriously to felicitate a madman, who has escaped from the protecting restraint and wholesome darkness of his cell, on his restoration to the enjoyment of light and liberty? Am I to congratulate a highwayman and murderer, who has broke prison, upon the recovery of his natural rights? This would be to act over again the scene of the criminals condemned to the galleys, and their heroic deliverer, the metaphysic knight of the sorrowful countenance.

When I see the spirit of liberty in action, I see a strong principle at work; and this, for a while, is all I can possibly know of it. The wild *gas*, the fixed air, is plainly broke loose: but we ought to suspend our judgment until the first effervescence is a little subsided, till the liquor is cleared, and until we see something deeper than the agitation of a troubled and frothy surface. I must be tolerably sure, before I venture publicly to congratulate men upon a blessing, that they have really received one. Flattery corrupts both the receiver and the giver ; and adulation is not of more service to the people than to kings. I should therefore suspend my congratulations on the new liberty of France, until I was informed how it had been combined with government ; with public force ; with the discipline and obedience of armies ; with the collection of an effective and well-distributed revenue ; with morality and religion ; with the solidity of property ; with peace and order ; with civil and social manners. All these (in their way) are good things too ; and, without them, liberty is not a benefit whilst it lasts, and is not likely to continue long. The effect of liberty to individuals is, that they may do what they please : we ought to see what it will please them to do, before we risk congratulations, which may be soon turned into complaints. Prudence would dictate this in the case of separate, insulated, private men ; but liberty, when men act in bodies, is *power*. Considerate people, before they declare themselves will observe the use which is made of *power* ; and particularly of so trying a thing as *new* power in *new* persons, of whose principles, tempers, and dispositions they have little or no experience, and in situations where those who appear the most stirring in the scene may possibly not be the real movers. . . .

All circumstances taken together, the French Revolution is the most astonishing that has hitherto happened in the world. The most wonderful things are brought about in many instances by means the most absurd and ridiculous ; in the most ridiculous modes ; and, apparently, by the most contemptible instruments. Everything seems out of nature in this strange chaos of levity and ferocity, and of all sorts of crimes jumbled together with all sorts of follies. In viewing this monstrous tragi-comic scene, the most opposite passions necessarily succeed, and sometimes mix with each other in the mind ; alternate contempt and indignation ; alternate laughter and tears ; alternate scorn and horror.

It cannot, however, be denied that to some this strange scene appeared in quite another point of view. Into them it inspired no other sentiments than those of exultation and rapture. They saw nothing in what has been done in France but a firm and temperate exertion of freedom ; so consistent, on the whole, with morals and with piety, as to make it deserving not only of the secular applause of dashing Machiavellian politicians, but to render it a fit theme for all the devout effusions of sacred eloquence.

[Burke proceeds to criticize a sermon given by Dr. Richard Price at a meeting house in Old Jewry in which it was claimed that the people of England have the right to choose their own kings, and that William III had been so chosen. He shows that the principle of hereditary succession had been most strictly followed, the only qualification introduced being succession in the Protestant line.]

So far is it from being true that we acquired a right by the Revolution to elect our kings, that if we had possessed it before, the English nation did at that time most solemnly renounce and abdicate it, for themselves, and for all their posterity for ever. These gentlemen may value themselves as much as they please on their Whig principles ; but I never desire to be thought a better Whig than Lord Somers ; or to understand the principles of the Revolution better than those by whom it was brought about ; or to read in the Declaration of Right any mysteries unknown to those whose penetrating style has engraved in our ordinances, and in our hearts, the words and spirit of that immortal law.

It is true that, aided with the powers derived from force and opportunity, the nation was at that time, in some sense, free to take what course it pleased for filling the throne ; but only free to do so upon the same grounds on which they might have wholly abolished their monarchy, and every other part of their constitution. However, they did not think such bold changes within their commission. It is indeed difficult, perhaps impossible, to give limits to the mere *abstract* competence of the supreme power, such as was exercised by parliament at that time ; but the limits of a *moral* competence, subjecting, even in powers more indisputably sovereign, occasional will to permanent reason, and to the steady maxims of faith, justice, and fixed fundamental policy, are perfectly intelligible, and perfectly binding upon those who exercise any authority, under any name, or under any title in the state. The House of Lords, for instance, is not morally competent to dissolve the House of Commons ; no, nor even to dissolve itself, nor to abdicate, if it would, its portion in the legislature of the kingdom. Though a king may abdicate for his own person, he cannot abdicate for the monarchy. By as strong, or by a stronger reason, the House of Commons cannot renounce its share of authority. The engagement and pact of society, which generally goes by the name of the constitution, forbids such invasion and such surrender. The constituent parts of a state are obliged to hold their public faith with each other, and with all those who derive any serious interest under their engagements, as much as the whole state is bound to keep its faith with separate communities. Otherwise competence and power would soon be confounded, and no law be left but the will of a prevailing force. On this principle the succession of the crown has always been what it now is, an hereditary succession by law : in the old line it was a succession by the common law ; in the new by the statute law, operating on the principles of the common law, not changing the substance, but regulating the mode, and describing the persons. Both these descriptions of law are of the same force, and are derived from an equal authority, emanating from the common agreement and original compact of the state, *communi sponsione reipublicæ*, and as such are equally binding on king and people too, as long as the terms are observed, and they continue the same body politic. . . .

I know that we are supposed a dull, sluggish race, rendered passive by finding our situation tolerable, and prevented by a mediocrity of freedom from ever attaining to its full perfection.

Your leaders in France began by affecting to admire, almost to adore, the British constitution ; but as they advanced, they came to look upon it with a sovereign contempt. The friends of your National Assembly amongst us have full as mean an opinion of what was formerly thought the glory of their country. The Revolution Society has discovered that the English nation is not free. They are convinced that the inequality in our representation is a " defect in our constitution *so gross and palpable,* as to make it excellent chiefly in *form* and *theory* ". That a representation in the legislature of a kingdom is not only the basis of all constitutional liberty in it, but of " *all legitimate government* ; that without it a *government* is nothing but an *usurpation* "—that " when the representation is *partial,* the kingdom possesses liberty only *partially* ; and if extremely partial, it gives only a *semblance* ; and if not only extremely partial, but corruptly chosen, it becomes a *nuisance* ". Dr. Price considers this inadequacy of representation as our *fundamental grievance* ; and though, as to the corruption of this semblance of representation, he hopes it is not yet arrived to its full perfection of depravity, he fears that " nothing will be done towards gaining for us this *essential blessing,* until some *great abuse of power* again provokes our resentment, or some *great calamity* again alarms our fears, or perhaps till the acquisition of a *pure and equal representation by other countries,* whilst we are *mocked* with the *shadow,* kindles our shame ". To this he subjoins a note in these words : " A representation chosen chiefly by the treasury, and a *few* thousands of the *dregs* of the people, who are generally paid for their votes ". . . .

It is no wonder, therefore, that with these ideas of everything in their constitution and government at home, either in church or state, as illegitimate and usurped, or at best as a vain mockery, they look abroad with an eager and passionate enthusiasm. Whilst they are possessed by these notions, it is vain to talk to them of the practice of their ancestors, the fundamental laws of their country, the fixed form of a constitution, whose merits are confirmed by the solid test of long experience, and an increasing public strength and national prosperity. They despise experience as the wisdom of unlettered men; and as for the rest, they have wrought underground a mine that will blow up, at one grand explosion, all examples of antiquity, all precedents, charters, and acts of parliament. They have " the rights of men ". Against these there can be no prescription; against these no agreement is binding : these admit no temperament, and no compromise ; anything withheld from their full demand is so much of fraud and injustice. Against these, their rights of men, let no government look for security in the length of its continuance, or in the justice and lenity of its administration. The objections of these speculatists, if its forms do not quadrate with their theories, are as valid against such an old and beneficent government, as against the most violent tyranny, or the greenest usurpation. They are always at issue with governments, not on a question of title. I have nothing to say to the clumsy subtility of their political metaphysics. But let them not break prison to burst like a *Levanter*, to sweep the earth with their hurricane, and to break up the fountains of the great deep to overwhelm us.

Far am I from denying in theory, full as far is my heart from withholding in practice (if I were of power to give or to withhold) the *real* rights of men. In denying their false claims of right, I do not mean to injure those which are real, and are such as their pretended rights would totally destroy. If civil society be made for the advantage of man, all the advantages for which it is made become his right. It is an institution of beneficence; and law itself is only beneficence acting by a rule. Men have a right to live by that rule ; they have a right to do justice, as between their fellows, whether their fellows are in public function or in ordinary occupation. They have a right to the fruits of their industry, and to the means of making their industry fruitful. They have a right to the acquisitions of their parents ; to the nourishment and improvement of their offspring ; to instruction in life, and to consolation in death. Whatever each man can separately do, without trespassing upon others, he has a right to do for himself ; and he has a right to a fair portion of all which society, with all its combinations of skill and force can do in his favour. In this partnership all men have equal rights ; but not to equal things. He that has but five shillings in the partnership, has as good a right to it, as he that has five hundred pounds has to his larger proportion. But he has not a right to an equal dividend in the product of the joint stock ; and as to the share of power, authority, and direction which each individual ought to have in the management of the state, that I must deny to be amongst the direct original rights of man in civil society ; for I have in my contemplation the civil social man, and no other. It is a thing to be settled by convention.

If civil society be the offspring of convention, that convention must be its law. That convention must limit and modify all the descriptions of constitution which are formed under it. Every sort of legislative, judicial, or executory power are its creatures. They can have no being in any other state of things ; and how can any man claim under the conventions of civil society, rights which do not so much as suppose its existence ? rights which are absolutely repugnant to it ? One of the first motives to civil society, and which becomes one of its fundamental rules, is, *that no man should be judge in his own cause.* By this each person has at once divested himself of the first fundamental right of uncovenanted man, that is, to judge for himself, and to assert his own cause. He abdicates all right to be his own governor. He inclusively, in a great measure, abandons the right of self-defence, the first law of nature. Men cannot enjoy the rights of an uncivil and of a civil state together. That he may obtain justice, he gives up his right of determining what it is in points the most essential to him. That he may secure some liberty, he makes a surrender in trust of the whole of it.

Government is not made in virtue of natural rights, which may and do exist in total independence of it ; and exist in much greater clearness, and in a much greater degree of abstract perfection : but their abstract perfection is their practical defect. By having a right to everything they want everything. Government is a contrivance of human wisdom to provide for human *wants*. Men have a right that these wants should be provided for by this wisdom. Among these wants is to be reckoned the want, out of civil society, of a sufficient restraint upon their passions. Society requires not only that the passions of individuals should be subjected, but that even in the mass and body, as well as in the individuals, the inclinations of men should frequently be thwarted, their will controlled, and their passions brought into subjection. This can only be done *by a power out of themselves* ; and not, in the exercise of its function, subject to that will and to those passions which it is its office to bridle and subdue. In this sense the restraints on men, as well as their liberties, are to be reckoned among their rights. But as the liberties and the restrictions vary with times and circumstances, and admit of infinite modifications, they cannot be settled upon any abstract rule ; and nothing is so foolish as to discuss them upon that principle.

The moment you abate anything from the full rights of men, each to govern himself, and suffer any artificial, positive limitation upon those rights, from that moment the whole organization of government becomes a consideration of convenience. This it is which makes the constitution of a state and the due distribution of its powers, a matter of the most delicate and complicated skill. It requires a deep knowledge of human nature and human necessities, and of the things which facilitate or obstruct the various ends, which are to be pursued by the mechanism of civil institutions. The state is to have recruits to its strength, and remedies to its distempers. What is the use of discussing a man's abstract right to food or medicine ? The question is upon the method of procuring and administering them. In that deliberation I shall always advise to call in the aid of the farmer and the physician, rather than the professor of metaphysics.

The science of constructing a commonwealth, or renovating it, or reforming it, is, like every other experimental science, not to be taught *a priori*. Nor is it a short experience that can instruct us in that practical science ; because the real effects of moral causes are not always immediate ; but that which in the first instance is prejudicial may be excellent in its remoter operation ; and its excellence may arise even from the ill-effects it produces in the beginning. The reverse also happens : and very plausible schemes, with very pleasing commencements, have often shameful and lamentable conclusions. In states there are often some obscure and almost latent causes, things which appear at first view of little moment, on which a very great part of its prosperity or adversity may most essentially depend. The science of government being therefore so practical in itself, and intended for such practical purposes, a matter which requires experience, and even more experience than any person can gain in his whole life, however sagacious and observing he may be, it is with infinite caution that any man ought to venture upon pulling down an edifice, which has answered in any tolerable degree for ages the common purposes of society, or on building it up again, without having models and patterns of approved utility before his eyes.

I am constantly of opinion that your French states, in three orders, on the footing on which they stood in 1614, were capable of being brought into a proper and harmonious combination with royal authority. This constitution by estates was the natural and only just representation of France. It grew out of the habitual conditions, relations, and reciprocal claims of men. It grew out of the circumstances of the country, and out of the state of property. The wretched scheme of your present masters is not to fit the constitution to the people, but wholly to destroy conditions, to dissolve relations, to change the state of the nation, and to subvert property, in order to fit their country to their theory of a constitution.

Until you make out practically that great work, a combination of opposing forces, " a work of labour long, and endless praise ", the utmost caution ought to have been used in the reduction of the royal power, which alone was capable of holding together the comparatively heterogeneous mass of your states. But, at this day, all these considerations are unseasonable. To what end should we discuss the limitations of royal power ? Your king is in prison. Why speculate on the measure and standard of liberty ? I doubt much, very much indeed, whether France is at all ripe for liberty on any standard. Men are qualified for civil liberty in exact proportion to their disposition to put moral chains upon their own appetites ; in proportion as their love to justice is above their rapacity, in proportion as their soundness and sobriety of understanding is above their vanity and presumption ; in proportion as they are more disposed to listen to the counsels of the wise and good, in preference to the flattery of knaves. Society cannot exist unless a controlling power upon will and appetite be placed somewhere, and the less of it there is within, the more there must be without. It is ordained in the eternal constitution of things that men of intemperate minds cannot be free. Their passions forge their fetters.

This sentence the prevalent part of your countrymen execute on themselves. They possessed not long since, what was next to freedom—a mild paternal monarchy. They despised it for its weakness. They were offered a well-poised free constitution. It did not suit their taste nor their temper. They carved for themselves. They flew out, murdered, robbed, and rebelled. They have succeeded, and put over their country an insolent tyranny made up of cruel and inexorable masters, and that too of a description hitherto not known in the world. The powers and policies by which they have succeeded are not those of great statesmen, or great military commanders, but the practices of incendiaries, assassins, housebreakers, robbers, spreaders of false news, forgers of false orders from authority, and other delinquencies, of which ordinary justice takes cognisance. Accordingly the spirit of their rule is exactly correspondent to the means by which they obtained it. They act more in the manner of thieves who have got possession of a house, than of conquerors who have subdued a nation.

Burke had no great regard for the political wisdom of the great mass of the people in his day, and rightly so, perhaps, in view of their lack of education and experience. But the demand for manhood suffrage, which had been growing steadily in the latter half of the eighteenth century, became more and more clamant in the nineteenth. It inspired the Chartists. But with typical British caution this ideal of modern democracy was achieved only by halting (but sure) steps spread over the whole century and more. It was the first step which counted the most. The first great Reform Bill was passed by the House of Commons in 1831, only to be promptly rejected by the Lords. A few days later, Macaulay made one of his greatest speeches in the House of Commons, a speech which raised the fundamental question: *Can a stable government be based on anything other than the consent of the governed?* Public opinion is a vague and slow-acting force, but it is immensely powerful, and sooner or later it makes itself felt in every village and in every street of every town. It is a power which has long been able to find expression in Western Civilization, and one which is now growing rapidly in some non-European regions of the world, while it is being as vigorously repressed, and prevented from finding its voice in others.

LORD MACAULAY

CONSENT OR FORCE IN GOVERNMENT

I DOUBT, sir, whether any person who had merely heard the speech of the right honourable Member for the University of Cambridge would have been able to conjecture what the question is which we are discussing, and what the occasion on which we are assembled. For myself, I can with perfect sincerity declare that never in the whole course of my life did I feel my mind oppressed by so deep and solemn a sense of responsibility as at the present moment. I firmly believe that the country is now in danger of calamities greater than ever threatened it, from domestic misgovernment or from foreign hostility. The danger is no less than this, that there may be a complete alienation of the people from their rulers. To soothe the public mind, to reconcile the people to the delay, the short delay, which must intervene before their wishes can be legitimately gratified, and in the meantime to avert civil discord, and to uphold the authority of law, these are, I conceive, the objects of my noble friend, the Member for Devonshire : these ought, at the present crisis, to be the objects of every honest Englishman. They are objects which will assuredly be attained, if we rise to this great occasion, if we take our stand in the place which the Constitution has assigned to us, if we employ, with becoming firmness and dignity, the powers which belong to us as trustees of the nation, and as advisers of the Throne. . . .

It is not my intention, sir, again to discuss the merits of the Reform Bill. The principle of that bill received the approbation of the late House of Commons after a discussion of ten nights ; and the bill, as it now stands, after a long and most laborious investigation, passed the present House of Commons by a majority which was nearly half as large again as the minority. This was little more than a fortnight ago. Nothing has since occurred to change our opinion. The justice of the case is unaltered. The public enthusiasm is undiminished. Old Sarum has grown no larger. Manchester has grown no smaller. In addressing this House, therefore, I am entitled to assume that the bill is in itself a good bill. If so, ought we to abandon it merely because the Lords have rejected it ? We ought to respect the lawful privileges of their House ; but we ought also to assert our own. We are constitutionally as independent of their Lordships as their Lordships

are of us. We have precisely as good a right to adhere to
our opinion as they have to dissent from it. In speaking
of their decision, I will attempt to follow that example of
moderation which was so judiciously set by my noble friend,
the Member for Devonshire. I will only say that I do not
think that they are more competent to form a correct judgment
on a political question than we are. It is certain that, on all
the most important points on which the two Houses have for
a long time past differed, the Lords have at length come over
to the opinion of the Commons. I am therefore entitled to
say, that with respect to all those points, the Peers themselves
being judges, the House of Commons was in the right and
the House of Lords in the wrong. It was thus with respect
to the Slave-trade ; it was thus with respect to Catholic
Emancipation ; it was thus with several other important
questions. I, therefore, cannot think that we ought, on the
present occasion, to surrender our judgment to those who
have acknowledged that, on former occasions of the same
kind, we have judged more correctly than they. . . .

The next question is this : ought we to make a formal
declaration that we adhere to our opinion ? I think that we
ought to make such a declaration ; and I am sure that we
cannot make it in more temperate or more constitutional
terms than those which my noble friend asks us to adopt. I
support the Resolution which he has proposed with all my
heart and soul : I support it as a friend to Reform ; but I
support it still more as a friend to law, to property, to social
order. No observant and unprejudiced man can look forward
without great alarm to the effects which the recent decision
of the Lords may possibly produce. I do not predict, I do
not expect, open, armed insurrection. What I apprehend is
this, that the people may engage in a silent, but extensive
and persevering war against the law. What I apprehend is,
that England may exhibit the same spectacle which Ireland
exhibited three years ago, agitators stronger than the magistrate,
associations stronger than the law, a Government powerful

enough to be hated, and not powerful enough to be feared, a people bent on indemnifying themselves by illegal excesses for the want of legal privileges. I fear that we may before long see the tribunals defied, the tax-gatherer resisted, public credit shaken, property insecure, the whole frame of society hastening to dissolution. It is easy to say, " Be bold ; be firm ; defy intimidation ; let the law have its course ; the law is strong enough to put down the seditious ". Sir, we have heard all this blustering before ; and we know in what it ended. It is the blustering of little men whose lot has fallen on a great crisis. Xerxes scourging the winds, Canute commanding the waves to recede from his foot-stool, were but types of the folly of those who apply the maxims of the Quarter Sessions to the great convulsions of society. The law has no eyes ; the law has no hands ; the law is nothing, nothing but a piece of paper printed by the King's printer, with the King's arms at the top, till public opinion breathes the breath of life into the dead letter. We found this in Ireland. The Catholic Association bearded the Government. The Government resolved to put down the Association. An indictment was brought against my honourable and learned friend, the Member for Kerry. The Grand Jury threw it out. Parliament met. The Lords Commissioners came down with a speech recommending the suppression of the self-constituted legislature of Dublin. A bill was brought in ; it passed both Houses by large majorities ; it received the Royal assent. And what effect did it produce ? Exactly as much as that old Act of Queen Elizabeth, still unrepealed, by which it is provided that every man who, without a special exemption, shall eat meat on Fridays and Saturdays, shall pay a fine of twenty shillings or go to prison for a month. Not only was the Association not destroyed ; its power was not for one day suspended ; it flourished and waxed strong under the law which had been made for the purpose of annihilating it. The elections of 1826, the Clare election two years later, proved the folly of those who think that nations are governed by wax

Q

and parchment : and, at length, in the close of 1828, the Government had only one plain choice before it, concession or civil war. Sir, I firmly believe that, if the people of England shall lose all hope of carrying the Reform Bill by constitutional means, they will forthwith begin to offer to the Government the same kind of resistance which was offered to the late Government, three years ago, by the people of Ireland, a resistance by no means amounting to rebellion, a resistance rarely amounting to any crime defined by the law, but a resistance nevertheless which is quite sufficient to obstruct the course of justice, to disturb the pursuits of industry, and to prevent the accumulation of wealth. And is not this a danger which we ought to fear ? And is not this a danger which we are bound, by all means in our power, to avert ?

I know only two ways in which societies can permanently be governed : by public opinion, and by the sword. A Government having at its command the armies, the fleets, and the revenues of Great Britain, might possibly hold Ireland by the sword. So Oliver Cromwell held Ireland ; so William the Third held it ; so Mr. Pitt held it ; so the Duke of Wellington might perhaps have held it. But to govern Great Britain by the sword ! So wild a thought has never, I will venture to say, occurred to any public man of any party ; and, if any man were frantic enough to make the attempt, he would find, before three days had expired, that there is no better sword than that which is fashioned out of a ploughshare. But, if not by the sword, how is the country to be governed ? I understand how the peace is kept at New York. It is by the assent and support of the people. I understand also how the peace is kept at Milan. It is by the bayonets of the Austrian soldiers. But how the peace is to be kept when you have neither the popular assent nor the military force, how the peace is to be kept in England by a Government acting on the principles of the present Opposition, I do not understand.

There is in truth a great anomaly in the relation between the English people and their Government. Our institutions are either too popular or not popular enough. The people have not sufficient power in making the laws ; but they have quite sufficient power to impede the execution of the laws when made. The legislature is almost entirely aristocratical ; the machinery by which the decrees of the legislature are carried into effect is almost entirely popular ; and, therefore, we constantly see all the power which ought to execute the law, employed to counteract the law. Thus, for example, with a criminal code which carries its rigour to the length of atrocity, we have a criminal judicature which often carries its lenity to the length of perjury. Our law of libel is the most absurdly severe that ever existed, so absurdly severe that, if it were carried into full effect, it would be much more oppressive than a censorship. And yet, with this severe law of libel, we have a Press which practically is as free as the air. In 1819 the Ministers complained of the alarming increase of seditious and blasphemous publications. They proposed a bill of great rigour to stop the growth of the evil ; and they carried their bill. It was enacted, that the publisher of a seditious libel might, on a second conviction, be banished, and that if he should return from banishment, he might be transported. How often was this law put in force ? Not once. Last year we repealed it : but it was already dead, or rather it was dead born. It was obsolete before *Le Roi le veut* had been pronounced over it. For any effect which it produced it might as well have been in the Code Napoleon as in the English Statute Book. And why did the Government, having solicited and procured so sharp and weighty a weapon, straightway hang it up to rust ? Was there less sedition, were there fewer libels, after the passing of the Act than before it ? Sir, the very next year was the year 1820, the year of the Bill of Pains and Penalties against Queen Caroline, the very year when the public mind was most excited, the very year when the public press was most scurrilous. Why, then, did not the Ministers use their new law ? Because they durst not ; because they could not. They had obtained it with ease ; for in obtaining it they had to deal with a subservient Parliament. They could not execute it : for in executing it they would have to deal with a refractory people. These are instances of the difficulty of carrying the law into effect when the people are inclined to thwart their rulers. The great anomaly, or, to speak more properly, the great evil which I have described, would, I believe, be removed by the Reform Bill. That bill would establish harmony between the people and the legislature. It would give a fair share in the making of laws to those without whose co-operation laws are mere waste paper. Under a reformed system we should not see, as we now often see, the nation repealing Acts of Parliament as fast as we and the Lords can pass them. As I believe that the Reform Bill would produce this blessed and salutary concord, so I fear that the rejection of the Reform Bill, if that rejection should be considered as final, will aggravate the evil which I have been describing to an unprecedented, to a terrible extent. To all the laws which might be passed for the collection of the revenue, or for the prevention of sedition, the people would oppose the same kind of resistance by means of which they have succeeded in mitigating, I might say in abrogating, the law of libel. There would be so many offenders that the Government would scarcely know at whom to aim its blow. Every offender would have so many accomplices and protectors that the blow would almost always miss the aim. The veto of the people, a veto not pronounced in set form like that of the Roman tribunes, but quite as effectual as that of the Roman tribunes for the purpose of impeding public measures, would meet the Government at every turn. The Administration would be unable to preserve order at home, or to uphold the national honour abroad ; and, at length, men who are now moderate, who now think of revolution with horror, would begin to wish that the lingering agony of the State might be terminated by one fierce, sharp, decisive crisis.

Is there a way of escape from these calamities ? I believe that there is. I believe that, if we do our duty, if we give the people reason to believe that the accomplishment of their wishes is only deferred, if we declare our undiminished attachment to the Reform Bill, and our resolution to support no Minister who will not support that bill, we shall avert the fearful disasters which impend over the country. . . .

The Constitution of England, thank God, is not one of those constitutions which are past all repair, and which must, for the public welfare, be utterly destroyed. It has a decayed part ; but it has also a sound and precious part. It requires purification ; but it contains within itself the means by which that purification may be effected. We read that in old times, when the villeins were driven to revolt by oppression, when the castles of the nobility were burned to the ground, when the warehouses of London were pillaged, when a hundred thousand insurgents appeared in arms on Blackheath, when a foul murder perpetrated in their presence had raised their passions to madness, when they were looking round for some captain to succeed and avenge him whom they had lost, just then, before Hob Miller, or Tom Carter, or Jack Straw, could place himself at their head, the King rode up to them and exclaimed, " I will be your leader ! " and at once the infuriated multitude laid down their arms, submitted to his guidance, dispersed at his command. Herein let us imitate him. Our countrymen are, I fear, at this moment, but too much disposed to lend a credulous ear to selfish impostors. Let us say to them, " We are your leaders ; we, your own House of Commons ; we, the constitutional interpreters of your wishes ; the knights of forty English shires, the citizens and burgesses of all your largest towns. Our lawful power shall be firmly exerted to the utmost in your cause ; and our lawful power is such, that when firmly exerted in your cause, it must finally prevail." This tone it is our interest and our duty to take. The circumstances admit of no delay. Is there one among us who is not looking with breathless anxiety for the next tidings which may arrive from the remote parts of the kingdom ? Even while I speak, the moments are passing away, the irrevocable moments pregnant with the destiny of a great people. The country is in danger; it may be saved; we can save it. This is the way; this is the time. In our hands are the issues of great good and great evil, the issues of the life and death of the State. May the result of our deliberations be the repose and prosperity of that noble country which is entitled to all our love; and for the safety of which we are answerable to our own consciences, to the memory of future ages, to the Judge of all hearts!

We need not trace the steps by which the franchise was extended in Great Britain, nor the other instances of freedom slowly broadening down "from precedent to precedent". But the occasion is perhaps not inopportune for a glance at a remarkable display not only of the power of public opinion throughout the whole British Commonwealth of Nations, but also of the extent to which our monarchy has become so limited that, in Winston Churchill's words, "the supremacy of Parliament over the Crown, the duty of the Sovereign to act in accordance with the advice of his ministers" is now an understood thing. Monarchies have not been popular since the rise of democracy, and there are very few left, but the King of England is enthroned more firmly than ever in the hearts of his subjects, both at home and overseas. *Why does the Crown in Britain, despite its loss of prerogatives, now stand for more than it ever did before?* An answer to this question will be found in the words of the Prime Minister who so ably and so tactfully upheld the traditions of the constitution when Edward VIII abdicated. This abdication brought into a clear light what the " divine right " of the king is to-day: that of being the willing servant of the people in his public life, and an example to them in his private life.

EARL BALDWIN

THE ABDICATION OF EDWARD VIII

[On December 10, 1936, at the close of Question time in the House of Commons, Mr. Baldwin rose, and amid a tense silence announced, "A message from His Majesty the King, signed by His Majesty's own hand".

He presented it to the Speaker, and the Speaker read aloud :—]

"AFTER long and anxious consideration, I have determined to renounce the Throne to which I succeeded on the death of my father, and I am now communicating this, my final and irrevocable decision. Realizing as I do the gravity of this step, I can only hope that I shall have the understanding of my peoples in the decision I have taken and the reasons which have led me to take it. I will not now enter into my private feelings, but I would beg that it should be remembered that the burden which constantly rests upon the shoulders of a Sovereign is so heavy that it can only be borne in circumstances different from those in which I now find myself. I conceive that I am not overlooking the duty that rests on me to place in the forefront the public interest when I declare that I am conscious that I can no longer discharge this heavy task with efficiency or with satisfaction to myself.

" I have accordingly this morning executed an Instrument of Abdication in the terms following :

" ' I, Edward VIII, of Great Britain, Ireland, and the British Dominions beyond the Seas, King, Emperor of India, do hereby declare my irrevocable determination to renounce the Throne for myself and for my descendants, and my desire that effect should be given to this Instrument of Abdication immediately.

" ' In token whereof I have hereunto set my hand this tenth day of December, nineteen hundred and thirty-six, in the presence of the witnesses whose signatures are subscribed.

" ' (Signed) EDWARD R.I.'

My execution of this Instrument has been witnessed by my three brothers, their Royal Highnesses the Duke of York, the Duke of Gloucester, and the Duke of Kent.

" I deeply appreciate the spirit which has actuated the

appeals which have been made to me to take a different decision, and I have, before reaching my final determination, most fully pondered over them. But my mind is made up. Moreover, further delay cannot but be most injurious to the peoples whom I have tried to serve as Prince of Wales and as King, and whose future happiness and prosperity are the constant wish of my heart.

" I take my leave of them in the confident hope that the course which I have thought it right to follow is that which is best for the stability of the Throne and Empire and the happiness of my peoples. I am deeply sensible of the consideration which they have always extended to me both before and after my accession to the Throne and which I know they will extend in full measure to my successor.

" I am most anxious that there should be no delay of any kind in giving effect to the Instrument which I have executed and that all necessary steps should be taken immediately to secure that my lawful successor, my brother, His Royal Highness the Duke of York, should ascend the Throne.

" (Signed) EDWARD R.I."

[Mr. Baldwin thereupon said :—]

I beg to move that His Majesty's most gracious Message be now considered.

No more grave message has ever been received by Parliament and no more difficult, I may almost say repugnant, task has ever been imposed upon a Minister. I would ask the House, which I know will not be without sympathy for one in my position to-day, to remember that in this last week I have had but little time in which to compose a speech for delivery to-day, so I must tell what I have to tell truthfully, sincerely, and plainly, with no attempt to dress up or to adorn.

[He went on to outline the uneasiness he had felt in the month of October at the comments about the King which

were then appearing in the American Press. He felt it essential
that someone should see the King and warn him about the
difficult situation which might arise, and that " someone "
could only be the Prime Minister. So he had sought an
audience and had seen the King on October 20.]

On the Tuesday morning I saw him. Sir, I may say before
I proceed to the details of the conversation that an adviser of
the Crown can be of no possible service to his master unless
he tells him at all times the truth as he sees it, whether that
truth be welcome or not.

And let me say here, as I may say several times before I
finish, when I look back on these talks there is nothing that I
have told His Majesty of which I felt he should not be aware.
Nothing.

But His Majesty's attitude all through has been—let me
put it in this way : Never has he shown any sign of offence,
of being hurt, at anything I have said to him, and the whole
of our discussions have been carried out, as I said, with an
increase, if possible, of the mutual respect and regard in
which we stood. I told His Majesty that I had two great
anxieties : one, the effect of a continuance of the kind of
criticism that at that time was proceeding in the American
Press, the effect it would have in the Dominions, and particularly in Canada, where it was widespread, the effect it
would have in this country.

That was the first anxiety. And then I reminded him of
what I had often told him and his brothers in years past, and
that is this : you take the British Monarchy—a unique institution. The Crown in this country through the centuries has been
deprived of many of its prerogatives, but to-day, while that is
true, it stands for far more than it ever has done in its
history.

The importance of its integrity is, beyond all question,
far greater than it has ever been, being, as it is, not only the
last link of Empire that is left but a guarantee in this

country, so long as it exists in that integrity, against many evils that have affected and afflicted other countries.

There is no man or woman in this country, to whatever party they belong, who would not subscribe to that. But while this feeling largely depends on the respect which has grown up in the last three generations for the Monarchy, it might not take so long, in the face of the kind of criticism to which it is being exposed, to lose that power far more rapidly than it was built up, and, once lost, I doubt if anything would restore it.

That was the basis of my talk on that aspect, and such criticism should not have cause to go on. I said that in my view no popularity in the long run would be weighed against the effect of such criticism. I told His Majesty that I, for one, had looked forward to his reign being a great reign in a new age—he has so many of the qualities necessary—and that I hoped we should be able to see our hopes realized. I told him I had come—naturally, I was his Prime Minister—but I wanted to talk it over with him as a friend to see if I could help him in this matter. . . .

I then pointed out the danger of the divorce proceedings, that if a verdict was given in that case that left the matter in suspense for some time, that period of suspense might be dangerous, because then everyone would be talking, and when once the Press began, as it must begin some time in this country, a most difficult situation would arise for me, for him, and there might well be a danger which both he and I had seen all through this—I shall come to that later—and it was one of the reasons why he wanted to take this action quickly— that is, that there might be sides taken and factions grow up in this country in a matter where no faction ought ever to exist.

It was on that aspect of the question that we talked for an hour, and I went away glad that the ice had been broken, because I knew that it had to be broken. . . . The next time I saw him was on Monday, November 16. That was at

Buckingham Palace. By that date the decree *nisi* had been pronounced in the divorce case. . . .

I felt it my duty to begin the conversation, and I spoke to him for a quarter of an hour or twenty minutes on the question of marriage. Again, we must remember that the Cabinet had not been in this at all. I reported to about four of my senior colleagues the conversation at Fort Belvedere. I saw the King on Monday, November 16, and I began by giving him my view of a possible marriage. I told him that I did not think that a particular marriage was one that would receive the approbation of the country. That marriage would have involved the lady becoming Queen. I did tell His Majesty once that I might be a remnant of the old Victorians, but that my worst enemy would not say of me that I did not know what the reaction of the English people would be to any particular course of action, and I told him that, so far as they went, I was certain that that would be impracticable. I cannot go farther into the details, but that was the substance.

I pointed out to him that the position of the King's wife was different from the position of the wife of any other citizen in the country; it was part of the price which the King has to pay. His wife becomes Queen; the Queen becomes the Queen of the country; and therefore, in the choice of a Queen the voice of the people must be heard. It is the truth that was expressed in those lines that may come to your minds :—

> " . . . his will is not his own ;
> For he himself is subject to his birth ;
> He may not, as unvalued persons do,
> Carve for himself ; for on his choice depends
> The safety and the health of the whole State."

Then His Majesty said to me—I have his permission to state this—that he wanted to tell me something that he had long wanted to tell me. He said : " I am going to marry Mrs. Simpson, and I am prepared to go ". I said : " Sir, that is most grievous news and it is impossible for me to make any comment on that to-day ". . . .

He sent for me again on Wednesday, November 25. In the meantime a suggestion had been made to me that a possible compromise might be arranged to avoid those two possibilities that had been seen, first in the distance, and then approaching nearer and nearer. The compromise was that the King should marry, that Parliament should pass an Act enabling the lady to be the King's wife without the position of Queen ; and when I saw His Majesty in November 25 he asked me whether that proposition had been put to me, and I said " Yes ".

He asked me what I thought of it. I told him that I had not considered it. I said : " I can give you no considered opinion ". If he asked me my first reaction informally, my first reaction was that Parliament would never pass such a Bill. But I said that if he desired it I would examine it formally. He said he did so desire. Then I said : " It will mean my putting that formally before the whole Cabinet and communicating with the Prime Ministers of all the Dominions ", and I asked was that his wish. He told me that it was. I said that I would do it.

On December 2 the King asked me to go and see him again. I had intended asking for an audience later that week, because such inquiries as I thought proper to make I had not completed. The inquiries had gone far enough to show that neither in the Dominions nor here would there be any prospect of such legislation being accepted. His Majesty asked me if I could answer his question. I gave him the reply that I was afraid it was impracticable for those reasons. I do want the House to realize this : His Majesty said he was not surprised at that answer. He took my answer with no question, and he never recurred to it again.

I want the House to realize that, because if you can put yourself in His Majesty's place and you know what His Majesty's feelings are you know how glad you would have been had this been possible. You must realize that he behaved there as a great gentleman. He said no more about it ; the matter was closed. I never heard another word about it from him. That decision was, of course, a formal decision, and that was the only formal decision of any kind taken by the Cabinet until I come to the history of yesterday.

When we had finished that conversation I pointed out that the possible alternatives had been narrowed, and that it really had brought him into the situation that he would be placed in a grievous situation between two conflicting loyalties in his own heart—either complete abandonment of the project on which his heart was set, and remaining as King, or doing as he intimated to me that he was prepared to do in the talk which I have reported, going, and later on contracting that marriage if it were possible. . . .

I would say a word or two on the King's position. The King cannot speak for himself. The King has told us that he cannot carry, and does not see his way to carry, these almost intolerable burdens of Kingship without a woman at his side —and we know that. This crisis, if I may use the word, has arisen now rather than later from that very frankness of His Majesty's character, which is one of his many attractions. It would have been perfectly possible for His Majesty not to have told me of this at the date when he did, and not to have told me for some months to come. But he realized the damage that might be done in the interval by gossip and rumours and talk ; and he made that declaration to me when he did on purpose to avoid what he felt might be dangerous, not only here but throughout the Empire, to the moral force of the Crown which we are all determined to sustain.

He told me his intentions and he has never wavered from them. I want the House to understand that. He felt his duty to take into his anxious consideration all the representations that his advisers might give him, and not until he had fully considered them did he make public his decision. There has been no sign of conflict in this matter. My efforts during these last days have been directed, as have the efforts of those most closely round him, in trying to help him to make the choice which he has now made. And we have failed. The King has made his decision to take this moment to send this gracious message because of his confident hope that by that he will preserve the unity of this country and of the whole Empire and avoid those factious differences which might so easily have arisen.

It is impossible, unfortunately, to avoid talking to some extent to-day about one's self. These last days have been days of great strain, but it was a great comfort to me, and I hope it will be to the House, when I was assured before I left him on Tuesday night, by that intimate circle that was with him at the Fort that evening, that I had left nothing undone that I could have done to move him from the decision at which he had arrived and which he has communicated to us. While there is not a soul among us who will not regret this from the bottom of his heart, there is not a soul here to-day that wants to judge. We are not judges. He has announced his decision. He has told us what he wants us to do, and I think we must close our ranks and do it.

At a later stage this evening I shall ask leave to bring in the necessary Bill so that it may be read the first time, printed, and made available to members. . . .

This House to-day is a theatre which is being watched by the whole world. Let us conduct ourselves with that dignity that His Majesty himself is showing in this hour of his trial.

Whatever be our regret at the contents of the message, let us fulfil his wishes, to do what he asks, and to do it with speed, and let no word be spoken to-day that the speaker or the utterer of that word may regret in days to come.

Let no word be spoken that causes pain to any soul, and let us not forget to-day the revered and beloved figure of Queen Mary.

Think what all this time has meant to her and think of her when we have to speak, if speak we must, during this debate.

We have, after all, as guardians of democracy in this little island, to see that we do our work to maintain the integrity of the Monarchy, that Monarchy which, as I said at the beginning of my speech, is now the sole link of our whole Empire and the guardian of our freedom.

BOOK IV

THE CHALLENGE
TO WESTERN CIVILIZATION

R

THE CHALLENGE TO WESTERN CIVILIZATION

In his book on *British Politics since 1900* D. C. Somervell suggests that while the mental stature of statesmen has remained much the same during the past century, the problems which they have had to solve have shown a steady increase in complexity and difficulty. Past civilizations have fallen when the men in power could not cope with their problems. Can our leaders meet the challenge to-day?

The problems they now have to face are undoubtedly of the first magnitude. They present a bigger threat to Western Civilization than anything recorded in history since the fall of Rome. It was war with the barbarians which brought down the Roman Empire. *How have two world wars affected the outlook for Europe?* Professor Toynbee, whose knowledge and understanding of history are probably unequalled in the modern world, provides an answer in the following lecture. He first dealt with the " dwarfing of Europe " in a lecture given in 1926, and he brought his argument up to date, following another major war, in his book, *Civilization on Trial,* from which our extract is taken. He mentions some of the more intense stresses which Europe is having to withstand. Some of these are internal, and are due to movements like the development of industrialism, and of the democratic spirit. Others are due to external forces, such as the impact on our Western Civilization of the propaganda and the actions of the Communist countries.

ARNOLD J. TOYNBEE

THE DWARFING OF EUROPE

BEFORE the war of 1914-18, Europe enjoyed an undisputed ascendancy in the world, and the special form of civilization which had been developing in Western Europe during the past twelve hundred years seemed likely to prevail everywhere.

The ascendancy of Europe was marked by the fact that five out of the eight great powers then existing—that is to say, the British Empire, France, Germany, Austria-Hungary, and

Italy—had their roots in European soil. A sixth, the Russian Empire, lay in the immediate continental hinterland of the European peninsula, and during the last two and a half centuries it had become welded onto Europe—partly by the growth of a great trade between agrarian Russia and industrial Europe (a trade which had developed *pari passu* with the industrialization of Western-and-Central European countries) ; partly by the political incorporation in Russia of a fringe of countries with a Western tradition of European civilization, such as Poland, Finland, and the Baltic Provinces ; and partly by the adoption of Western technique, institutions, and ideas on the part of the Russians themselves. The two remaining great powers—Japan and the United States—were geographically non-European, and for that very reason they took little part, before the first world war, in the play of international politics—a play which was performed at that time on a European stage. It may be pointed out, however, that Japan, like Russia, had only risen to the rank of a great power through a partial adoption of that Western civilization of which Western Europe was the home. As for the United States, she was the child of Western Europe, and down to 1914 she was still drawing heavily upon European capital—human capital in the form of immigrants and material capital in the form of goods and services financed by European loans—in order to develop her latent natural resources.

This ascendancy of Europe in the world went hand in hand with the spread of Western civilization. The two movements were complementary, and it would be impossible to say that either was the cause or the effect of the other. Naturally, the spread of Western civilization was facilitated by the ascendancy of Europe, because the strong and efficient are always imitated by the weak and inefficient—partly out of necessity and partly from admiration (whether this admiration is avowed or not). On the other hand, the spread of Western civilization gave those peoples among whom it was indigenous an inestimable advantage in competition with those among whom it was exotic. During the century ending in 1914 the world was conquered economically not only by the new Western industrial system but by the Western nations among whom that system had been invented ; and the advantage possessed by an inventor in a battle fought with his own weapons was illustrated strikingly in the first world war itself. The fact that the war of 1914-18 was fought on the lines of Western military technique—which was, of course, an application of Western industrial technique—gave Germany an absolute military superiority over Russia, though German man-power was only half as great as Russian at the time. Had the Central-Asian, and not the Western, technique of warfare been predominant in the world during the years 1914-1918, as it had been during the Middle Ages, the Russian Cossacks might have overwhelmed the Prussian Uhlans. (Both these types of cavalry had a Central-Asian origin which is betrayed by their Turkish names—*oghlan* being the Turkish for " boy ", and *qazaq* for " digger ".)

The predominance of the Western civilization throughout the world on the eve of the fateful year 1914 was, indeed, both recent and unprecedented. It was unprecedented in this sense—that, though many civilizations before that of Europe had radiated their influence far beyond their original home-lands, none had previously cast its net right round the globe.

The civilization of Eastern Orthodox Christendom, which grew up in mediæval Byzantium, had been carried by the Russians to the Pacific ; but, so far from spreading westwards, it had itself succumbed to Western influence since the close of the seventeenth century. The civilization of Islam had expanded from the Middle East to Central Asia and Central Africa, to the Atlantic coast of Morocco and the Pacific coasts of the East Indies, but it had obtained no permanent foothold in Europe and had never crossed the Atlantic into the New World. The civilization of ancient Greece and Rome had extended its political dominion into North-Western Europe under the Roman Empire, and its artistic inspiration into India

and the Far East, where Græco-Roman models had stimulated
the development of Buddhist art.   Yet the Roman Empire
and the Chinese Empire had co-existed on the face of the same
planet for two centuries with scarcely any direct intercourse,
either political or economic.   Indeed, so slight was the contact
that each of these two societies saw the other, through a glass
darkly, as a half-mythical fairyland.   In other words, the
Græco-Roman civilization and the contemporary Far Eastern
civilization each expanded to their full capacity, in the same
age, without coming into collision.   It was the same with the
other ancient civilizations.   Ancient India radiated her religion,
her art, her commerce, and her colonists into the Far East
and the East Indies, but never penetrated the West.   The
civilization of the Sumerians in the Land of Shinar exerted
an influence as far afield as the Indus valley and Transcaspia
and South-eastern Europe ; but attempts to prove that it was
the parent of the early Chinese civilization on the one side,
or of the Egyptian on the other, have miscarried.   There is a
brilliant and rather militant school of English anthropologists
who maintain that all known civilizations—including those of
Central America and Peru—can be traced back to an Egyptian
origin.   And these anthropologists point to the present world-
wide extension of our Western civilization as an analogy in
support of their thesis.   If our own civilization has become
world-wide in our own time, they argue, why should not the
Egyptian civilization have achieved an equal extension a few
thousand years earlier ?   This thesis is interesting, but it is
the subject of acute controversy and must be regarded as non-
proven.   As far as we know for certain, the only civilization
that has ever yet become world-wide is ours.

Moreover, this is a very recent event.   Nowadays we are
apt to forget that Western Europe made two unsuccessful
attempts to expand before she eventually succeeded.

The first of these attempts was the mediæval movement in
the Mediterranean, for which the most convenient general name
is the Crusades.   In the Crusades, the attempt to impose the

political and economic dominion of West Europeans upon other peoples ended in a complete failure, while, in the interchange of culture, the West Europeans received a greater impress from the Muslims and Byzantines than they imparted to them. The second attempt was that of the Spaniards and Portuguese in the sixteenth century of our era. This was more or less successful in the New World—the modern Latin American communities owe their existence to it—but, elsewhere, Western civilization, as propagated by the Spaniards and Portuguese, was rejected after about a century's trial. The expulsion of the Spaniards and Portuguese from Japan, and of the Portuguese from Abyssinia, in the second quarter of the seventeenth century, marked the failure of this second attempt.

The third attempt was begun in the seventeenth century by the Dutch, French, and English, and these three West European nations were the principal authors of the world-wide ascendancy that our Western civilization was enjoying in 1914. The English, French, and Dutch peopled North America, South Africa, and Australasia with new nations of European stock which started life with the Western social heritage, and they brought the rest of the world within the European orbit. By 1914 the network of European trade and European means of communication had become world-wide. Almost the whole world had entered the Postal Union and the Telegraphic Union, and European devices for mechanical locomotion— the steamship, the railway, the motor-car—were rapidly penetrating everywhere. On the plane of politics, the European nations had not only colonized the New World but had conquered India and tropical Africa.

The political ascendancy of Europe, however, though outwardly even more imposing than her economic ascendancy, was really more precarious. The daughter-nations overseas had already set their feet firmly on the road towards independent nationhood. The United States and the Latin American republics had long since established their independence by revolutionary wars ; and the self-governing British Dominions were in process of establishing theirs by peaceful evolution. In India and tropical Africa, European domination was being maintained by a handful of Europeans who lived there as pilgrims and sojourners. They had not found it possible to acclimatize themselves sufficiently to bring up their children in the tropics ; and this meant that the hold of Europeans upon the tropics had not been made independent of a European base of operations. Finally, the cultural influence of the West European civilization upon Russians, Muslims, Hindus, Chinese, Japanese, and tropical Africans was so recent a ferment that it was not yet possible to predict whether it would evaporate without permanent effect, or whether it would turn the dough sour, or whether it would successfully leaven the lump.

This then, in very rough outline, was the position of Europe in the world on the eve of the war of 1914-18. She was in the enjoyment of an undisputed ascendancy, and the peculiar civilization which she had built up for herself was in process of becoming world-wide. Yet this position, brilliant though it was, was not merely unprecedented and recent ; it was also insecure. It was insecure chiefly because, at the very time when European expansion was approaching its climax, the foundations of West European civilization had been broken up and the great deeps loosed by the release and emergence of two elemental forces in European social life—the forces of industrialism and democracy, which were brought into a merely temporary and unstable equilibrium by the formula of nationalism. It is evident that a Europe which was undergoing the terrible double strain of this inward transformation and outward expansion—both on the heroic scale—could not with impunity squander her resources, spend her material wealth and man-power unproductively, or exhaust her muscular and nervous energy. If her total command of resources was considerably greater than that which any other civilization had ever enjoyed, these resources were relative to the calls upon them ; and the liabilities of

Europe on the eve of 1914, as well as her assets, were of an unprecedented magnitude. Europe could not afford to wage even one world war ; and when we take stock of her position in the world after a second world war and compare it with her position before 1914, we are confronted with a contrast that is staggering to the imagination.

In a certain sense, Europe still remains the centre of the world ; and in a certain sense, again, the world is still being leavened by that Western civilization of which Western Europe is the original home ; but the sense in which these two statements are still true has changed so greatly that the bare statements are misleading without a commentary. Instead of being a centre from which energy and initiative radiate outwards, Europe has become a centre upon which non-European energy and initiative converge. Instead of the world being a theatre for the play of European activities and rivalries, Europe herself—after having been the cockpit in two world wars in which the world did its fighting on European soil—is now in danger of becoming for a third time an arena for conflicts between non-European forces. An arena still may be defined as a central, public place, but it is hardly a place of honour or security.

It is true, again, that the influence of our Western civiliza-tion upon the rest of the world is still at work. Indeed, its action has become intensified, if we measure it in purely quantitative terms. For example, before the two wars, the new facilities for travel were only available for a wealthy minority of Europeans and Americans. During the wars, these facilities were turned to account to transport not only Euro-peans and Americans but Asiatics and Africans, *en masse*, to fight, or to labour behind the front, in war zones all over the world. During the last twenty or thirty years, additional means of mechanical communication have been made avail-able, not merely for a minority but for large sections of society. The motor-car has learnt to conquer the desert ; the aeroplane has out-sped the motor-car ; and the radio has reinforced the telephone and telegraph as a means of instantaneous long-distance intercourse. Unlike the railway and the telegraph, the motor-car and the radio-set can be owned and employed by private individuals—a feature which greatly enhances their efficacy as media of communication. With the wholesale intermingling of peoples during the two wars, and with these new mechanical aids to communication after them, it is not surprising to find that the leaven of Western civilization is penetrating the world more widely, deeply, and rapidly now than before.

At this moment we see peoples like the Chinese and the Turks, who, within living memory, seemed bound hand and foot by the Confucian and the Islamic social heritage, adopting not merely the material technique of the West (the industrial system and all its works) and not merely the externals of our culture (trifles like felt hats and cinemas) but our social and political institutions : the Western status of women, the Western method of education, the Western machinery of parliamentary representative government. In this, the Turks and Chinese are only conspicuous participants in a movement which is spreading over the whole of the Islamic world, the whole of the Hindu world, the whole of the Far East, the whole of tropical Africa ; and it looks almost as though a radical Westernization of the entire world were now inevitable. Insensibly, our attitude towards this extraordinary process has changed. Formerly, it caught our attention in the two apparently isolated cases of Japan and Russia, and we thought of these two cases as " sports "—due, perhaps, to some exceptional quality in the social heritage of these two countries which made their people specially susceptible to Westernization ; or due, perhaps, alternatively, to the personal genius and forcefulness of individual statesmen like Peter the Great and Catherine and Alexander the Liberator and that group of Japanese elder statesmen who deliberately imposed the adoption of Western ways upon the mass of their fellow-countrymen from the eighteen-sixties onwards. Now we see that Japan and Russia were simply forerunners of a movement which was to become universal. As Europeans observe this process of the Westernization of the world and watch it gathering momentum under their eyes, they may be inclined to exclaim almost in a spirit of exaltation : " What does it matter if Europe really has lost her ascendancy in the world, if the whole world is becoming European ? *Europæ si monumentum requiris, circumspice !* "

That mood of exaltation, however, if it did for a moment capture European minds, would rapidly be dispelled by doubts. The propagation of Western culture from Europe over the world may be a great thing quantitatively, but what about quality ? If at this instant Europe were to be blotted out of the book of life, would the Western civilization be able to maintain its European standard in the foreign environments to which it has been transplanted ? If Europe were blotted out altogether, could the Western civilization even survive ? And with Europe still alive, but deposed from her former position of supremacy—which is manifestly the fate that has overtaken her—will the Western civilization, though saved from extinction, escape degeneration ?

Still more alarming doubts suggest themselves when we contemplate the modern history of Russia—and Russia is the most instructive case to consider, because in Russia the process of Westernization has had longer than elsewhere to work itself out. In Russia, the leaven of Western Europe has been at work for two centuries longer than in Japan or China, and for a century longer than among the Muslims and the Hindus. Thus, the point to which the current of Westernization has carried Russia by now enables us to foresee, by analogy, at any rate, one of the possibilities that lie before the Far East, Islam, India, and Africa in the course of the next few generations. This possibility, which is revealed by the case of Russia—and of course it is no more than one possibility among a number of alternatives—is a disconcerting one for Western minds to contemplate.

The Europeans have regarded themselves as the Chosen People—they need feel no shame in admitting that; every past civilization has taken this view of itself and its own heritage—and, as they have watched the Gentiles, one after another, casting aside their own heritage in order to take up Europe's instead, they have unhesitatingly congratulated both themselves and their cultural converts. " One more sinner " Europeans have repeated to themselves devoutly " has repented of the filthy devices of the heathen and become initiated into the True Faith."

Now the first effects of the conversion—at any rate among the peoples converted to Western civilization before the wars— appeared to bear out this pious and optimistic view. For half a century after the Revolution of 1868 Japan seemed to have come unscathed through the tremendous transformation to which she had committed herself; and Russia would have been pronounced by a detached observer who took stock of her in 1815, or even as lately as 1914, to have been set by Peter the Great upon the road of progress—though in her case the road might have appeared to be longer, steeper, and more toilsome than in the case of Japan. A fair-minded observer of Russia, at either of those dates, would have admitted that the standard of Western civilization in a recently Westernized Russia was far lower than in a Europe where that civilization was at home ; but he would have pleaded that, in spite of this backwardness, and in spite of disappointingly frequent setbacks, Russia was rapidly catching up the European vanguard in the march of Western civilization. " Remember " he would have said " that, in this forward march, Europe had ten centuries' start, and you will admit that the pace at which Russia is catching up to Europe is very creditable."

But what would the same fair-minded observer say about Russia to-day ? I do not propose to speculate on the moral judgment that he would pass—that is irrelevant to my subject —but, whatever his judgments of value might be, I think he could hardly avoid making the two following judgments of fact : first, that the gospel according to Lenin and Stalin draws its inspiration from the West every bit as much as the gospel according to Peter and Alexander ; and, second, that the effect of the West upon Russia has changed over from positive to negative. The Russian prophets of the first dispensation were inspired by a set of Western ideas which attracted them towards the social heritage of our Western civilization ; the Russian prophets of the second dispensation have been attracted by another set of ideas which are also of Western origin, but which lead them to regard the West as a kind of apocalyptic Babylon. We cannot comprehend the total effect of Westernization upon Russia up to date unless we see this Bolshevik reaction of the twentieth century and the Petrine reaction of the seventeenth century in perspective— as successive, and perhaps inseparable, phases in a single process which the encounter between two different civilizations has set up. In this perspective we shall come to regard the process of Westernization with less complacency, and shall find ourselves reciting the parable :

> " When the unclean spirit is gone out of a man, he walketh through dry places, seeking rest ; and, finding none, he saith : ' I will return unto my house whence I came out '. And when he cometh he findeth it swept and garnished. Then goeth he and taketh to him seven other spirits more wicked than himself, and they enter in and dwell there ; and the last state of that man is worse than the first."

From a Western standpoint, " the unclean spirit " which originally possessed Russia was her Byzantine social heritage. When Peter the Great went on his pilgrimage to Europe and beheld Solomon in all his glory, there was no more spirit left in him. Byzantinism did not, indeed, go out of Russia, but it did go underground, and for ten generations the Russian people walked through dry places, seeking rest and finding none. Unable to endure existence in a swept and garnished house, they flung their doors wide open and summoned all the spirits of the West to enter in and dwell there ; and in crossing the threshold these spirits have turned into seven devils.

The moral seems to be that a social heritage will not readily bear transplantation. Culture spirits which are the tutelary geniuses, the *lares* and *penates*, of the house where they are at home, and where there is a pre-established harmony between them and the human inhabitants, become demons of malevolence and destruction when they enter into a house inhabited by strangers ; for these strangers are naturally ignorant of the subtle rites in which their new gods' souls delight. As long as the Ark of Jehovah remained in Israel among Jehovah's Chosen People, it served them as their talisman, but, when the Ark was captured by the Philistines, the hand of the Lord was heavy upon every city in which it rested, and the Chosen People themselves were infected with the plague by which the Gentiles were requited for their sacrilege.

If this analysis is right, Europeans cannot take much comfort for the dethronement of Europe in the prospect that the influence of European civilization may yet become the dominant force in the world. They will be less impressed by the fact that this mighty force has been generated in Europe than by the equally evident fact that, at a certain stage in its operation, it is apt to take a violently destructive turn. Indeed, this destructive recoil of European influence abroad upon Europe herself seems to be one of the signal dangers to which Europe is exposed in the new position in which she finds herself since the wars. In order to estimate the other principal danger to which Europe is now exposed, we must turn our attention from the relations between Europe and Russia to the relations between Europe and the United States.

The reversal in the relations between Europe and the United States since 1914 gives the measure in which the world-movement centring in Europe has become centripetal instead of centrifugal. The United States, as she was in 1914, was a monument of the outward radiation of European energies during the previous three centuries. Her population of over one hundred millions had been created by the man-power of Europe, and the volume of migration across the Atlantic was expanding, on a steeply ascending curve, down to the very year in which the first world war broke out. Again, the development of the material resources of the vast territory of the United States—a territory comparable in area to the whole of Europe, excluding Russia—was dependent not merely upon the influx of European man-power but upon the importation of European goods and the application of European services. The positive current of economic circulation, in the form of emigrants and goods and services, was flowing before 1914 from Europe into the United States ; the negative current, in the form of remittances and payments of interest for goods and services supplied on credit, was flowing from the United States to Europe. As a result of the two wars, the direction of the current has been dramatically reversed.

The facts are so notorious, they are so constantly and so deeply impressed upon our consciousness, that I almost feel that I ought to apologize to my readers for recalling them. From the moment when the first world war broke out, the stream of European emigrants to America ceased to flow ; and, by the time the first war was over, the United States— who had previously not only welcomed European immigrants but whose employers of labour sought them in the highways and hedges of Europe and compelled them to come in—had learnt to feel that European immigration was not a national asset but a national danger : that it was a transaction in which the balance of advantage was with the immigrant and not with the country which received him. This momentous change of attitude in the United States towards European immigration was promptly given practical expression in the two restriction acts of 1921 and 1924. The effect upon the economic life of Europe—or, more accurately, of those European countries from which the largest contingents of emigrants to the United States had latterly been drawn—was very far-reaching.

Take the classic case of Italy. In 1914 the number of Italian immigrants into the United States was 283,738 ; by contrast, the Italian annual quota proclaimed by President Coolidge on June 30, 1924, in pursuance of the Act of that year, was 3845. In consequence, the stream of Italian emigrants was partly damned up and partly diverted from the vacuum of the United States—a vacuum which had existed because America was a new world in process of development—to the vacuum in France—a vacuum which had been created because Europe was an old world devastated by having been made into the battle-field of an œcumenical war. In the eighteenth century, French and English armies crossed the Atlantic in order to fight on the banks of the Ohio and the St. Lawrence for the possession of the North American continent. In the twentieth century, American armies have crossed the Atlantic in order to decide the destinies of the world on European battle-fronts. Till 1914, the fertilizing stream of European emigration to America was still increasing in volume. From 1921 onwards, this stream was being deliberately checked, and during the inter-war years it was replaced by an uneconomic trickle of American tourists to Europe.

Of course, this inter-war trickle of American tourists to Europe, though small and unproductive compared to the mighty river of emigrants which had formerly flowed from Europe to America, was very large compared to any other movement of travel for uneconomic purposes that there had ever been ; and the fact that this tourist traffic could be financed brings me to the second point in which the relations between Europe and the United States have been reversed—a point which is so obvious that I shall simply state it without dwelling on it. The United States had changed, almost in the twinkling of an eye, from being the greatest debtor country in the world to being the greatest creditor country ; and, in spite of their traditional aversion to European entanglements,

Americans were driven, by the necessities of the new economic situation, to seek markets on credit, in Europe, for American goods and services. But there was an unfortunate difference in kind between pre-war European investment in the United States and the inter-war American investment in Europe. Before 1914 Europe provided the United States with credits for productive outlay. During the two wars Europe borrowed from America the means of working her own destruction ; and to-day she is borrowing desperately from America again, not in order to develop new European resources, but merely to repair some part of the ravages which two world wars have inflicted on her.

Confronted with this painful reversal in their relations with the United States, Europeans naturally ask themselves : " Is this an accidental, and therefore retrievable and merely temporary, misfortune—an incidental consequence of exceptional catastrophes ? Or has it older and deeper causes, the effect of which it will be less easy to counteract ? " I venture to suggest that this second possibility appears to be the more probable of the two—that, although the two wars have precipitated this reversal of relations and have given it a revolutionary and dramatic outward form, some such reversal was nevertheless inherent in the previous situation, and would have taken place—though no doubt more gently and gradually —even if these wars had never been fought.

In his book from which the above lecture is taken, Dr. Toynbee goes on to illustrate the views just outlined by reference to the industrial system of Europe. He shows that the national state, such as France or Great Britain, is too small a unit for the industrial system of to-day. So that " Europe as a whole is in process of being dwarfed by the overseas world . . . while the national states of Europe, singly, are being dwarfed by the federal states of this new world ". This brings the business man to the front as a key man in the preservation of our civilization. *What should the Business Mind of the Future be like ?*

S

Technology and commerce have long been characteristic of our civilization, and its future welfare may well depend on what kind of business mentality becomes common in it. The question is well answered in the following brief extract from a lecture on " Foresight " which A. N. Whitehead gave to the Harvard Business School. He shows why business men should be philosophers—lovers of wisdom—and why a co-ordinating philosophy of life spread through all the community is necessary if our civilization is to survive.

A. N. WHITEHEAD

THE BUSINESS MAN OF THE FUTURE

I WILL conclude this chapter by a sketch of the Business Mind of the Future. In the first place, it is fundamental that there be a power of conforming to routine, of supervising routine, of constructing routine, and of understanding routine both as to its internal structure and as to its external purposes. Such a power is the bedrock of all practical efficiency. But for the production of the requisite Foresight, something more is wanted. This extra endowment can only be described as a philosophic power of understanding the complex flux of the varieties of human societies : for instance, the habit of noting varieties of demands on life, of serious purposes, of frivolous amusements. Such instinctive grasp of the relevant features of social currents is of supreme importance. For example, the time-span of various types of social behaviour is of the essence of their effect on policy. A widespread type of religious interest, with its consequent modes of behaviour, has a dominant life of about a hundred years, while a fashion of dress survives any time between three months and three years. Methods of agriculture change slowly. But the scientific world seems to be on the verge of far-reaching biological discoveries. The assumption of slow changes in agriculture must therefore be scanned vigilantly. This example of time-spans can be generalized. The quantitative aspect of social changes is of

the essence of business relations. Thus the habit of transforming observation of qualitative changes into quantitative
estimates should be a characteristic of business mentality.

I have said enough to show that the modern commercial
mentality requires many elements of discipline, scientific and
sociological. But the great fact remains that details of relevant
knowledge cannot be foreseen. Thus even for mere success,
and apart from any question of intrinsic quality of life, an
unspecialized aptitude for eliciting generalizations from particulars and for seeing the divergent illustration of generalities
in diverse circumstances is required. Such a reflective power
is essentially a philosophic habit : it is the survey of a society
from the standpoint of generality. This habit of general
thought, undaunted by novelty, is the gift of philosophy in
the widest sense of that term.

But the motive of success is not enough. It produces a
short-sighted world which destroys the sources of its own
prosperity. The cycles of trade depression which afflict the
world warn us that business relations are infected through and
through with the disease of short-sighted motives. The
robber barons did not conduce to the prosperity of Europe
in the Middle Ages, though some of them died prosperously
in their beds. Their example is a warning to our civilization.
Also we must not fall into the fallacy of thinking of the business
world in abstraction from the rest of the community. The
business world is one main part of the very community which
is the subject-matter of our study. The behaviour of the
community is largely dominated by the business mind. A
great society is a society in which its men of business think
greatly of their functions. Low thoughts mean low behaviour,
and, after a brief orgy of exploitation, low behaviour means a
descending standard of life. The general greatness of the
community, qualitatively as well as quantitatively, is the first
condition for steady prosperity, buoyant, self-sustained, and
commanding credit. The Greek philosopher who laid the
foundation of all our finer thoughts ended his most marvellous

dialogue with the reflection that the ideal state could never arrive till philosophers are kings. To-day, in an age of democracy, the kings are the plain citizens pursuing their various avocations. There can be no successful democratic society till general education conveys a philosophic outlook.

Philosophy is not a mere collection of noble sentiments. A deluge of such sentiments does more harm than good. Philosophy is at once general and concrete, critical and appreciative of direct intuition. It is not—or at least should not be—a ferocious debate between irritable professors. It is a survey of possibilities and their comparison with actualities. In philosophy, the fact, the theory, the alternatives, and the ideal are weighed together. Its gifts are insight and foresight, and a sense of the worth of life ; in short, that sense of importance which nerves all civilized effort. Mankind can flourish in the lower stages of life with merely barbaric flashes of thought. But when civilization culminates, the absence of a co-ordinating philosophy of life spread throughout the community spells decadence, boredom, and the slackening of effort.

Every epoch has its character determined by the way its populations react to the material events which they encounter. This reaction is determined by their basic beliefs—by their hopes, their fears, their judgments of what is worth while. They may rise to the greatness of an opportunity, seizing its drama, perfecting its art, exploiting its adventure, mastering intellectually and physically the network of relations that constitutes the very being of the epoch. On the other hand, they may collapse before the perplexities confronting them. How they act depends partly on their courage, partly on their intellectual grasp. Philosophy is an attempt to clarify those fundamental beliefs which finally determine the emphasis of attention that lies at the base of character.

Mankind is now in one of its rare moods of shifting its outlook. The mere compulsion of tradition has lost its force. It is our business—philosophers, students, and practical men

—to re-create and re-enact a vision of the world, including those elements and order without which society lapses into riot, and penetrated through and through with unflinching rationality. Such a vision is the knowledge which Plato identified with virtue. Epochs for which, within the limits of their development, this vision has been widespread are the epochs unfading in the memory of mankind.

Our discussion has insensibly generalized itself. It has passed beyond the topic of Commercial Relations to the function of a properly concrete philosophy in guiding the purposes of mankind.

Yes, man does not live by bread alone. We can rely on the business man and the technologist to satisfy the physical needs of our civilization (although the world's supply of food *will* present increasing difficulties as the population grows), but where shall we find " the concrete philosophy in guiding the purposes of mankind " ? How will the needs of the mind be met ?

Hitherto Western Civilization has been intensely *personal*. Two thousand three hundred years ago Aristotle stated his ideal of the " good life ", and suggested that the first objective of political organization should be to make it possible for this good life to be lived by all men fit to achieve it. The first essential in the good life is the regular and free use of the intellect—the habit of thinking for oneself. The Renaissance fixed this habit in Western culture. The Reformation brought religious freedom of thought to all who wanted it. The Great Rebellion in England and the Revolution in France brought political freedom within the ambition of the people, and nineteenth-century liberalism placed it within their grasp. Thus Aristotle's ideal was worked out through the ages by Western Civilization and given concrete form. Then, thanks to the industrial revolution, to progress in technology, and to education, it was made a possibility, not merely for the select few, but for all the people.

The twentieth century, however, has seen the growth of a new ideal in the heart of Western Civilization, a new heresy which derides this idea of the good life for the individual, declaring that the state is all-important. This is the doctrine of Fascism, a doctrine which is shared by Communism. *What is the appeal of Fascism?* What made the youth of Italy and Germany, hot for certainties amid all the perplexities of the years between the wars, welcome this dusty answer so readily? Let us listen to Mussolini, speaking at the height of his power, and see if we can imagine the kind of mentality to which this political philosophy would appeal.

BENITO MUSSOLINI

THE DOCTRINE OF FASCISM

LIKE all sound political systems, Fascism has a practical as well as a theoretical aspect; the practical side embodies the theory, and the theory springs from certain historical forces on which it is grafted and within which it works. . . . Fascism does not see in the world only those superficial, material aspects in which man appears as a self-centred individual, standing alone, subject to natural laws and instincts which urge him towards a life of selfish momentary pleasure; it does not only see the individual, but also the nation and the country; individuals and generations bound together by a moral law, moral traditions, and a mission which, repressing the instinct for life enclosed in a brief circle of pleasure, builds up a higher life founded on duty, a life free from the limitations of time and space, in which the individual may achieve that purely spiritual existence in which his worth as a man consists, by self-sacrifice, the renunciation of self-interest, by death itself.

The idea is therefore a spiritual one, and arises from a general reaction of the present century against the flaccid materialist positivism of the nineteenth century. Anti-positivist, yet positive; this is neither a sceptical nor an agnostic, neither a pessimistic nor a supinely optimistic system, as are most of the negative doctrines which place the centre of life outside man; for indeed man can, and must, form his own world by the exercise of his own free will.

Fascism wants men to be active and to engage in activity with all their energy ; it requires that they should be manfully aware of the difficulties besetting them and ready to face them. Life is conceived as a struggle in which a man is bound to win for himself a really worthy place, first of all by fitting himself physically, morally, and intellectually, and to have the necessary qualities for winning it. As it is for the individual, so is it for the nation and for all mankind. Hence the high value of culture in all its forms, religious, scientific, and artistic, and the outstanding importance of education. Hence also the essential value of work, by which man subdues Nature and creates the human world in its economic, political, ethical, and intellectual aspects.

This positive conception of life is obviously an ethical one. It covers the entire field of reality as well as the human activities which master it. No action is exempt from moral judgment ; no activity can be deprived of the value which a moral purpose confers on all things. Therefore life, as conceived by the Fascist, is serious, austere, religious ; all its manifestations take place in a world sustained by moral forces and subject to spiritual responsibilities. The Fascist disdains an easy-going life.

In the Fascist theory of history, man is such only by virtue of the spiritual process to which he contributes as a member of the family, the social group, the nation, and in his relation to history to which all nations have contributed. Hence the great value of tradition in records, in language, in customs, and in the rules of social life. Apart from history, man is a nonentity. Fascism is therefore opposed to all individualistic abstractions based on eighteenth-century materialism ; and it is opposed to all Jacobin utopias and innovations. It does not believe in the possibility of happiness on earth as conceived by eighteenth-century economic writers, and therefore rejects the teleological notion that at some future time the human family will secure a final settlement of all its difficulties. This notion runs counter to experience, which teaches that life is in continual motion and undergoing a process of evolution. In politics Fascism aims at realism ; in practice it desires to deal only with those problems which are the spontaneous product of historic conditions and which find or suggest their own solution. Only by experiencing reality and getting a firm hold on the forces at work within it, may man influence other men and Nature.

Being anti-individualistic, the Fascist system of life stresses the importance of the State and recognizes the individual only in so far as his interests coincide with those of the State, which stands for the consciousness and the universality of man as an historic entity. It is opposed to classic Liberalism, which arose as a reaction to absolutism and exhausted its historical function when the State became the expression of the consciousness and will of the people. Liberalism denied the State in the name of the individual ; Fascism reasserts the rights of the State as expressing the real essence of the individual. And if liberty is to be the attribute of living men and not that of abstract dummies invented by individualistic Liberalism, then Fascism stands for liberty and for the only liberty worth having, the liberty of the State and of the individual within the State. The Fascist conception of the State is all-embracing ; outside of it no human or spiritual values may exist, much less have any value. Thus understood, Fascism is totalitarian and the Fascist State, as a synthesis and a unit which includes all values, interprets, develops, and lends additional power to the whole life of a people.

No individuals or groups, political parties, associations, economic unions, social classes are to exist apart from the State. Fascism therefore opposes Socialism which rejects unity within the State, obtained by the fusion of all classes into a single ethical and economic reality, since it sees in history nothing more than the class struggle. Fascism likewise opposes trade-unionism as a class weapon. But Fascism recognizes the real needs which gave rise to Socialism and trade-unionism, when they are brought within the orbit of the

State, giving them due weight in the corporative system through which widely different interests are co-ordinated and harmonized for the unity of the State.

Grouped according to their several interests, individuals form classes ; they form trade unions when they are organized according to their various economic callings ; but first and foremost they form the State, which is no mere matter of numbers, the sum-total of individuals forming a majority. Fascism therefore opposes the form of democracy which entrusts the nation to a majority, debasing it to the level of the largest number ; but, if the Nation be considered, as it should be, from the point of view of quality instead of quantity, as an idea, it is the purest form of democracy, the mightiest because it is the most ethical, the most coherent, the truest, the expression of a people through the conscience and will of the few, if not indeed of a single man, tending to express itself as the consciousness and the will of the mass, as of the whole group ethnically moulded by natural and historical conditions into a nation, advancing as a single conscience and a single will along the selfsame geographically defined region, but a people historically perpetuating itself ; a multitude unified by an idea and imbued with the will to live, the " will to power ", a consciousness and a personality of its own.

In so far as it is embodied in a State, this higher personality becomes a Nation. It is not the Nation which produces the State ; that is an old-fashioned naturalistic idea which afforded a basis for nineteenth-century publicists in favour of national governments. It is rather the State which forms the Nation, by lending strength and power and real life to a people conscious of its own moral unity. . . .

Fascism, in short, is not only a lawgiver and a founder of institutions, but an educator and a promoter of spiritual life. It does not merely aim at remoulding the forms of life, but also their content, man, his character and his faith. To achieve this purpose it enforces discipline and makes use of authority, entering into the mind and ruling with undisputed sway. Therefore it has chosen as its emblem the lictors' rods, the symbol of unity, strength, and justice.

Fascism is now clearly defined not only as a regime but as a doctrine. This means that Fascism, exercising its critical faculties on itself and on others, has studied from its own special standpoint and judged by its own standards all the problems affecting the material and intellectual interest now causing grave anxiety to the nations of the world, and it is ready to deal with them by its own methods.

As far as concerns the future development of mankind, quite apart from all present-day political considerations, Fascism does not, on the whole, believe in the possibility or utility of perpetual peace. Pacifism is therefore rejected as a cloak for cowardly supine renunciation as against self-sacrifice. War alone keys up all the energies of man to their greatest pitch and sets the mark of nobility on those nations which have the bravery to face it. All other tests are substitutes which never place a man face to face with himself before the alternative of life and death. Therefore all doctrines which postulate peace at any price as their premise are incompatible with Fascism. Equally foreign to the spirit of Fascism, even though they may be accepted for their utility in meeting special political situations, are all internationalist or League organizations, which, as history amply proves, crumble to the ground whenever the heart of nations is stirred deeply by sentimental, idealist, or practical considerations. Fascism carries this anti-pacifist attitude into the life of the individual. " I don't care a damn " (*me ne frego*), scrawled on his bandages by a wounded man, became the proud motto of the storm-troopers, and it is not only an act of philosophical stoicism, it sums up a doctrine which is not merely political ; it is the evidence of a fighting spirit which accepts all risks. It stands for a new mode of life of the Italians. The Fascist accepts and loves life ; he rejects and despises suicide as cowardly. Life as he understands it means the fulfilment of duty, moral improvement, conquest ; life must be lofty and full, it must be lived for oneself but above all for others, both near by and far off, present and future.

The demographic policy of the regime is a consequence of these premises. The Fascist loves his neighbour, but that word does not stand for a vague and incomprehensible idea. Love of one's neighbour does not exclude necessary educational severity; still less does it exclude differentiation and rank. Fascism will have nothing to do with universal embraces; as a member of the community of nations it looks other peoples straight in the eyes; it is vigilant, on its guard; it follows others in all their activities and takes note of any change in their interests; and it does not allow itself to be deceived by changing and deceptive appearances.

Such a conception of life makes of Fascism the resolute negation of the doctrine underlying so-called scientific and Marxist Socialism, the doctrine of historic materialism which would explain the history of mankind in terms of the class struggle and of changes in the processes and means of production, to the exclusion of all else.

That the vicissitudes of economic life, the discovery of raw materials, new technical processes, scientific inventions, have their importance nobody denies; but that they are sufficient to explain human history to the exclusion of other factors is absurd. Fascism believes now and always in sanctity and heroism, that is to say, in acts wherein no economic motive, immediate or remote, is at work. Having denied historic materialism, which sees in men mere puppets on the fringes of history, appearing and disappearing on the crest of the waves while the real directive forces move and work in the depths, Fascism also denies the immutable and irreparable character of class struggle, which is the natural outcome of that economic conception of history; above all, it denies that class struggle is the principal agent in social transformations.

Besides Socialism, Fascism points its guns at the whole block of democratic ideologies and rejects both their premises and their practical application and methods. Fascism denies that numbers, as such, may be the determining factors in human society ; it denies the right of numbers to govern by means of periodical consultations ; it asserts the incurable and fruitful and beneficent inequality of men, who cannot be levelled by any such mechanical and external device as universal suffrage. Democratic regimes may be described as those under which the people are deluded from time to time into the belief that they are exercising sovereignty, while all the time real sovereignty belongs to and is exercised by other forces, sometimes irresponsible and secret. Democracy is a kingless regime infested by many kings, who are sometimes more exclusive, tyrannical, and destructive than a single one, even if he is a tyrant.

As an appendix to Mussolini's doctrine, here are brief extracts from two of Hitler's speeches. The first shows quite clearly the emphasis on the " national " side of his national-socialism, while the second demonstrates the complete identity of thought and aims with the Italian Fascists.

ADOLF HITLER

NAZI IDEALS

[(1) From the speech to the Reichstag on the fourth anniversary of the Nazi revolution, January 30, 1937.]

FOUR years have passed since the moment when the greatest national revolution and reformation which Germany ever experienced began. These are the four years I asked for as a trial period. It is not possible to mention all that might be regarded as the most remarkable events of this astonishing epoch in the life of our people. This rather is the work of the Press and propaganda.

[But he went on to summarize them as follows :

1. There is now only one representative of German sovereignty—the people itself.
2. The will of the people finds its expression in the Party as its political organization.
3. Therefore there is only one legislative body.
4. There is only one executive authority.

It follows that the people are the basis of everything, and Party, State, Army, Industry, Justice, and so on are only the means of maintaining the people.]

In a new German penal code, German justice will be placed on a basis which will put justice for all time into the service of maintaining the German race.

The restoration of Germany's equality of status exclusively concerns Germany herself. We have never taken anything from any people or harmed any people. In this sense I will deprive the German railways and the Reichsbank of their former character, and place both, without reservation, under the sovereignty of the government.

[(2) From his speech in Rome, May 8, 1938 :]

Duce, with deep emotion I thank you for the moving words of the greeting you have addressed to me. Since the moment when I first set foot on Italian soil I have been conscious everywhere of an atmosphere of friendship and sympathy which rejoices me deeply. . . . Germany and Italy have similar interests and are closely bound to one another by their common ideology. There has been created in Europe a block of 120,000,000 people resolved to safeguard their right to live and to defend themselves against all forces which might venture to oppose their natural development. . . . Now that we have become immediate neighbours, taught by the experience of 2000 years, we both acknowledge those natural frontiers which Providence and history have drawn between our two peoples. They will give Italy and Germany not only the possibility of peaceful and permanent collaboration through a clear division of their spheres of activity, but will provide a bridge for mutual help and support. It is my irrevocable will and my legacy to the German people that the frontier of the Alps shall be regarded for ever as unchangeable. Duce, just as you and your people kept friendship for Germany in a moment of crisis, so I and my people are ready to show Italy the same friendship in times of stress.

The Fascist doctrine of force seems to be the direct negation of all that Western Civilization has striven to achieve. It will never do for our guiding philosophy of social life. What alternative is there? *Does Communism fit in with Western Civilization?* An answer to this question was provided in a sermon preached by the Archbishop of York at the annual service of the Industrial Christian Fellowship in 1948. It is an answer remarkable for its fairness and for its tolerance—both high virtues of our culture—and it carries all the greater conviction to the thoughtful mind because of this sincere regard for truth. Dr. Garbett does not " trespass on the grounds of the statesman who has to take precautions to safeguard his nation ", but he says enough to show that Communism ranks with Fascism as a foe to all those values which have made Western Civilization what it is.

CYRIL F. GARBETT

CHRISTIANITY AND COMMUNISM

I HAVE been asked to speak to you on Christianity and Communism. I did not choose the subject. It is so controversial, and passion often rises so high in discussing it that, left to myself, I should have preferred to have taken some other subject. But the very fact that the word " communism " often excites an immediate reaction, makes it important that the Christian should be careful and discriminating in his judgment on it.

We must be clear, at any rate, what we mean by communism.

And if the Christian passes judgment on it, it must be on religious and moral grounds, leaving it to those who have special knowledge of the subject to approve or to condemn its economic and political implications. Let me therefore make it as plain as I can at the very outset that I am carefully and deliberately avoiding any discussion of the economic merits or demerits of communism; nor shall I trespass on the grounds of the statesman who has to take precautions to safeguard his nation from any threat to its order and stability which may come from communism either from without or from within its borders.

The general definition of communism in its widest meaning is a universal classless society in which all are equal, and in which all share alike through the common ownership of the means of production and distribution. All communists would, I think, agree that this is their aim; though some would qualify it by saying that at present universal communism is impossible, and that they must be content to work for communism in their own country and its immediate neighbours. Some, too, would say that within a communist society there is still room for private property on a small scale, so that the individual can retain and use as he thinks best anything he has earned by his personal skill or labour. For instance, on a collective farm I visited in Russia, I was told that, apart from the land on which they all worked, each farmer had a plot of ground about an acre in extent, the produce from which belonged to him personally, and he could save or sell it as he liked.

Nor does equality under communism mean that everyone receives exactly the same amount; the worker who does most receives most. Steps would, however, soon be taken either by taxation or by confiscation to prevent individuals from accumulating wealth, or from leaving any considerable portion of their savings to their children.

With these and some other qualifications, the definition I have given of communism holds good—a classless and equal society made possible through the ownership by the community of the means of production and distribution. Communism thus defined as an ideal is open to destructive criticism on the grounds that it is impractical, that economically it would lead to ruin, that politically it is unworkable ; but the ideal is not un-Christian, and ought not to be condemned as such.

In actual practice communism takes very different shapes. In its simplest form it is found in the Acts of the Apostles, where we read of the early converts in Jerusalem :

" Neither said any of them that ought of the things which he possessed was his own ; but they had all things in common. . . . Neither was there any among them that lacked : for as many as were possessors of lands or houses sold them, and brought the prices of the things which were sold, and laid them down at the apostles' feet : and distribution was made unto every man according as he had need."

From time to time, both in Europe and in America, there have been groups of men and women who have literally followed this example. The monastic orders are the most striking examples of this. But with the exception of the monasteries, all these attempts have come to grief after a short period. The communism described in the Acts was the result of the voluntary action of a small group of enthusiasts : the experiment soon came to an end and left the Church of Jerusalem so impoverished that the Gentile Churches had to send money for its relief. It would be absurd to regard it as a precedent to be followed on a world-wide scale under industrial and economic conditions entirely different from those which existed in Palestine in the first century.

Communism, as we know it to-day, is an economic and social system imposed on the individual by the State. The various industries with their factories, the mines, the land, the means of communication and distribution are taken, owned, and managed by the State, and used as the State directs. Everyone in the nation, whether he likes it or not, thus comes under a communist regime. He has no choice about this, after he has once cast his vote for a fractional share in a member of Parliament. The voluntary element so essential to primitive communism and its later imitations has disappeared. But different as modern communism is as an economic or political system from the communism described in the Acts, it need not be inconsistent with Christian faith and life. There are many Christians who are convinced that there is much more in common between Christianity and communism than between Christianity and capitalism. In Russia there are millions of Orthodox who are loyal citizens of a communist State; they accept its economic and social system, while rejecting its materialistic basis. In Poland there are convinced communists who regularly attend Mass. In Czechoslovakia, among the members of some of the reformed Churches, there are to be found convinced communists. A Chinese bishop told me that in China there are Christians who are communists, and the same is true in Australia. The Church, therefore, should avoid an indiscriminate condemnation of communism, which would compel many, especially of the younger generation, to feel that they must choose between Christianity and communism.

But while it is possible to be a Christian and a communist, it is not possible to be a Christian and a Marxian communist without disloyalty either to Christ or to Marx, for Marxian communism is far more than a political or economic theory; it has a doctrine behind it which leaves no room for Christianity or for any form of theism. It teaches that the world is material; that the material world is the only reality; that the mind is only the product of matter. In accordance with this, Marx taught that human progress has been due, not to the conflict of ideas which led to a further apprehension of truth, but to the clash between economic forces due to class warfare which will eventually lead to a higher economic and social order through

T

the destruction of capitalism and the bourgeois, as in the past it resulted in the destruction of feudalism. This " dialectical materialism ", to use a most cumbrous phrase, describes progress as due to an incessant economic warfare which, governed by iron laws, is remorseless and inevitable in its results. Such a deterministic and materialistic philosophy is openly and avowedly atheistic. Lenin made this plain when he wrote :

" The saying of Marx, ' Religion is the opium of the people ', is the corner-stone of the Marxist point of view on the matter of religion. All contemporary religion and churches, all and every kind of religious organization Marxism has always viewed as organs of bourgeois reaction, serving as a defence of exploitation and the drugging of the working class."

And this materialistic philosophy is opposed not only to every form of supernatural and spiritual religion, but it is also a denial of all the ethical and moral values which have helped to form Western civilization. In the *Communist Manifesto* even Christian Socialism is described as " the holy water with which the priest consecrates the heart-burnings of the aristo-crat ". It is Marxian communism which to-day is far and away the most powerful form of communism in the world. It is the communism of the governing parties in Russia and its satellite states. It is militant and aggressive, and is preached and propagated by its adherents with the fervour of the missionaries of a new religion. It is the most dangerous rival to Christianity, and directly and uncompromisingly challenges its faith and morals.

It does not necessarily persecute the Church : in Russia the Orthodox and the Protestant Churches are given to-day as much freedom as they had under the Czars, but always on the implicit understanding that no opposition is offered to the State. It is thus possible for Russian Christians to live quietly in a Marxian state, accepting its economic and political system, but rejecting its philosophical and anti-theistic ideology.

There are three fundamental differences between Christianity and Marxian communism.

(1) Christianity believes in a personal God, all powerful, of perfect holiness, goodness, and love. The Marxian communist denies the existence of God and of the spiritual world. As He does not exist He can neither be Sovereign, Judge, nor Father, and as there is no other world than this, there can be no life after death. Faith in God to the Marxian communist is the result of wishful thinking. He looks upon belief in God as a harmless delusion which gives comfort to the weak and ignorant, or as a dangerous and mischievous superstition which must be destroyed by the teaching of science, or, if necessity demands, by physical force.

(2) The Christian who has faith in a righteous God believes in a moral law, binding at all times, and in all places. Man does not always see this law clearly, often he misunderstands and misinterprets it, and when he sees it he frequently fails to obey it ; but the laws of justice, mercy, and truth remain the same with their absolute claim for obedience. But to the Marxian there is no eternal moral law. Morality is always relative to the State. Good is what promotes the welfare and power of the State ; evil is what hinders or injures it. Morality, therefore, changes according to the necessities of the State. Lying, deceit, the breach of treaties, treachery, violence, may all be used without any moral guilt or blame in the interests and service of the State.

(3) And from the denial of God there follows the denial of the dignity and rights of man. As the Christian believes that God is the Father of all, all men, whatever their colour or race, are of value in His sight ; as responsible to their Creator they must have freedom to use fully the talents He has given them. Marxian communism denies the dignity of man, and declares that he comes from the earth and will return to the earth as if he had never been, that he has no rights beyond those which the State confers upon him. He has no individuality of his

own ; he must act, speak, and think as the State directs. He is a means to an end. The Christian looks on man as the child of God, the Marxian as a tool for the use of the State. If man thus exists for the State, the State has the right to send him to labour camps, to enslave and torture him, and to kill him without remorse if this should seem expedient for its advantage or security.

William Temple summed up these differences in a sentence:

" The great and profound difference between Christian civilization and the kind of civilization which the Communists are aiming at lies in our affirmation that the primary fact of the world is God, that each individual man is the child of God, that at the root of his being he is a child of God, and that he is a child of God before he is a citizen of any national community."

Christianity and Marxianism are thus opposed on matters of faith and ethics on which there can be no compromise. The Marxian methods of establishing communism are equally inconsistent with the Christian way of life. They consist of class warfare leading to revolution, and the establishment of the dictatorship of the proletariat.

In the *Communist Manifesto* Marx and Engels foresee a fierce struggle between the possessing and non-possessing classes, ending in a revolution which would place the proletariat in power. Class warfare has been one of the weapons of communism. Its leaders from Marx to Stalin have urged that it should be waged in every country so as to weaken the forces of law and order, and prepare the way to revolution. The *Communist Manifesto* ends by declaring :

The Communists everywhere support every revolutionary movement against the existing social and political order of things. . . . They openly declare that their ends can be attained only by the forcible overthrow of all existing social conditions.

When this war has been suspended, it has only been for a short period for tactical reasons, and presently it has been resumed with greater violence. To-day this cold war is waged in every country from the Far East to the West. At the moment it is conducted with exceptional vigour in Western Europe, where Marshall Aid and the reconstruction of Europe would be fatal to the plan for world-wide communism. Deliberately communism is setting itself to retard recovery and so increase want and misery, in the hope that by so doing it may prepare the way for the revolutions which already have won for it strongholds in Eastern Europe. These weapons of class warfare and revolution are directly opposed to the Christian teaching on fellowship, peace, and love.

And when the revolution has been successful, the dictatorship of the proletariat follows. The party which has taken the lead in seizing power forms itself into a dictatorship, and, on the excuse that the revolution must be firmly established, suppresses free speech, free discussion, and a free press. By a gigantic system of spies and informers it removes by imprisonment, exile, or death any who venture to criticize its policy or actions. By complete control of education, the press, and the wireless, the dominant party gradually moulds the opinions and actions of the people into conformity with its own. It becomes a ruthless tyranny under which liberty is impossible. It establishes a reign of terror. The lights of freedom are extinguished and darkness spreads over the land. Its spokesmen defend this dictatorship as a temporary expedient which later on will pass away when communism has been firmly established. But the appetite for power grows, and the possibility of relinquishing it becomes less as the years pass. Fear of vengeance from those over whom they have tyrannized and of the envy of rivals make guilty men cling to their posts of power. For if they are expelled from them they know the fate that awaits them.

The police State is the denial of all that Christianity holds most sacred—the value of the individual, personal freedom, mercy, and justice. The struggle between the police State and democracy is even more fundamental than that between communism and capitalism.

The doctrines and methods of Marxian communism, of the communism which is not dominant and which is creating unrest and strife in almost every part of the world, are a challenge to the Church of God. But in repudiating communism I would stress once again the duty of discrimination both between different types of communism and between individuals who call themselves communists. We should be both unjust to many communists and do a lasting disservice to Christianity if we followed those who ask us to engage in a so-called Holy War against all forms of communism, and to brand as atheists all who accept its economic and political teaching. To agree to do this would mean a fatal breach with millions of our fellow Christians in Russia and elsewhere, who are loyal both to the Christian faith and to the communist State under which they live.

Discrimination must also be shown in criticism of communism as a working system ; it is not all evil, nor have all its results been evil. It has swept away much injustice. It was for this reason that the Lambeth Conference urged Church people to study the theory and practice of communism, so that they might know which elements in it are contrary to the Christian view of man, and which are a true judgment on the existing economic order. Nor must we forget that communism has brought not only fear, but also new hope, to millions once despairing, and has given them education and material benefits which at one time were denied them.

But when I have said this I go on to add that the Church must make it plain that the doctrines and methods of Marxian communism are contrary to Christian faith and practice. The Marxian would assert this uncompromisingly, and the Christian would be foolish to try to disguise it. There can be no common ground between Marxian and Christian doctrine and ethics ; they are fundamentally opposed. And the methods of violence, deceit and cruelty used by communism to gain its ends are the cause of incalculable misery and fear throughout the world. There can be no agreement between militant communism and a Church which has peace and good-will as its aim. The relationship between Christianity and communism is summed up in the resolution of the Lambeth Conference, which declares : " that Marxian communism is contrary to Christian faith and practice, for it denies the existence of God, Revelation and a future life ; it treats the individual man as a means and not an end ; it encourages class warfare ; it regards the moral law not as absolute but as relative to the needs of the State ".

We must not, however, be content with a bare denunciation of communism. We must take account of the new hope and confidence it has given to millions. This comes from its protest against social injustice. All through the *Communist Manifesto* there rings the cry of passionate indignation against social wrong. The same is largely true of Karl Marx's *Capital*. When I read it as an undergraduate (my tutor asked me why I wasted my time in reading such an out-of-date book !) I was not in the least impressed by its economic theory, but I was deeply moved by its account of the cruelties and hardships suffered in mines and factories by underpaid workers at the time of the Industrial Revolution. Wherever there is great poverty, and especially when there is a glaring contrast between luxury and want, wherever there is squalor and misery there is fertile ground for the seed of communism. Communism is a judgment on the social and economic sins of Western civilization. The best defence against communism is the removal of the social wrongs in which it flourishes. The Church must take a firm stand against any form of economic domination, whether capitalistic or communistic, which denies the rights of the individual.

It must protest at all times against social injustice wherever it exists, against unfair conditions of labour, against industrial systems which treat the worker as an unintelligent cog in a machine, and against bad housing. It must demand that all are given opportunities of useful employment, a just reward for their labours, some voice in the work in which they are engaged, and houses in which privacy, health, and comfort are possible.

If the Church at the time of the Industrial Revolution had denounced social wrong and had demanded justice for the working classes in the days of their weakness and oppression, many of the evils against which communism is a revolt would never have arisen. The *Communist Manifesto* declared : " The proletarians have nothing to lose but their chains " ; when this is true, revolution is not far off. It is not true of this country, where the working classes are gaining social and economic, as well as political, rights. It is, however, still true of other countries, and while it is true of them, embers are glowing which may be fanned into revolution.

Marxian communism must be defeated not only by argument and condemnation, but by showing that injustice and poverty can be removed by better methods than those of violence and revolution. Christian love for all men, as children of the same Father, should prove a more inspiring motive for the creation of a new universal order of justice and fellowship than the motives of hate and anger.

The Church is not afraid of the challenge of Marxian communism, it knows it cannot succeed, for it ignores both God and the true nature of man. It is building its house on sand which will be swept away by the tempest. But the Church has no right to look forward to this day, unless it is doing all in its power to hasten the coming of the time when human rights will be recognized throughout the world, and when peace and justice will be firmly established.

What can the more orthodox thinkers of our Western Civilization set against these heresies of Fascism and Communism ? Only the ancient tradition of liberalism, born of the give and take, the live and let-live, of " commerce " in the widest sense of that word. That is the authentic message ; there speaks the true voice. We heard it in the

Funeral Speech of Pericles; it inspired the pleas of Erasmus; it justified Luther's defiance of authority, and John Knox's too. It spoke again through Eliot and Hampden and Pym; it was the inward voice of Milton, the soul of Locke's philosophy, the guide of Pitt's policy, the flame of Burke's eloquence. It rings through the satires of Voltaire and the oratory of Mirabeau; it inspires the lectures of Guizot, and the great surge of liberal humanitarianism in the nineteenth and twentieth centuries.

What is the essence of the liberal philosophy? It lies, says Bertrand Russell, " not in *what* opinions are held, but in *how* they are held; instead of being held dogmatically, they are held tentatively, and with a consciousness that new evidence may at any moment lead to their abandonment ". And he goes on to say that, in these days of the atom bomb, " only through a revival of Liberal tentativeness and tolerance can our world survive ". What he gives is perhaps a somewhat negative definition of liberalism, although it does stress the world's crying need for it. Perhaps the nineteenth-century apostle of individualism, John Stuart Mill, will provide a fuller answer. It was Mill's task to humanize the rather bloodless Utilitarianism of the Benthamites, and to make " the greatest happiness of the greatest number " a practical political philosophy. His words may have a nostalgic appeal to some readers in these days of the Welfare State, but they are still the best expression of the gospel of individualism, and therefore the most characteristic statement of the philosophy of Western Civilization.

JOHN STUART MILL

THE INDIVIDUAL AND THE STATE

THERE is no recognized principle by which the propriety or impropriety of Government interference is customarily tested. People decide according to their personal preferences. Some, whenever they see any good to be done, or evil to be remedied, would willingly instigate the Government to undertake the business; while others prefer to bear almost any amount of social evil rather than add one to the departments of human interests amenable to governmental control. And men range themselves on one or the other side in any particular case, according to this general direction of their sentiments ; or according to the degree of interest which they feel in the particular thing which it is proposed that the Government should do, or according to the belief they entertain that the Government would, or would not, do it in the manner they prefer ; but very rarely on account of any opinion to which they consistently adhere, as to what things are fit to be done by a Government. And it seems to me that in consequence of this absence of rule or principle, one side is at present as often wrong as the other ; the interference of Government is, with about equal frequency, improperly invoked and improperly condemned.

The present object is to assert one very simple principle, as entitled to govern absolutely the dealings of society with the individual in the way of compulsion and control, whether the means used be physical force in the form of legal penalties, or the moral coercion of public opinion. That principle is, that the sole end for which mankind are warranted, individually or collectively, in interfering with the liberty of action of any of their number, is self-protection. That the only purpose for which power can be rightfully exercised over any member of a civilized community, against his will, is to prevent harm to others.

His own good, either physical or moral, is not a sufficient warrant. He cannot rightfully be compelled to do or forbear because it will be better for him to do so, because it will make him happier, because, in the opinions of others, to do so would be wise, or even right. These are good reasons for remonstrating with him, or reasoning with him, or persuading him, or entreating him, but not for compelling him, or visiting him with any evil in case he do otherwise. To justify that, the conduct from which it is desired to deter him must be calculated to produce evil to someone else. The only part of the conduct of anyone, for which he is amenable to society, is that which concerns others. In the part which merely concerns himself, his independence is, of right, absolute. Over himself, over his own body and mind, the individual is sovereign.

It is, perhaps, hardly necessary to say that this doctrine is meant to apply only to human beings in the maturity of their faculties. We are not speaking of children, or of young persons below the age which the law may fix as that of manhood or womanhood. Those who are still in a state to require being taken care of by others must be protected against their own actions as well as against external injury. For the same reason, we may leave out of consideration those backward states of society in which the race itself may be considered as in its nonage. The early difficulties in the way of spontaneous progress are so great that there is seldom any choice of means for overcoming them; and a ruler full of the spirit of improvement is warranted in the use of any expedients that will attain an end perhaps otherwise unattainable.

Despotism is a legitimate mode of government in dealing with barbarians, provided the end be their improvement, and the means justified by actually effecting that end. Liberty, as a principle, has no application to any state of things anterior to the time when mankind have become capable of being improved by free and equal discussion. Until then, there is nothing for them but implicit obedience to an Akbar or a Charlemagne, if they are so fortunate as to find one.

But as soon as mankind have attained the capacity of being guided to their own improvement by conviction or persuasion (a period long since reached in all nations with whom we need here concern ourselves), compulsion, either in the direct form or in that of pains and penalties for non-compliance, is no longer admissible as a means to their own good, and justifiable only for the security of others.

It is proper to state that I forgo any advantage which could be derived to my argument from the idea of abstract right, as a thing independent of utility. I regard utility as the ultimate appeal on all ethical questions; but it must be utility in the largest sense, grounded on the permanent interests of a man as a progressive being. Those interests, I contend, authorize the subjection of individual spontaneity to external control only in respect to those actions of each which concern the interest of other people. If anyone does an act hurtful to others, there is a *prima facie* case for punishing him by law, or, where legal penalties are not safely applicable, by general disapprobation. There are also many positive acts for the benefit of others which he may rightfully be compelled to perform ; such as to give evidence in a court of justice ; to bear his fair share in the common defence, or in any other joint work necessary to the interest of the society of which he enjoys the protection ; and to perform certain acts of individual beneficence, such as saving a fellow-creature's life, or interposing to protect the defenceless against ill-usage, things which, whenever it is obviously a man's duty to do, he may rightfully be made responsible to society for not doing.

A person may cause evil to others not only by his actions but by his inaction, and in either case he is justly accountable to them for the injury. The latter case, it is true, requires a much more cautious exercise of compulsion than the former. To make anyone answerable for doing evil to others is the rule ; to make him answerable for not preventing evil is, comparatively speaking, the exception. Yet there are many cases clear enough and grave enough to justify that exception. In all things which regard the external relations of the individual, he is *de jure* amenable to those whose interests are concerned, and, if need be, to society as their protector. There are often good reasons for not holding him to the responsibility ; but these reasons must arise from the special expediencies of the case : either because it is a kind of case in which he is on the whole likely to act better, when left to his own discretion, than when controlled in any way in which society have it in their power to control him ; or because the attempt to exercise control would produce other evils, greater than those which it would prevent. When such reasons as these preclude the enforcement of responsibility the conscience of the agent himself should step into the vacant judgment-seat and protect

those interests of others which have no external protection ;
judging himself all the more rigidly because the case does not
admit of his being made accountable to the judgment of his
fellow-creatures.

But there is a sphere of action in which society, as distinguished from the individual, has, if any, only an indirect
interest ; comprehending all that portion of a person's life and
conduct which affects only himself, or if it also affects others,
only with their free, voluntary, and undeceived consent and
participation. When I say only himself, I mean directly, and
in the first instance ; for whatever affects himself may affect
others through himself ; and the objection which may be
grounded on this contingency will receive consideration in the
sequel. This, then, is the appropriate region of human liberty.
It comprises, first, the inward domain of consciousness ;
demanding liberty of conscience in the most comprehensive
sense : liberty of thought and feeling ; absolute freedom of
opinion and sentiment on all subjects, practical or speculative,
scientific, moral, or theological.

[And here are the reasons which Mill gives, later on in his
essay, for " the necessity to the mental well-being of mankind
(on which all their other well-being depends) of freedom of
opinion and freedom of expression of opinion ":]

First, if any opinion is compelled to silence, that opinion
may, for aught we can certainly know, be true. To deny this
is to assume our own infallibility.

Secondly, though the silenced opinion be an error, it may,
and very commonly does, contain a portion of truth ; and
since the general or prevailing opinion on any subject is rarely
or never the whole truth, it is only by the collision of adverse
opinions that the remainder of the truth has any chance of
being supplied.

Thirdly, even if the received opinion be not only true, but
the whole truth ; unless it is suffered to be, and actually is,

vigorously and earnestly contested, it will, by most of those who receive it, be held in the manner of a prejudice, with little comprehension or feeling of its rational grounds. And not only this, but, fourthly, the meaning of the doctrine itself will be in danger of being lost, or enfeebled, and deprived of its vital effect on the character and conduct ; the dogma becoming a mere formal profession, inefficacious for good, but cumbering the ground, and preventing the growth of any real and heartfelt conviction, from reason or personal experience.

The liberty of expressing and publishing opinions may seem to fall under a different principle, since it belongs to that part of the conduct of an individual which concerns other people ; but, being almost of as much importance as the liberty of thought itself, and resting in great part on the same reasons, is practically inseparable from it. Secondly, the principle requires liberty of tastes and pursuits ; of framing the plan of our life to suit our own character ; of doing as we like, subject to such consequences as may follow : without impediment from our fellow-creatures, so long as what we do does not harm them, even though they should think our conduct foolish, perverse, or wrong. Thirdly, from this liberty of each individual follows the liberty, within the same limits, of combination among individuals ; freedom to unite for any purpose not involving harm to others : the persons combining being supposed to be of full age, and not forced or deceived.

No society in which these liberties are not, on the whole, respected, is free, whatever may be its form of government ; and none is completely free in which they do not exist absolute and unqualified. The only freedom which deserves the name is that of pursuing our own good in our own way, so long as we do not attempt to deprive others of theirs or impede their efforts to obtain it. Each is the proper guardian of his own health, whether bodily, *or* mental and spiritual. Mankind are greater gainers by suffering each other to live as seems good to themselves than by compelling each to live as seems good to the rest.

Though this doctrine is anything but new, and, to some persons, may have the air of a truism, there is no doctrine which stands more directly opposed to the general tendency of existing opinion and practice. Society has expended fully as much effort in the attempt (according to its lights) to compel people to conform to its notions of personal as of social excellence. The ancient commonwealths thought themselves entitled to practise, and the ancient philosophers countenanced, the regulation of every part of private conduct by public authority, on the ground that the State had a deep interest in the whole bodily and mental discipline of every one of its citizens ; a mode of thinking which may have been admissible in small republics surrounded by powerful enemies, in constant peril of being subverted by foreign attack or internal commotion, and to which even a short interval of relaxed energy and self-command might so easily be fatal that they could not afford to wait for the salutary permanent effects of freedom.

In the modern world, the greater size of political communities, and, above all, the separation between spiritual and temporal authority (which placed the direction of men's consciences in other hands than those which controlled their worldly affairs), prevented so great an interference by law in the details of private life ; but the engines of moral repression have been wielded more strenuously against divergence from the reigning opinion in self-regarding than even in social matters ; religion, the most powerful of the elements which have entered into the formation of moral feeling, having almost always been governed either by the ambition of a hierarchy, seeking control over every department of human conduct, or by the spirit of Puritanism. And some of those modern reformers who have placed themselves in strongest opposition to the religions of the past have been no way behind either churches or sects in their assertion of the right of spiritual domination. . . .

Apart from the peculiar tenets of individual thinkers, there is also in the world at large an increasing inclination to stretch unduly the powers of society over the individual, both by the force of opinion and even by that of legislation ; and as the tendency of all the changes taking place in the world is to strengthen society and diminish the power of the individual, this encroachment is not one of the evils which tend spontaneously to disappear, but, on the contrary, to grow more and more formidable. The disposition of mankind, whether as rulers or as fellow-citizens, to impose their own opinions and inclinations as a rule of conduct on others, is so energetically supported by some of the best and by some of the worst feelings incident to human nature, that it is hardly ever kept under restraint by anything but want of power ; and as the power is not declining but growing, unless a strong barrier of moral conviction can be raised against the mischief, we must expect, in the present circumstances of the world, to see it increase.

What has made the European family of nations an improving instead of a stationary portion of mankind ? Not any superior excellence in them—which, when it exists, exists as the effect, not as the cause—but their remarkable diversity of character and culture. Individuals, classes, nations, have been extremely unlike one another : they have struck out a great variety of paths, each leading to something valuable ; and, although at every period those who travelled in different paths have been intolerant of one another and each would have thought it an excellent thing if all the rest could have been compelled to travel his road, their attempts to thwart each other's development have rarely had any permanent success, and each has, in time, endured to receive the good which the others have offered. Europe is, in our judgment, wholly indebted to this plurality of paths for its progressive and many-sided development. But it already begins to possess the benefit in a considerably less degree. It is decidedly advancing towards the Chinese ideal of making all people alike. . . .

What, then, is the rightful limit to the sovereignty of the individual over himself? Where does the authority of society begin? How much of human life should be assigned to individuality, and how much to society?

Each will receive its proper share, if each has that which more particularly concerns it. To individuality should belong the part of life in which it is chiefly the individual that is interested; to society, the part which chiefly interests society.

Is liberalism (in the broad sense in which we are using the word) as dead as Mussolini pretended? It is not even dormant. It is the real political philosophy of millions of people, both in the British Commonwealth and in America. In the twentieth century it has given the vote to all adults. And the vast increase in the State's care for its less fortunate citizens is an expression of the spirit of liberal humanitarianism, no matter what political party may have introduced the various acts. There can be no doubt that the social security thus built up is the strongest of all barriers against the infiltrating tide of communism. Communism flourishes amid poverty and hopelessness. *Who planned the great offensive against poverty in England?* This honour rightly belongs to Lloyd George, and here are some passages from his epoch-making speech when, in 1909, he introduced what he called his "war budget" against poverty. This budget was the first "official" attempt to use taxation to redress some of the gross inequalities of wealth. That "slow sunrise of a thousand years", of which we read in the first book, showed an appreciable brightening when insurance against ill-health and against unemployment became part of the accepted policy of the countries in the West.

EARL LLOYD GEORGE

THE ATTACK ON POVERTY

I COME to the consideration of the social problems which are urgently pressing for solution—problems affecting the lives of the people. The solution of all these questions involves
U

finance. What the government have to ask themselves is this : can the whole subject of further social reform be postponed until the increasing demands made upon the National Exchequer by the growth of armaments has ceased ? Not merely *can* it be postponed, but ought it to be postponed ? Is there the slightest hope that if we deferred consideration of the matter, we are likely within a generation to find any more favourable moment for attending to it ?

And we have to ask ourselves this further question : If we put off dealing with these social sores, are the evils which arise from them not likely to grow and to fester, until finally the loss which the country sustains will be infinitely greater than anything it would have to bear in paying the cost of an immediate remedy ? There are hundreds of thousands of men, women, and children in this country now enduring hardships for which the sternest judge would not hold them responsible ; hardships entirely due to circumstances over which they have not the slightest command ; the fluctuations and changes of trade— even of fashions ; ill-health and the premature breakdown or death of the breadwinner. Owing to events of this kind, all of them beyond human control—at least beyond the control of the victims—thousands, and I am not sure I should be wrong if I said millions, are precipitated into a condition of acute distress and poverty.

How many people there are of this kind in this wealthy land the figures of Old Age Pensions have thrown a very unpleasant light upon. Is it fair, is it just, is it humane, is it honourable, is it safe to subject such a multitude of our poor fellow countrymen and countrywomen to continued endurance of these miseries until nations have learnt enough wisdom not to squander their resources on these huge machines for the destruction of human life ? I have no doubt as to the answer which will be given to that question by a nation as rich in humanity as it is in store. . . .

What are the dominating causes of poverty amongst the

industrial classes ? For the moment I do not refer to the poverty which is brought about by a man's own fault. I am only alluding to causes over which he has no control : old age, premature breakdown in health and strength, the death of the breadwinner, and unemployment due either to the decay of industries and seasonable demands, or the fluctuations or depressions in trade. The distress caused by any or either of these causes is much more deserving of immediate attention than the case of a healthy and vigorous man of sixty-five years of age, who is able to pursue his daily avocation, and to earn without undue strain an income which is quite considerable enough to provide him and his wife with a comfortable subsistence. When Bismarck was strengthening the foundations of the new German Empire, one of the very first tasks he undertook was the organization of a scheme which insured the German workmen and their families against the worst evils which ensue from these common incidents of life. And a superb scheme it is. It has saved an incalculable amount of human misery to hundreds of thousands and possibly millions of people who never deserved it.

Wherever I went in Germany, north or south, and whomsoever I met, whether it was an employer or a workman, a Conservative or a Liberal, a Socialist or a Trade Union Leader—men of all ranks, sections, and creeds, of one accord joined in lauding the benefits which have been conferred upon Germany by this beneficent policy. Several wanted extensions, but there was not one who wanted to go back. The employers admitted that at first they did not quite like the new burdens it cast upon them ; but they now fully realized the advantages which even they derived from the expenditure, for it had raised the standard of the workmen throughout Germany. By removing that element of anxiety and worry from their lives it had improved their efficiency. Benefits which in the aggregate amounted to forty millions a year were being distributed under this plan. When I was there, the Government were contemplating an enlargement of its operation which

would extend its benefits to clerks and to the widows and
orphans of the industrial population. . . .

At the present moment there is a network of powerful
organizations in this country, most of them managed with
infinite skill and capacity, which have succeeded in inducing
millions of workmen in this country to make something like
systematic provision for the troubles of life. But in spite of
all the ability which has been expended upon them, in spite of
the confidence they generally and deservedly inspire, unfortunately there is a margin of people in this country, amounting in the aggregate to several millions, who either cannot be
persuaded or perhaps cannot afford to bear the expense of
the systematic contributions which alone make membership
effective in these great institutions. And the experience of
this and of every other country is that no plan or variety of
plans short of an universal compulsory system can ever hope
to succeed in adequately coping with the problem. In this
country we have trusted until recently to voluntary effort, but
we found that for old age and accidents it was insufficient. In
Belgium they have resorted to the plan of granting heavy
subsidies to voluntary organizations, and they have met with a
certain amount of success. But whether here or in Belgium,
or in any other land, success must be partial where reliance is
absolutely placed upon the readiness of men and women to look
ahead in the days of abounding health and strength and
buoyancy of spirit to misfortunes which are not even in sight,
and which may be ever averted.

The Government are now giving careful consideration to
the best methods for making such a provision. We are
investigating closely the plans adopted by foreign countries,
and I hope to circulate papers on the point very soon. We
have put ourselves into communication with the leaders of
some of the principal friendly societies in the country with a
view to seeking their invaluable counsel and direction. We
could not possibly get safer or more experienced advisers. We
are giving special attention to the important reports of

the Poor Law Commission, both majority and minority, which advise that the leading principle of poor-law legislation in future shall be the drawing of a clear and definite line between those whose poverty is the result of their own misdeeds and those who have been brought to want through misfortune.

All I am in a position now to say is that, at any rate in any scheme which we may finally adopt, we shall be guided by these leading principles or considerations.

The first is that no plan can hope to be really comprehensive or conclusive which does not include an element of compulsion.

The second is that for financial as well as for other reasons, which I do not wish to enter into now, success is unattainable in the near future except on the basis of a direct contribution from the classes more immediately concerned.

The third is that there must be a State contribution substantial enough to enable those whose means are too limited and precarious to sustain adequate premiums to overcome that difficulty without throwing undue risks on other contributors.

The fourth and by no means the least important, is that in this country, where benefit and provident societies represent such a triumph of organization, of patience and self-government as probably no other country has ever witnessed, no scheme would be profitable, no scheme would be tolerable, which would do the least damage to those highly beneficent organizations. On the contrary, it must be the aim of every well-considered plan to encourage, and, if practicable, as I believe it is, to work through them.

That is all I propose to say on that particular subject at this juncture. I have gone into it at this length merely to indicate that here also is a source of contingent liability which I am bound to take into account in my financial scheme. In this country we have already provided for the aged over seventy. We have made pretty complete provision for accidents. All we have now left to do in order to put ourselves on a level with Germany—I hope our competition with Germany will not be in armaments alone—is to make some further provision for the sick, for the invalid, for widows and orphans. In a well-thought-out scheme, involving contributions from the classes directly concerned, the proportion borne by the State need not, in my judgment, be a very heavy one, and is well within the compass of our financial capacity without undue strain upon the resources of the country.

The Government are also pledged to deal on a comprehensive scale with the problem of unemployment. The pledges given by the Prime Minister on behalf of the Government are specific and repeated. I do not wish to encourage any false hopes. Nothing that a government can do, at any rate with the present organization of society, can prevent the fluctuations and the changes in trade and industry which produce unemployment. A trade decays, and the men who are engaged in it are thrown out of work. We have had an illustration within the last few days, to which Lord Rosebery has so opportunely called our attention, in the privation suffered by the horse-cab driver owing to the substitution of mechanical for horse traction. That is only one case out of many constantly happening in every country. Then there are the fluctuations of business which at one moment fill a workshop with orders which even overtime cannot cope with, and at another moment leave the same workshops with rusting machinery for lack of something to do.

Trade has its currents, and its tides, and its storms and its calms like the sea, which seem to be almost just as little under human control, or, at any rate, just as little under the control of the victims of these changes, and to say that you can establish by any system an equal equilibrium in the trade and concerns of the country is to make a promise which no man of intelligence would ever undertake to honour. You might as well promise to flatten out the Atlantic Ocean. But still, it is poor seamanship that puts out to sea without recognizing its

restlessness, and the changefulness of the weather, and the
perils and suffering thus produced. These perils of trade
depression come at regular intervals, and every time they
arrive they bring with them an enormous amount of distress.
It is the business of statesmanship to recognize that fact
and to address itself with courage and resolution to provide
against it.

Lloyd George's speech showed that the State had at last recognized
the fact that poverty was not a crime ; that some people might be in
dire need of assistance through no fault at all of their own ; and that
it was then the duty of the State to assist them without depriving
them of political rights, or placing on them the stigma attached to
" pauperism ". Winston Churchill gave valuable assistance to this new
crusade. " If I had to sum up the immediate future of democratic
politics in a single word " said Churchill in 1909 " I should say ' Insurance '. . . . By sacrifices which are inconceivably small, which are all
within the power of the very poorest man in regular work, families
can be secured against catastrophes which would otherwise smash
them up for ever." Britain led the world in 1911 with the first compulsory unemployment insurance scheme. How far we have travelled
since that time may be gauged from the Beveridge report of December
1942. Sir William Beveridge (as he was then) was asked to undertake
an inquiry into social insurance in June 1941, when Britain, or rather
the British Commonwealth of Nations, stood alone against the victorious
Axis. He " felt a little sad " at being asked to do this. He " wanted
to do something directly helping the war ". Gradually (he tells us in
his book, *Pillars of Security*) he " came to realize the intense interest
of the citizens of this country in the problem of security after the war.
I had a lesson in democracy, and of what is needed to make a democracy
whole-hearted in war. Democracies make war for peace, not war for
its own sake. They fight better if they know what they are fighting
for after the war." So he made the Report a personal but fundamental
document, signed by himself alone because it called for action and
decision by the government as a whole. In the Report, he says, " the
British people become articulate about what they want in the way of
social security ". Here are some of the opening paragraphs.

BARON BEVERIDGE

SOCIAL INSURANCE IN BRITAIN

THE schemes of social insurance and allied services which the Inter-departmental Committee have been called on to survey have grown piecemeal. Apart from the Poor Law, which dates from the time of Elizabeth, the schemes surveyed are the product of the last 45 years, beginning with the Workmen's Compensation Act, 1897. That Act, applying in the first instance to a limited number of occupations, was made general in 1906. Compulsory health insurance began in 1912. Unemployment insurance began for a few industries in 1912 and was made general in 1920. The first Pensions Act, giving non-contributory pensions subject to a means test at the age of seventy, was passed in 1908. In 1925 came the Act which started contributory pensions for old age, for widows, and for orphans. Unemployment insurance, after a troubled history, was put on a fresh basis by the Unemployment Act of 1934, which set up at the same time a new national service of Unemployment Assistance. Meantime, the local machinery for relief of destitution, after having been exhaustively examined by the Royal Commission of 1905-1909, has been changed both by the new treatment of unemployment and in many other ways, including a transfer of the responsibilities of the Boards of Guardians to Local Authorities. Separate provision for special types of disability—such as blindness— has been made from time to time. Together with this growth of social insurance and impinging on it at many points have gone developments of medical treatment, particularly in hospitals and other institutions; developments of services devoted to the welfare of children, in school and before it; and a vast growth of voluntary provision for death and other contingencies, made by persons of the insured classes through Industrial Life Offices, Friendly Societies, and Trade Unions.

In all this change and development, each problem has been

dealt with separately, with little or no reference to allied problems. The first task of the Committee has been to attempt for the first time a comprehensive survey of the whole field of social insurance and allied services, to show just what provision is now made and how it is made for many different forms of need. The picture presented is impressive in two ways. First, it shows that provision for most of the many varieties of need through interruption of earnings and othei. causes that may arise in modern industrial communities has already been made in Britain on a scale not surpassed and hardly rivalled in any other country of the world. In one respect only of the first importance, namely limitation of medical service, both in the range of treatment which is provided as of right and in respect of the classes of persons for whom it is provided, does Britain's achievement fall seriously short of what has been accomplished elsewhere; it falls short also in its provision for cash benefit for maternity and funerals and through the defects of its system for workmen's compensation. In all other fields, British provision for security, in adequacy of amount, and in comprehensiveness, will stand comparison with that of any other country; few countries will stand comparison with Britain. Second, social insurance and the allied services, as they exist to-day, are conducted by a complex of disconnected administrative organs, proceeding on different principles, doing invaluable service but at a cost in money and trouble and anomalous treatment of identical problems for which there is no justification. In a system of social security, better on the whole than can be found in almost any other country, there are serious deficiencies which call for remedy.

Thus limitation of compulsory insurance to persons under contract of service and below a certain remuneration if engaged on non-manual work is a serious gap. Many persons working on their own account are poorer and more in need of State insurance than employees; the remuneration limit for non-manual employees is arbitrary and takes no account of family responsibility. There is, again, no real difference between the income needs of persons who are sick and those who are unemployed, but they get different rates of benefit involving different contribution conditions and with meaningless distinctions between persons of different ages. An adult insured man with a wife and two children receives 38s. per week should he become unemployed ; if after some weeks of unemployment he becomes sick and not available for work his insurance income falls to 18s. On the other hand, a youth of seventeen obtains 9s. when he is unemployed, but should he become sick his insurance income rises to 12s. per week. There are, to take another example, three different means tests for non-contributory pensions, for supplementary pensions and for public assistance, with a fourth test—for unemployment assistance—differing from that for supplementary pensions in some particulars.

Many other such examples could be given ; they are the natural result of the way in which social security has grown in Britain. It is not open to question that, by closer co-ordination, the existing social services could be made at once more beneficial and more intelligible to those whom they serve and more economical in their administration.

In proceeding from this first comprehensive survey of social insurance to the next task—of making recommendations —three guiding principles may be laid down at the outset.

The first principle is that any proposals for the future, while they should use to the full the experience gathered in the past, should not be restricted by consideration of sectional interests established in the obtaining of that experience. Now, when the war is abolishing landmarks of every kind, is the opportunity for using experience in a clear field. A revolutionary moment in the world's history is a time for revolutions, not for patching.

The second principle is that organization of social insurance should be treated as one part only of a comprehensive policy of social progress. Social insurance fully developed may provide income security ; it is an attack upon Want. But Want is one only of five giants on the road of reconstruction, and in some ways the easiest to attack. The others are Disease, Ignorance, Squalor, and Idleness.

The third principle is that social security must be achieved by co-operation between the State and the individual. The State should offer security for service and contribution. The State, in organizing security, should not stifle incentive, opportunity, responsibility ; in establishing a national minimum, it should leave room and encouragement for voluntary action by each individual to provide more than that minimum for himself and his family.

The Plan for Social Security set out in this Report is built upon these principles. It uses experience but is not tied by experience. It is put forward as a limited contribution to a wider social policy, though as something that could be achieved now without waiting for the whole of that policy. It is, first and foremost, a plan of insurance—of giving in return for contributions benefits up to subsistence level, as of right and without means test, so that individuals may build freely upon it.

Under the scheme of social insurance, which forms the main feature of this plan, every citizen of working age will contribute in his appropriate class according to the security that he needs, or as a married woman will have contributions made by the husband. Each will be covered for all his needs by a single weekly contribution on one insurance document. All the principal cash payments—for unemployment, disability, and retirement will continue so long as the need lasts, without means test, and will be paid from a Social Insurance Fund built up by contributions from the insured persons, from their employers, if any, and from the State. This is in accord with two views as to the lines on which the problem of income maintenance should be approached.

The first view is that benefit in return for contributions, rather than free allowances from the State, is what the people of Britain desire. This desire is shown both by the established popularity of compulsory insurance, and by the phenomenal growth of voluntary insurance against sickness, against death, and for endowment, and most recently for hospital treatment. It is shown in another way by the strength of popular objection to any kind of means test. This objection springs, not so much from a desire to get everything for nothing, as from resentment at a provision which appears to penalize what people have come to regard as the duty and pleasure of thrift, of putting pennies away for a rainy day. Management of one's income is an essential element of a citizen's freedom. Payment of a substantial part of the cost of benefit as a contribution irrespective of the means of the contributor is the firm basis of a claim to benefit irrespective of means.

The second view is that whatever money is required for provision of insurance benefits, so long as they are needed, should come from a fund to which the recipients have contributed and to which they may be required to make larger contributions if the fund proves inadequate. The plan adopted since 1930 in regard to prolonged unemployment and sometimes suggested for prolonged disability, that the State should take this burden off insurance, in order to keep the contribution down, is wrong in principle. The insured persons should not feel that income for idleness, however caused, can come from a bottomless purse. The Government should not feel that by paying doles it can avoid the major responsibility of seeing that unemployment and disease are reduced to the minimum. The place for direct expenditure and organization by the State is in maintaining employment of the labour and other productive resources of the country, and in preventing and combating disease, not in patching an incomplete scheme of insurance.

The State cannot be excluded altogether from giving direct assistance to individuals in need, after examination of their means. However comprehensive an insurance scheme, some, through physical infirmity, can never contribute at all, and some will fall through the meshes of any insurance. The making of insurance benefit—without means test—unlimited in duration, involves of itself that conditions must be imposed at some stage or another as to how men in receipt of benefit shall use their time, so as to fit themselves or to keep themselves fit for service ; imposition of any condition means that the condition may not be fulfilled and that a case of assistance may arise. Moreover, for one of the main purposes of social insurance—provision for old age or retirement—the contributory principle implies contribution for a substantial number of years ; in the introduction of adequate contributory pensions there must be a period of transition during which those who have not qualified for pension by contribution but are in need, have their needs met by assistance pensions. National assistance is an essential subsidiary method in the whole Plan for Social Security, and the work of the Assistance Board shows that assistance—subject to means test—can be administered with sympathetic justice and discretion, taking full account of individual circumstances. But the scope of assistance will be narrowed from the beginning and will diminish throughout the transition period for pensions. The scheme of social insurance is designed of itself when in full operation to guarantee the income needed for subsistence in all normal cases.

In the first general election in Britain after the war, the people returned to power the party which they thought most likely to implement the provisions of the Beveridge Report. Social security is now the policy of all the countries of our Western Civilization, although they naturally differ as to the extent to which such security is feasible and desirable. Social developments of the modern Welfare State have revitalized the study of Sociology, just as other aspects have produced new theories in Economics. The important fact for our present study is that this social security has given a new solidity to the political foundations of the West, and one which will enable our civilization to resist any challenge which might come from within.

There remains the challenge from communist countries. In the twentieth century, use of propaganda has become one of the principal weapons in the hands of totalitarian governments. It was used in the thirties by Hitler, who succeeded in no small measure in bewildering sections of the British peoples by his unrelenting half-truth attacks on the Commonwealth, and the injustice of the Peace Treaties. The same weapon is now being subtly handled by communism in its persistent undermining of confidence in the Western democracies, its main theme being that the Western way of life is reactionary and on the decline. It would be as well boldly to face this question: *Is the Western way of life reactionary?* The answer was given in a lecture delivered at Yale University by Erwin D. Canham, Chairman of the United States Advisory Commission on Information and Editor of the *Christian Science Monitor*. This pronouncement, which was repeated at several universities, earned the distinction of receiving special mention in the United States Senate, and was subsequently made available through the United States Embassies.

ERWIN D. CANHAM

THE AUTHENTIC REVOLUTION

LET me tell you my thesis bluntly at the outset.

It is that the struggle for the salvation of free society in our time will be lost unless we in the West—and particularly we in the United States—awaken to and project the fact that we are the great revolutionaries in world history, and that our revolution is basically a spiritual one which we have already proved in action.

We have let most of the world think that the American achievement is primarily materialistic. This is the great gap between ourselves and those who yearn for much more than materialism. And we are the first victims ourselves of the misunderstanding.

The misunderstanding concerning America which is so

pervasive in the world to-day is the key to the future of
Western society. For, as Dr. Charles Malik, Minister of
Lebanon to the United States, has well said :

" To the superficial observer who is unable to penetrate
to the core of love and truth which is still at the heart of the
West, there is little to choose between the soulless materialism
of the West and the militant materialism of the East."

And, as Dr. Malik further told us in the West :

" If your only export in these realms is the silent example
of flourishing political institutions and happy human relations, you cannot lead. If your only export is a distant
reputation for wealth and prosperity and order, you cannot
lead. Nor can you really lead if you send forth to others
only expert advice and technical assistance. To be able to
lead and save yourself and others, you must, above everything else, address your mind and soul. Your tradition,
rooted in the glorious Græco-Roman-Hebrew-Christian-
Western-European humane outlook, supplies you with all
the necessary presuppositions for leadership. All you have
to do is to be the deepest you already are."

There is the challenge of the hour. It is not a challenge
requiring the postulating of new fundamentals. It calls for
no panaceas. It is a call to awakening and to articulation.
The basic need is to understand and to proclaim the truth.
The West must find its voice.

Let us, therefore, ask ourselves a few fundamental questions. Let us proclaim the truth on the issues which confront
the world. Mankind to-day is being told it must choose
between revolution and reaction. It is told that communism
represents revolution, and that our system—which is oppro-
briously called capitalism—represents reaction. In such a
confrontation, there would be no choice. Mankind must go
forward. But this statement of the issue is an explicit reversal
of the truth.

The fact is that communism—like totalitarianism in any form—represents the blackest of reactions. The fact is that the free system, of which capitalism is only a small and modified part, represents the authentic revolution—not a subversive revolution, but a revolution which sets men free.

We in the western world are the true standard-bearers of a great and emancipating doctrine. But we have allowed ourselves to be thrust into the indefensible position of seeking to protect the *status quo*. The free system is by no means the same thing as the *status quo*. Our tradition is not static, but is constantly dynamic. Our tradition strikes off chains. Totalitarianism would put them back on again.

The stirring battle cry which ends the *Communist Manifesto* is itself a delusion. Marx and Engels wrote : " The proletarians have nothing to lose but their chains. They have a world to win." Where, in to-day's world, are most people in chains ? Is it in the United States, where what is perhaps the most enlightened labour contract in history was recently signed by our largest industrial corporation and one of our largest trade unions ? Or is it in the world's most extensive communist state, the Soviet Union, where tragic millions, suffering and dying, are bearing the literal chains of slave labour ? Is it in Britain, where labour's own government is in power and is carrying through the most extensive peaceful and gradual social revolution in history ? Where are the chains to-day ? Where are the mental chains ? Are they in the free universities and the free churches of the Western world ? Or are they in the communist states, where man's right to think is now denied on behalf of the omnipotent state, and free science or free religion has ceased to exist ?

These are among the facts to which we must awaken. But let us come at our task in an orderly way. Let us first ask ourselves, in the most searching possible fashion, what are the chief claims of communism, and let us confront these statements with the best truth we know. Then let us examine the two doctrines—communism and western democracy—in actual practice, to test their words by their works. And, finally, let us chart a plan of campaign in this great battle of truth against falsehood.

First, what are communism's basic postulates ?

The primary claim of communism—the foundation stone on which it rests—is that of dialectical materialism. It is the assertion that ultimate reality lies in matter, and in matter alone. But the truth as we know it is that superior to matter in every way is the reality of mind and of spirit. In our time an awakening to the metaphysical bankruptcy of materialism is beginning to sweep over thoughtful mankind. The awakening is most striking among the natural scientists. They are finding, in the realm of the very little and of the very large— of the infinitesimal and of the infinite—that old materialistic assumptions are no longer valid. Reality is now by them recognized to be related to consciousness. Time and space are seen to be dependent upon consciousness. Reality is emerging more and more, to to-day's thinker, as the basic essence which lies behind and beneath the material manifestation. In short, not the chair of wood and wicker, but the idea of chair existing in consciousness, is seen to come closer to ultimate reality.

There is an even more striking and topical proof of the bankruptcy of materialism. Men have wrought the most powerful engines in their experience : from gunpowder and steam and electricity they have progressed to atomic power. And yet they now see that the power to help or harm mankind lies not in the atom itself, not in the uranium or plutonium or tritium, but in the thinking that motivates the finger which does or does not push the button that does or does not set off these fearful engines of destruction. In the words of a great Yale natural scientist, Dr. Edmund W. Sinnott, " Man, not matter, is the chief problem of mankind to-day ".

The second great lie of communism walks hand in hand with the first. It is that there is no God. To-day we have the

X

opportunity of knowing as never before that there is indeed a God, who is the loving Father of all mankind. We do not necessarily have to identify God merely with the single three-letter name, G-o-d. Perhaps it is useful to re-define God as the central Principle of the universe. Perhaps it helps to think of Him as eternal Truth and Life and Love. These things cannot be denied. We know the universe is orderly. We know that it works according to established rules and principles, some of which we have been able partially to define. It seems to me to be rationally impossible to recognize the reality of an orderly universe and to deny God.

Still further to disprove communist dialectic, take the assertions that there is no objective and eternal truth, and that only the transient and the temporal exist. I am sure that we in the Western world can readily prove to our satisfaction that there is Truth, and that it is transcendent. Again we can prove it in the working of the laws of the universe. Or we can prove it in the vast and noble reaches of the mind and the heart. There is abundant evidence of the existence of permanent and immanent values. These are accessible to mankind through a humble search for understanding. They come through the path of reason as well as down the road of revelation. They lift mankind out of its own confusions and perversities. They are to be confirmed not only in the religious convictions and teachings of mankind, but in the positive philosophical traditions of Plato and Aristotle, of Hegel and Whitehead.

Finally we come to another great communist falsehood: that the individual exists for the sake of society and the state. This lie follows logically from the assertion of materialism and the denial of eternal truth and order. It is the specific doctrine which enslaves mankind. And yet the truth as we know it and prove it in action daily is that the state and society exist for the sake of the individual. It is this communist lie which stifles the spirit of man. It is totalitarian. It is contrary to nature and to man.

Again in the eloquent words of Dr. Malik :

" That the State, the mere organ of government and order, is the source of every law, every truth, every norm of conduct, every social and economic relationship ; that no science, no music, no economic activity, no philosophy, no art, no theology, is to be permitted except if it is state-licensed and state-controlled : all this is so false, so arrogant, so autocratic and tyrannical that no man who has drunk deep from the living waters of the Western Platonic-Christian tradition can possibly accept it. The State does not come in first place ; it comes in tenth or fifteenth place. The University is higher than the State ; the tradition of free inquiry is higher than the State ; the Church is higher than the State ; the family is higher than the State ; natural law is higher than the State ; God is higher than the State ; within limits, free economic activity is higher than the State."

It is good that Dr. Malik should have recognized not only the spiritual importance of Church and University and family, but of free economic activity as well. For this brings us to the crux of our problem to-day. It is the free economic activity of the West which is most under fire in the contemporary world. It is this free economic activity which is used by those who hate it or misunderstand it to brand the West with the stigma and curse of materialism. The need, therefore, is for an awakening to the spiritual obligation and heritage of the free economic system.

Let us, then, proceed to the second of our main points : an examination of communism and the free economic system as they reveal themselves in action.

It is not necessary, first of all, to belittle the actual achievements of the Soviet state. Historic objectivity requires us to recall the importance of the transition from Czardom, the achievement of partial industrialization in the face of two wars. In a certain narrow framework the Soviet state has accepted a large obligation to the individuals who make it up. It has gone a long way toward harmonizing the diverse interests of widely separated and scattered racial and cultural groups. In the second world war the Red Army under Marshal Stalin helped greatly in resisting and defeating a powerful aggressor.

It is important to recognize, also, that we have to live with the Russians, and many of the things we find dangerous in the present Soviet state are traits and trends which long antedate communism. We must find ways of adjusting ourselves to life with an awakened Eurasian continent. It is, perhaps, a blessing for mankind that the awakening and industrialization of this vast area has come about under a system which inevitably handicaps and limits its potential achievement. Sometimes one is appalled at the aggressive possibilities of a Russian empire organized with the efficiency and power of industrialized Britain in the nineteenth century or the United States in the twentieth century. A great natural scientist, Dr. Merle Tuve, recently remarked that the greatest single discovery of the second world war was the efficiency of the free system. That kind of efficiency, coupled with the natural resources and the immense racial dynamism of the people now under the hammer and sickle, would make a world force of incalculable potential.

Communism has partly liberated and partly stifled this great capacity. On balance, at the point of the mid-century, there is far more of stifling than there is of liberation. When, as I believe to be inevitable, the Russian peoples are finally and genuinely liberated, we must be ready with a universal system of peace and order. Otherwise, they will be an explosive force against which to-day's communism will be a pallid squib. Fortunately, there is also in the Russian people a great and magnificent spiritual and universal yearning. The free Russian soul, in all its exuberance, longs for human brotherhood and bears a heavy burden of anguish for the spiritual failure of humankind. These deep impulses have helped to support communism. They would be far more effective in support of a free system wrought for the benefit of all mankind. The Russian need for religion has partially and temporarily accepted communism as a religion. When the Russian spirit is ultimately freed, it must find its way fully into the spiritual pastures of the great Western tradition of truth and love. Otherwise, Russia might remain the world's great challenge for long and turbulent years—far more dangerously than in our own time, when Russia is self-curbed by a hopelessly inefficient and inhibiting system. Even under the present limitations, it is unnecessary to add that the Russian achievement is considerable.

But on balance the system remains one of chains and of slavery. It remains reaction, of the pattern of all the tyrannies that have sought to bind the free spirit of man and to withhold his natural rights down through the millennia. The fact is that communism in its works is both spiritually and materially sterile. It is fundamentally a failure, because it is unable to utilize more than the merest fraction of the forces which are available. It is the most profligate destroyer of human resources. Its concentration camps and its mass graves are filled with the richest of human talent. Those who survive are denied the immense productive force of free inquiry, of objective experiment, and of full self-analysis.

Against all this, contrast the actual achievement of the free system of the West. The American economy—derided and attacked by its enemies—is to-day holding the line against world collapse. With all the faults which we know full well lie within our society and in its economic organization, the fact remains that the world to-day would be in chaos without the stability and productivity of the United States.

I am not here seeking to put a halo around the profit motive : far from it. The first and most important thing to say about the free economic system is that it can survive only to the degree that the individuals and combinations that make it up accept their social obligation.

Moreover, there is considerable difference between much of the economic organization that passes by the name of capitalism in some parts of the world and the best of the free economic system which enlightened leadership has brought into being in the United States and elsewhere. In many places overseas, when we defend capitalism we defend a feudal or a cartelist concept which would appal the thoughtful American business enterpriser. In some places, it is true, a sense of social obligation has dawned. We are not necessarily committed to the task of putting Humpty-Dumpty together again. But it is essential for us to put the importance of social obligation first, and not place ourselves in the position of advocating the return of industrial or financial feudalism.

The free economic system in the United States, and measurably in many other parts of the world—including, particularly, the smaller states where neutrality and/or co-operation have supported much real equality and high standards of living—can be objectively left to stand or fall on its own merits. It stands. It stands because it has given more opportunity to the individual than any other system ever tried. It stands because it is perfectible. It is not dogmatic—or should not be. It should always recognize the imperatives of self-criticism and of change. It should remember the paramountcy of human values. But these are not values of social security alone.

There are serious shortcomings in the idea of security, taken as an ultimate value. No society which enshrined security as an end in itself was able long to continue the march of progress. Dissatisfaction, adversity, risk—these are the imperatives of progress. Furthermore, to enshrine security as an end in itself, and to place its procurement and maintenance in the hands of the State, is to say that the State is above the individual. That is the road of slavery ; of social suicide. We must keep the individual and the individual-based forms of organization as our primary values : man and church and school, along with family and free economic activity. The State owes nobody a living. At the same time, it is necessary and effective to organize through the State the various functions which the individual or private organizations cannot accomplish. It goes without saying that insurance barriers against the hazards of the economic system—old age or unemployment—are accepted and legitimate parts of collective responsibility. That form of social security can be kept in its proper place.

But the increasing sense of dependence of the individual upon the State is not the obverse of the needful recognition of social obligation. It is, however, often the result of the failure of free enterprise to recognize its social obligation. In an industrial society, dominated by mass production, the individual is peculiarly insecure. He will seek the means of survival through collective action. For the labourer and artisan, protection comes through unions and government. Sometimes it comes through a co-operative relationship with his employer, which is best of all. For the employer, protection also comes through collective action, sometimes private and sometimes in governmental laws and procedures. But we have made great progress in evolving forms which are consistent both with free enterprise and with the special hazards of an industrial society. And again I must emphasize that these forms work best when they are founded upon a voluntary and perceptive acceptance of social obligation. That is the final and indispensable bulwark of the free system.

The fruits of the system are expressed in material and spiritual terms. Altogether too often we have remembered only the material rewards. We boast of our standard of living, and when we go abroad the dollars clink in our pockets. We are sometimes obsessed with material gain and with unrestrained selfishness. We have been our own worst salesmen, for we have convinced most of the rest of the world that we are money-mad materialists. But the greatest fruitage of the free system is spiritual. It stands in the recognition of the essential dignity of man which is implicit in equality of opportunity. It lies in the concept of legitimate service.

Perhaps you will understand me when I say, not too

whimsically, that the American filling station is a very good illustration of the triumph of the free system. It is not the mechanical excellence of the filling station which is its chief virtue. It is its spirit. There are an enthusiasm and a self-respect which have infused the filling station and made it one of the most successful of our various institutions. I do not altogether know why this is so. I merely point out that our free economic system at its best has gone a long way towards the enshrining of human values and the attainment of a genuinely democratic relationship between server and served. I do not think anyone will deny that this is a spiritual value.

Something of the same achievement was illustrated the other day by the words of a German editor who recently had an opportunity to visit the United States. He was taken to a small eastern city as the guest of a local newspaper. I asked him how he liked it and what he had learned. He put it in these words : " The best thing was that they introduced me to everybody, and they introduced me to the lift-boy just the same way they introduced me to the mayor ".

Awareness of the individual importance of man is our greatest achievement. It lies at the heart of the matter. Recognizing the significance of individual man, we have been able to mobilize and utilize the vast and still uncounted and uncountable resources of the human spirit. This is an accomplishment of revolutionary importance. It springs from the circumstances under which Europeans first came to the New World; it is based upon the political and ideological and spiritual roots of our society. It is genuine democracy. Established in the midst of the natural resources of a continent, it has enabled us to become a material and spiritual bastion for the safeguarding of Western civilization. We have been able to achieve the adequate blending of natural and human resources, and while we have wasted natural resources often in profligate manner, we have come to utilize human resources within enterprising but humane bounds. This is illustrated by our rejection of child labour on the one hand and our increasingly wide opportunities for women on the other. But I would not gild the lily. There are plenty of dark spots in our human experience, as we have moved towards fuller light. There are dark spots to-day. They are part of the challenge, part of the incentive, part of the unfinished business without which we would decline and perish.

And that brings us to our third point : a plan of campaign in the war of ideas. The first necessity is manifestly self-awakening. We must re-discover the ideas by which we live. The ideology of communism is well known and widely proclaimed. It is passionately believed by many of those who proclaim it. This awareness and intensity is integrated and guided. There is no comparable intensity or co-ordination of ideas among those who believe in the free system. There will not be until we look at our heritage in fundamental terms and arouse ourselves to its revolutionary import to-day. The obligation of every citizen, of every leader, is to awaken himself and to awaken his fellow-man to the significance of to-day's challenge.

The second necessity, after the awakening, is the voice. Already there are various small voices from the free nations—voices seeking to penetrate the void of human thinking. They must rise to full articulation. We possess to-day mighty machines for disseminating ideas to every corner of the globe. But we have not yet learned what we have to say. In fact, the message we must say is the same old message of truth down the ages : the significance of man under God, of his brotherhood, of his birthright of freedom.

The third necessity, along with the awakening and the voice, is the fuller demonstration of the free system in action. There is contagion in falsehood. Some of the lies of totalitarianism and materialism have penetrated into our own thinking. We must not let them stay there. In this unhealthy atmosphere of no peace, no war, we have yielded some citadels to the enemy. Some have sought to weaken or destroy the free spirit of inquiry and of teaching in our schools and universities. Happily, enough have seen the truth clearly and have prevented the sabotage of our educational institutions. In these bewildering times we have yielded to distrust of human character, and the cloud of suspicion—often of slander—hangs heavy over the human spirit. We must learn again to trust character, because free institutions depend upon respect for fellow man. We must spurn the corrosive doubts which do far more harm to our body politic than the dangers to which they pertain. We must, as I have said earlier, manifest social responsibility throughout our economic system. We must make swifter progress towards the removal of racial and religious barriers which prevent true community. These are but a few of our items of unfinished business—of our ways of proving in action the truth by which alone we live.

And, finally, let us regain perspective, let us cast off the inferiority complex with which communism has bemused us, let us reaffirm a consciousness of our birthright.

We stand in human history as the greatest revolutionaries of all time. Not just we Americans—but all of us in the Western world.

We are the guardians of a sacred and dynamic heritage. We have come a long way. We have a long way to go.

We have discovered long since the eternal truth of love and peace and brotherhood. We have discovered, and in a measure applied, the enormous potency of the free man.

We have lifted part way the heavy burden of toil that has crushed humanity down through the years, and more gloriously we have begun to lift the curtain of ignorance which has blanketed the human mind.

We are on the march.

And to-day we are challenged. For the challenge we may be infinitely grateful. Because our society to-day faces adversity. There is a hill up which we must climb. We will not decline in slothful ease. We will pit ourselves against the lies which in our time assault the deep foundations of truth.

These lies cannot prevail, even to the extent of setting civilization into a relapse, if we are worthy of our heritage.

And we can and will be worthy of that heritage if and as we awaken. The voice of no one of us is powerful enough to awaken all the slumberers in to-day's world.

It is our individual and collective duty to think these things through for ourselves, and in our free way to help our brother man to his needful awareness. Let us pass along the message of freedom. One day it will reach critical mass and a chain reaction will begin.

Meanwhile, we must preserve the physical defences of the Western world by keeping military aggression at bay; we must strengthen the economic sinews and the stability of the free world; we must lead our civilization to higher plateaus of demonstrated freedom and achievement.

And from the valley below, those who have accepted the false doctrines of totalitarianism of the right or the left will one day see the heights which we have ascended and will join us on the continuous pathway ahead.

BIOGRAPHICAL NOTES

JOHN QUINCY ADAMS (1767-1848), the sixth President of the United States, was the son of John Adams, the second President. Coming from a talented family, he was a precocious child. He accompanied his father to Europe while still in his early teens, and studied in Paris and at the University of Leyden. He graduated at Harvard in 1787, and was admitted to the bar three years later. He served as United States minister to the Netherlands, to Portugal, and to Prussia, but returned home in 1800, was elected to the Massachusetts Senate, and then to the Senate at Washington. In 1814 he played an important part in the negotiation of the peace treaty which brought the 1812 war with Great Britain to an end, and for the next three years he was U.S. minister in London. He strongly supported President Monroe in his famous policy of the Monroe doctrine, and he was elected President by the House of Representatives in 1824. His term of office was not very happy, and he spent the remainder of his life in working against slavery.

EARL BALDWIN OF BEWDLEY (1867-1947) was always shown in cartoons busy smoking a pipe. The cartoonists may or may not be right in assuming that a pipe-smoker is a man of slow but sure solidity, but it was in this character that Baldwin appealed to the English people. In actual fact he saw much farther ahead than most people on most questions. He was a cousin of Rudyard Kipling, and future generations will amuse themselves with idle discussions as to which of the two showed the greater imaginative foresight. His great-grandfather built up the important family coal and iron company in Worcestershire, and for twenty years after graduating at Trinity College, Cambridge, he devoted himself to this business. In 1908 he succeeded his father as Chairman of Baldwin's, Director of the Great Western Railway, and M.P. for Bewdley. In 1916 he became Parliamentary Private Secretary to Bonar Law, and thenceforth his political progress was regular and rapid. In 1922, following the famous Carlton Club Conference at which Baldwin had led the Conservatives away from further coalition with the Liberals, a Conservative Government was elected, with Bonar Law in charge, and Baldwin at the Exchequer. Bonar Law soon resigned owing to ill-health, and, to the surprise of most people, Baldwin took over the Premiership. At that time Great Britain was in the depths of a post-war depression. Baldwin believed that it could

317

only be cured by Protection, and he quickly appealed to the country for a vote of confidence on this issue. The country said "No!" In 1924 he was again Premier, but pledged not to introduce Protection. Throughout the financial crisis of 1931 he loyally served under Ramsay MacDonald in the National Government, and in 1935 was again Premier, and this time with the country solidly behind him. He lost a lot of prestige over the failure of Britain to push forward a strong League of Nations policy, but this was recovered by his tactful handling of the difficult and delicate situation arising out of Edward VIII's determination to abdicate. As soon as George VI was crowned, Baldwin resigned his position as Premier and his seat in the Commons, and retired from active politics with the title of Earl Baldwin of Bewdley.

SIR ERNEST BARKER (1874-   ), Professor of Political Science in Cambridge University from 1928 to 1939, laid the foundations of his wide scholarship on the classics, then turned to modern history, and so to political science. He went to Manchester Grammar School, thence to Balliol College, Oxford, where he was Classical Scholar. From 1898 to 1920 he held posts of ever-increasing responsibility at various Oxford Colleges, and then moved to London to become Principal of King's College. After the second world war he went to Cologne University for a year to restore sanity to the teaching of political science there. His numerous publications include *Greek Political Theory*; *Ideas and Ideals of the British Empire*; *Reflections on Government*; *Britain and the British People*; and a very readable autobiography, *Father of the Man*.

LORD BEVERIDGE (1879-   ) will long be remembered as Chairman of the Inter-departmental Committee on Social Insurance and Allied Services which produced the famous "Beveridge Report". But his record of public service goes back to a much earlier date. He was born in Bengal, and educated at Charterhouse and Balliol College, Oxford, where he took a triple First. Like Mr. Attlee he gained his first experience of the problems of poverty at Toynbee Hall in London's dockland. He was leader-writer for the *Morning Post* from 1906 to 1908, and then he joined the Board of Trade to work out the new unemployment insurance scheme. A C.B. in 1916 and a K.C.B. in 1919 were witness to the official appreciation of his services. Then he left the Civil Service for a more academic life, and from 1919 to 1937 he was a Director of the London School of Economics and Political Science. He went to Oxford in 1937 as Master of University College, and in 1941 while he was there he accepted the Chairmanship of the

Social Insurance Committee appointed by Mr. Greenwood. His own books include: *Unemployment: a Problem for Industry*; *Insurance for All*; *Planning under Socialism*; *Pillars of Security*; *Full Employment in a Free Society*; *The Price of Peace*; and *Power and Influence*.

JAMES HENRY BREASTED (1865-1935), a Professor of Egyptology and Oriental History in the University of Chicago from 1905 to 1933, was present with Howard Carter when the tomb of King Tutankhamen was opened. He was educated at Chicago, Yale, Berlin, and Oxford, and played an important part in many archæological expeditions in Egypt and in Mesopotamia. His numerous publications include: *A History of Egypt*; *Ancient Records of Egypt*; *Historical Documents*; *The Early World*; *Ancient Times*; *Survey of the Ancient World*; *The Conquest of Civilization*; and *The Edwin Smith Surgical Papyrus*.

EDMUND BURKE (1729-97), the " Shakespeare of English orators ", was born in Dublin, the second of the fifteen children of an Irish attorney. Burke himself was never strong. His education, which received its greatest impetus at Trinity College, Dublin, continued throughout his lifetime, and he retained to a remarkable degree the childhood ability to learn facts quickly. He came to London in 1750 and quickly made a reputation as a writer and a supporter of the Whig party. His *Thoughts on the Cause of the Present Discontents* in 1770 severely criticized the court intrigues and the unconstitutional methods of the Government, and in the next few years he devoted all his energies to an attempt to make the Government see the folly of trying to impose taxes on the North American colonies. He next turned his attention to India, and in 1785 began the attack which led to the impeachment of Warren Hastings. The French Revolution came as a great shock to him, and thenceforth, as his *Reflections* show, he was a conservative rather than a reformer. His speeches in Parliament usually emptied the House, and Goldsmith describes him as one

> Who, too deep for his hearers, still went on refining,
> And thought of convincing while they thought of dining.

But they are still read, both for their historical value and for their style.

ERWIN D. CANHAM (1904-   ), Editor of *The Christian Science Monitor*, is well known to radio-listeners, television-viewers, and to readers in the United States. He was born in Auburn, Maine, and took his first degree in 1925. After some years on the reporting staff of the *Christian Science Monitor* he came to Oxford as a Rhodes Scholar, graduating there in 1936. He has also received many honorary degrees and distinctions. He became General News Editor of the *Monitor* in 1939, Managing Editor in 1941, and took his present post as Editor in 1945. He is Chairman of the United States Advisory Commission on Information, and a Vice-President of the Executive Committee of the United States National Commission for U.N.E.S.C.O.

SIR JOHN ELIOT (1592-1632), a martyr in the cause of English liberty, graduated at Oxford and studied law in London before entering Parliament in 1614, and taking his first lesson in resistance to unconstitutional demands under King James I. The part which he played in the later struggle with Charles I is outlined in Green's lecture on " The King and the Parliament " in this volume. Charles never forgave him his bold attack on Buckingham, and his share in the Petition of Right, and on the dissolution of Parliament in 1629 he was arrested, sentenced to pay a fine of £2000 and to remain in prison until he should acknowledge himself guilty of conspiracy against the King. His health failed, but he was allowed no alleviation of his confinement, and he died in the Tower rather than admit he had been in the wrong.

QUEEN ELIZABETH (1533-1603) was the daughter of Henry VIII and Anne Boleyn. She followed her half-sister, Mary, on the throne under her father's will. Of the other things inherited from her father we can mention a remarkable " toughness " of character, an iron determination to make England great, whatever the personal cost to herself might be, and a gift for choosing men of the highest talent to serve her purposes. The difficulties she had to face were enormous. Her mother's marriage was declared invalid just before Anne was executed in 1536; her childhood was lonely and loveless; her position while Mary was on the throne was most insecure, and she was even charged with complicity in Wyatt's rebellion. When she became Queen in 1558 she had to face the rivalry at home of Mary Queen of Scots (whose claim to the throne was the better founded), and the growing antagonism abroad of Philip of Spain. Elizabeth managed to avoid any open warfare for twenty-five years, and during this time men like Drake and Grenville laid the foundations of naval and commercial supremacy. They knew that the man-of-war requires sailors and not soldiers on board, and when the Armada came they proved their contention. Elizabeth had a remarkable gift for evoking the enthusiastic loyalty of her Protestant subjects, and her reign was a golden age in many respects for the country which she loved so much.

DESIDERIUS ERASMUS (1466-1536) was probably born at Rotterdam, but it is doubtful how far the account of his birth given in *The Cloister and the Hearth* can be regarded as true. After his school-days were over he became an Augustinian monk, and entered the service of the Bishop of Cambrai. His thirst for knowledge led him to spend a roving life, moving from one university town to another. He first visited England at the invitation of Lord Mountjoy, who had been one of his pupils in Paris. Most of his later years were spent at Basle. He wrote a number of books of maxims and anecdotes culled from Latin and Greek authors, together with moral reflections on them, and he brought out critical editions of the works of many of the Early Fathers of the Church. But his greatest service to scholarship and to religion alike was his edition of the New Testament, containing the Greek Text, together with a Latin translation, and many critical notes. It is better to think of him as a scholar of the Renaissance rather than a theologian of the Reformation, and this in spite of the immense influence which he had on the latter, and which led to the popular saying : " Erasmus laid the egg and Luther hatched it ".

H. A. L. FISHER (1865-1940) was awarded the Order of Merit in 1937 " in recognition of his eminent position as an historian and of his services to Literature ". His work as Minister of Education in bringing in the Act of 1918 might also have been included in the tribute. As an historian his position would be secure by virtue of his *History of Europe* alone, although he has written many other books, more especially on Napoleon Bonaparte and his times. His Education Act of 1918 made " a national system of public education available for all persons capable of profiting thereby " an established aim of our social legislation. Fisher was educated at Winchester and at New College, Oxford, where he became a Fellow. He was appointed Vice-Chancellor of Sheffield University in 1912, and entered Parliament in 1916. He was Member for the Combined Universities from 1918 to 1926, when he was elected Warden of New College and retired from active politics.

JAMES ANTHONY FROUDE (1818-94), the great historian of the sixteenth century, was born at Dartington Rectory in Devonshire. He was very unhappy at Westminster School, and after three years he left and had some private tuition before going to Oriel College, Oxford, where he became a Fellow. The tide of faith which was receding in the nineteenth century soon left Froude among the agnostics, and he resigned his Fellowship and supported himself by writing for the London reviews while he worked at his monumental *History of England*

Y

from the Fall of Wolsey to the Defeat of the Spanish Armada. The first volume appeared in 1856, with others at intervals until 1870. In 1868 Froude was elected Rector of St. Andrews, beating Disraeli by fourteen votes. He was active in other fields as well. He travelled as Government Commissioner to South Africa in 1874-5 to study the question of federation, and ten years later he visited Australia and then the West Indies. In 1892 he was appointed to the Chair of Modern History at Oxford in place of his ancient rival and critic, Professor Freeman.

CYRIL F. GARBETT, G.C.V.O. (1875-1955), Archbishop of York 1942-55, died on the last day of 1955, and thus missed the barony coming in the New Year's Honours List. The son of a vicar, he went to Portsmouth Grammar School, and to Keble College, where he took honours in History, and then to Cuddesdon College, Oxford. He was President of the Oxford Union in 1898. From 1900 to 1919 he worked hard as a parish priest in Portsea, first as Assistant Curate and then as Vicar. He was consecrated Bishop of Southwark in 1919, and in 1932 became Bishop of Winchester. Ten years later he was translated to York. Dr. Garbett has written many books on the religious and social problems of our time. Among them we may mention: *The Work of a Great Parish*; *Secularism and Christian Unity*; *What is Man?*; *We would see Jesus*; *Physician, heal Thyself*; and *Watchman, What of the Night?*

JOHN RICHARD GREEN (1837-83), the author of the *Short History of the English People*, was by birth and education a product of Oxford. He entered the Church, but ill-health caused him to abandon parish work, and he turned his talents to writing for the *Saturday Review*. His later years were spent entirely in historical study. His masterpiece was the first historical book which set kings and wars in the background and the social life of the people in the foreground. This, and its great charm of style, have made it probably the most popular of all history books. More scholarly works of his are *The Making of England* and *The Conquest of England*, both of which deal with the Anglo-Saxon period.

FRANÇOIS GUIZOT (1787-1874), famous alike as historian, statesman, and orator, was born at Nîmes. He came to Paris in 1805 intending to devote himself to history and literature, but he was drawn into politics, and throughout the rest of his life he was kept alternating between helping to make the history of his own times, and writing and lecturing about past history. He held liberal and progressive views at first, but gradually became more and more conservative, mainly, perhaps, because of his objection to a republic, which was the chief demand of the left wing in France. In 1847 he was the leader of the Cabinet, under Louis-Philippe, which fell in the Revolution of 1848, and, when the Second Republic was proclaimed, he retired to London. He was in Paris again in 1850, and once more active in politics, but the *coup d'état* of Louis Napoleon put an end to his public career.

HENRY VIII (1491-1547), the second son of the Tudor Henry VII who restored order and prosperity to England after the Wars of the Roses, became Prince of Wales on the death of his elder brother in 1502, and succeeded to the throne in 1509 amid universal acclamations called forth by his outstanding merits, both mental and physical. He died in 1547, hated and feared by almost all. He lived in troubled times. There were the wars with France and with Scotland, the breach with Rome, and the six marriages. But through all the worries and the distractions he kept one clear aim in view : the handing down to the heirs of his body of a powerful and a united England.

ADOLF HITLER (1889-1945), responsible for " a more hideous total of human suffering and misery " than any other man in history, was born in the Austrian border town of Branau, the son of Alois Schickel-gruber, a customs officer. His boyhood was unhappy. He hated his father, he hated his country, and if he had any warm feelings at all they were for the great German fatherland across the River Inn. His father died when he was thirteen, his mother two years later, and he was left to make his way alone. He wanted to be an artist, but could make only a bare pittance by commercial work. The first world war solved his problems for a time, and he enlisted in the Bavarian army. He won the Iron Cross and a corporal's stripes, was wounded on the Somme in 1916, and gassed at Ypres shortly before the armistice. The defeat of Germany led him to think that he had a mission to restore the former glories of his adopted country, and he took the first step usual in such cases—that of finding people to blame for its misfortunes. In June 1919 he became member No. 7 of a new German Workers' Party. He discovered his power as a speaker, and soon became leader, attracting bigger and bigger crowds to hear his crude denunciations of the Jews, the Marxists, and the Treaty of Versailles. His party flourished in the days of German inflation and commercial ruin ; it lost ground in the more prosperous years, and then came to the forefront again in the depression of 1929. Middle-classes and the unemployed both looked to Hitler for salvation, and in speech after speech he promised it. The 1933 elections,

Y 2

with the Reichstag fire to sway the anti-communists, proved a triumph for the Nazis, and Hitler became Führer, an absolute dictator. The persecution of the Jews followed ; then the dissolution of the trades unions, the proscription of all other parties, and the reorganization of the whole state to foster Nazi ideas. Then the aggression abroad started. The Rhineland was reoccupied, Austria annexed, the Sudetenland taken over, and the rest of Czechoslovakia. Memel and Poland followed, and the second world war. Hitler committed suicide in his Berlin air-raid shelter on April 30, 1945.

VICTOR HUGO (1802-85) is perhaps best known as the author of *Les Misérables*, but from his school-days until he had passed his eightieth year his mind was incredibly active and enormously productive. He wrote odes, ballads, romantic tragedies, melodramas, novels, reviews, political diatribes, criticisms, travels, newspaper editorials—everything in fine which he thought calculated to inspire or to direct the intellect of France. To him France was the leader of civilization, Paris the leader of France, and he himself meant to become, and in fact became, as the leader of the romantic school, the dictator of Paris in all matters concerned with literature. He also played an active part in politics in the second half of his life. No man with his keen sympathy for " les misérables " could remain aloof, and he became the prophet of the progressive republicans. His antagonism to Louis Napoleon led to his proscription after the *coup d'état* of December 2, 1851, and he fled to Brussels, and then to the Channel Islands (to which we owe *The Toilers of the Sea*). When " Napoleon the Little " was brought crashing down by the Franco-Prussian War, Hugo returned to Paris in triumph. His last years were mainly devoted to the writing of philosophical poems.

JUNIUS was the *nom de plume* of the writer of a series of political letters which appeared in the *Public Advertiser*, London, from 1767 to 1772. Scholars still argue about his identity, although the majority opinion is in favour of Sir Philip Francis (1740-1818). Junius, whoever he may have been, certainly had a good inside knowledge of the politics of his time, and of events at court.

JOHN KNOX (1505-72), reformer and revolutionary, came of a family of poor people, but at Glasgow University and elsewhere he secured an education far above that of the average cleric of his day. He was born near Edinburgh, but came to England in 1551, and helped in the revision of the Prayer Book under Edward VI. He fled to the Continent under Queen Mary, and spent much time at Geneva, where he came strongly under Calvin's influence. He returned to Scotland in 1559, and from that time until his death he was engaged in one hazardous contest after another with what he considered " the powers of darkness ". As a result of his work the Presbyterian Church, as he organized it, became the Established Church of Scotland.

EARL LLOYD GEORGE (1863-1945), the great Liberal leader, and the man to whom Britain owed almost as much during the first world war as it did to Winston Churchill in the second, was a Welshman through and through, although he did happen to be born at Manchester. He studied law, and in 1890 he won an astonishing victory in the Parliamentary election for Carnarvon—a constituency he represented continually until his retirement in 1944. An excellent and vigorous speaker, and a man of great brains and energy, he made his reputation at the Board of Trade, where he proved remarkably successful in reconciling the claims of capital and labour in the industrial disputes of that period. Under Asquith's Government he introduced his first budget in 1909, an epoch-making event, since it marked the first gentle attempt at some contribution towards an equalization of wealth through the Finance Act. It was thrown out by the Lords, mainly on the Land Tax proposals, and, on the appeal to the country, Lloyd George won, with the help of the Irish and the Labour Members. During the war he put all his energy into the supply of munitions, and then became Premier in 1916. He had a huge majority in the 1919 election, but from 1922 onwards was in opposition. His *War Memoirs* are an invaluable record of the events of 1914-20.

JOHN LOCKE (1632-1704), the philosopher, was the son of a Somersetshire lawyer who fought for the Parliament in the Civil War. He went to Christ Church College at Oxford, where he became a tutor and studied Medicine and Science. In 1666 he became Private Secretary to the Earl of Shaftesbury, an association which lasted for fifteen years. Under William III he began to write his political and philosophical treatises. His *Essay Concerning Human Understanding* gives his ideas on the theory of knowledge, while his two *Treatises on Government* give the case for that ultimate sovereignty of the people which is the basis of modern democracy. His four *Letters Concerning Toleration* are arguments in favour of freedom of thought.

MARTIN LUTHER (1483-1546), the greatest figure in the Reformation, was born at Eisleben and spent a lonely childhood under strict discipline. He went to the University of Erfurt in 1501 and took his master's degree. Soon afterwards, being greatly concerned about his soul's salvation, he entered a monastery. Peace of mind came, however, not from fasts and penances and ritual prayers, but from a deep study of the Pauline epistles. From these he derived a conviction that salvation was freely offered to all who believed, and he at once began to preach this doctrine of salvation through faith—though still as a Catholic and a monk. He was transferred to the University of Wittenberg in 1508, and while he was there a friar appeared, selling papal indulgences, a common enough custom then, but, as Luther now perceived, directly opposed to his theory that forgiveness of sins was freely available for all penitents. He proposed, therefore, to lead an open discussion on this practice of selling indulgences, and in accordance with the usual custom he posted up his theses, the 95 steps of his argument. The appearance of these in 1517 may well be taken as marking the beginning of the Reformation.

LORD MACAULAY (1800-59) had a very successful career, but he might have risen to even greater heights if he had had to struggle against adversity and opposition. He was educated at Trinity College, Cambridge, and entered public life as a Member of Parliament in 1830, thenceforth dividing his time and energies between public affairs and literature. He was a member of the Supreme Council of India for a time, and on his return home served twice in the Cabinet. Admired as no other English essayist and historian had ever been, commanding unprecedented prices for his work, listened to with respect in the Cabinet and with rapt attention in the Commons, surrounded at home by well-loved books, whose contents he assimilated without an effort, devoted to his work in literature, and full of broad sympathies with progress, he certainly found life good. He never married. He was raised to the peerage as Baron Macaulay of Rothley in 1857. His *Lays of Ancient Rome* still attract the school-boy, and his *Essays* and his *History of England from the Accession of James II* can still be read with pleasure by the more mature mind.

JOHN STUART MILL (1806-73), the apostle of philosophical radicalism, was the son of James Mill, the philosopher and economist. His father subjected him to an extraordinary system of education in which the study of Greek began at the age of three, solid reading in history a few years later, and algebra and Latin at the age of eight. The boy's intellect was sufficiently robust to survive this course of treatment, partly because it was administered solely by his father. It was the latter's ambition to make his son an enthusiastic disciple of Bentham, yet holding his opinions in the true radical manner, independently of the suggestion of authority, parental or otherwise. He succeeded, although John Stuart's utilitarianism was a much more humane system than James Mill's. Mill worked for the East India Company from 1820 to 1858, and wrote many of his books in his spare time. His *Political Economy* appeared in 1848, and attempted to systematize and complete the theories of Adam Smith and Ricardo. It is important for its pioneer stressing of the vital connexion between economic theory and social development. In collaboration with his wife he wrote four powerful works : *On Liberty* ; *On Parliamentary Reform* ; *Subjection of Women* ; and *Utilitarianism*. Mill was an advanced radical in his later years, but the passage of time has brought public opinion very largely into agreement with his views.

JOHN MILTON (1608-74), author of the greatest epic poem in the English language, was born in Cheapside and carefully educated by his father during his early years, then by a private tutor and at St. Paul's School. At the age of 16 he entered Christ's College, Cambridge where he remained for seven years and took an M.A. degree. He had intended to become a clergyman, but his liberal and freedom-loving mind could not tolerate the tyrannous church system of Laud. When the Civil War broke out he proved a staunch supporter of Parliament, and during the Commonwealth he was Latin Secretary, the equivalent of our Foreign Secretary, since Latin was the diplomatic language of the day. His outspoken republican writings meant that he was in very grave danger at the Restoration, and for a long time he had to live in hiding. It is probable that friends at court secured his pardon, and he spent his last years in quiet retirement, blind, but with friends to read to him, and to take down, at his dictation, *Paradise Lost*.

COMTE DE MIRABEAU (1749-91), the great orator of the French Revolution, was a man of " hideously magnificent aspect ". He came of an aristocratic family, but when the States-General met in 1789, the Third Estate at once found in him a ready-made leader. Under his inspiration they refused to accept orders for adjournment, and formed themselves into the National Assembly. Mirabeau's aim was probably a strong constitutional monarchy, somewhat similar to that of England, and free not only from the arbitrary control of the king and the aristocracy but also from the anarchy of short-sighted control by the ignorant masses. In a country, and at a time when the great majority of the people were for the second of these alternatives against the first (though they naturally did not realize the inevitable shortcomings of such an uneducated popular government) he rapidly became unpopular with both sides, and was, perhaps with some justification, accused of treachery by the Third Estate. Mirabeau had wasted his youth in riotous living. Had it not been so, he might have had the strength to carry out a comparatively bloodless French Revolution, but, as it was, the task he took upon his shoulders proved too great for his own constitution, and he died in 1791.

BENITO MUSSOLINI (1883-1945), the Fascist leader, was a socialist agitator in his youth. He was arrested and given five months' imprisonment for his active resistance to the Italian Government's military occupation of the Turkish province of Tripolitania in North Africa. He became Editor of the *Avanti*, the left-wing paper, in 1912, the general theme of his editorials being that Italy needed a blood-bath, followed by the taking over of the Government by the revolutionary socialists. Most of these socialists objected to Italy's entry into the 1914 war, so Mussolini founded his own daily, *Il Popolo d' Italia*, to advance his view that if Italy helped the Allies to victory, more power would be given to the proletariat all over Europe. During the war he drifted further and further away from his socialist antecedents, and in 1919 he founded his new Fascist party. Ample funds were provided by industrialists and big landowners—who were afraid of the rising tide of socialism—and these were used to form armed groups of men. The Premier allowed these to exist because they were used to maintain order and suppress socialist riots. But they quickly passed over to the offensive, and the march on Rome took place in October 1922. Mussolini became Prime Minister, and so remained until his downfall under the Italian defeats of 1943. The Germans rescued him from prison, but his death came at the hands of Italian partisans in April 1945. He gave the people an efficient, but completely anti-democratic Government. Abroad he seized every opportunity for aggression. His ambition flourished on the weakness of the democratic governments, but it was unfortunate for him that his example inspired in Hitler an even more unscrupulous and irresponsible foe of freedom.

WILLIAM PENN (1644-1718), the Quaker founder of Pennsylvania, was born in London and educated at Oxford until he joined the Quakers, when he was expelled. He spent some years abroad, and on his return was prominent again in Quaker activities, being twice imprisoned. He inherited a fortune from his father, Admiral Sir William Penn, and helped to found a Quaker colony in New Jersey in 1676. In 1681 he secured a grant of the territory which is now Pennyslvania, and as Governor gave it a liberal constitution with freedom of worship. He was in Pennsylvania from 1682 to 1684, and again from 1699 to 1701, but his later years were spent in furthering the welfare of the Society of Friends in England.

PERICLES (c. 495-429 B.C.) was leader of the Democratic party in Athens, and virtual ruler of the city from about the middle of the fifth century B.C. The age of Pericles is celebrated as the climax of Athenian civilization. The great tragic poets, Æschylus, Sophocles, and Euripides, all belong to this period, while its architecture is represented by the Parthenon, and its sculpture by the Acropolis statues of Pheidias. Pericles was instrumental in persuading the Athenians to develop their sea-power, and the wealth which paid for all these great works of art was mainly amassed by overseas trade.

WILLIAM PITT, EARL OF CHATHAM (1708-78), was " The Great Commoner ", until his acceptance of the title sacrificed much of his popularity with the people. He entered Parliament in 1735, and right from the first stood out for an integrity of conduct in public and private affairs which seemed very strange to most of the politicians of that era. When the Seven Years War broke out, the incompetence of the New-castle Government forced it to arrange a coalition with Pitt. In this, " Newcastle said what he liked and Pitt did what he liked ", and, as a result, Great Britain emerged from the war as the greatest power in the world. Sea-power was built up to an unprecedented degree, and her colonies in North America and in India were safe against the attacks of any other European power, but only a few years later the folly of George III and his ministers forced the New England colonies to break away. Pitt sympathized with their claim that there should be no taxation without representation, but he did not want to see them leave the Empire, and he made his famous last speech in protest against a peace treaty which would allow this.

JOHN PYM (1584-1643) was, in some respects, the most remarkable of the parliamentarian champions in the struggle against Charles I. He had a keener intellect than Hampden, and a power of sustained thought of which Cromwell was never capable. He was born in Somersetshire, and entered Parliament in 1621, two years after leaving Oxford University. He was one of the promoters of Buckingham's impeachment in 1626, and actively supported the Petition of Right in 1628. He was prominent again in 1640, taking part in the impeachment of Strafford and of Laud. Charles I tried to sent him to the Tower in 1642, but was defeated by the firm stand which the House of Commons took against any invasion of its privileges.

EARL OF ROSEBERY (1847-1929) the " Orator of Empire " and a hero to two generations of British working men, was educated at Eton and Oxford, but left the latter city when the university authorities of the time insisted on his relinquishing his racing stud. His powers of fluent and original expression soon brought him into prominence as a politician, and he took his first seat in the Cabinet under Gladstone in 1884. He became Secretary of State for Foreign Affairs in 1886, and even Bismarck found him " very sharp ". It was at this time that he did his best work for the Commonwealth by helping to forge those strong links between the Colonies, which were soon to become Dominions, and the Mother Country—links which he foretold would stand the strain of a great war. He was Prime Minister for a little over a year in 1894-5, and thereafter, with the exception of some brief but brilliant excursions, he held aloof from party politics. He wrote a *Life of Pitt* and an essay on the last days of Napoleon entitled *The Last Phase*.

GIROLAMO SAVONAROLA (1452-98) was a Dominican monk with a strong streak of Puritanism in his make-up. He aroused great enthusiasm by his denunciation of the abuses in the Church, and crowds went to hear him warning them of the wrath to come. His influence in Florence became so great that when the Medici were driven out he assumed supreme power. He told the people he was going to set up the kingdom of God in Florence, and he introduced an austere rule even more severe than that of Calvin later on in Geneva. But he did not allow for human nature. For a time the people put up with it, but his enemies cleverly exposed the weakness of his claim to have Divine authority for all he did in Florence, and then their growing hatred of all his austerities quickly brought about his downfall. He was brought to trial as an impostor and a heretic, and he paid the penalty for trying to force the people to live up to ideals impossible of attainment.

JOHN ALEXANDER SMITH (1869-1939), classical scholar and Waynflete Professor of Moral and Metaphysical Philosophy at Oxford from 1910 to 1936, was educated at Edinburgh University and at Balliol College, Oxford, where he took a double First, and held the Jowett Lecturership in Philosophy from 1896-1910. With Sir W. D. Ross he was responsible for the supervisory editing of the Oxford edition of the English translation of Aristotle's works.

OSWALD SPENGLER (1880-1936), the German philosopher and historian, was born at Blankenberg in the Harz Mountain district. He studied mathematics, biology, history, and art, and used his rare grasp of all these subjects to throw a multicoloured light on the history and the philosophy of Western civilization. His great masterpiece, *The Decline of the West*, was written between 1911 and 1918, and aroused the keenest interest among all students of history. His later works dealt mainly with political problems.

JOHN ADDINGTON SYMONDS (1840-93) spent eleven years in writing his greatest work, *The Renaissance in Italy*. He was born at Bristol and educated at Harrow and Balliol College, Oxford, where he won the Newdigate Prize and an open Fellowship at Magdalen. His health was undermined by his studies, and after a few years at Clifton, where he did some lecturing, he had to go abroad, and the last years of his life were spent mostly at Davos Platz. In addition to his work on the Renaissance he wrote studies of the Greek poets and of Dante, lives of Shelley, Sidney, Ben Jonson, and Michelangelo, a book on early English drama, and translations of Cellini's *Autobiography* and of other Italian works.

ARNOLD JOSEPH TOYNBEE, C.H. (1889-   ) was for thirty years Director of Studies in the Royal Institute of International Affairs, and Research Professor of International History in the University of London. He has received honorary degrees from many universities, both British and American. He went to school at Winchester, and then to Balliol College, Oxford, where he was Fellow and Tutor from 1912 to 1915. For the next four years he was busy with government work in connexion with the war, and from 1919 to 1924 he was Professor of Byzantine and Modern Greek at London. During the second world war he added the Directorship of Foreign Research and Press Service in the Royal Institution to his other duties. He was a member of the British Delegation to the Peace Conference in Paris in 1946. His publications include *The New Europe*; *Greek Historical Thought*; *The World after the Peace Conference*; *A Survey of International Affairs, 1920-38*; and his world-famous, ten-volume masterpiece, *A Study of History*. The first three volumes of this came out in 1934, three more in 1939, and the last in 1954. A one-volume summary by D. C. Somervell has been highly approved by all competent judges.

ROBERT VAUGHAN (1795-1868), an eloquent and popular Congregational minister and public lecturer, was born in the West of England of Welsh descent. He early showed a taste for historical reading, and, having gained a high reputation by his books on Wycliffe and on the Stuart Dynasty, he was appointed to the Chair of History in University College, London, in 1834. The art of appealing to the public, which he had cultivated as a preacher, was put to equally good service in his lectures, and the public ones were often attended by social notabilities. In 1843 he went to Manchester as President and Professor of Theology in the Lancashire Independent College. He brought out the first number of the *British Quarterly* in 1845, and edited this journal for the next twenty years. Resigning his presidency in 1857, he retired to St. John's Wood, where he wrote his best historical work, *Revolutions in English History*.

ALFRED NORTH WHITEHEAD, O.M. (1861-1947), Professor of Philosophy at Harvard University from 1924 to 1937, was well described in *The Times* obituary notice as " the latest and greatest of the Cambridge Platonists ". He linked together the finest and deepest thoughts of Plato and Aristotle with the discoveries of modern science on matter and energy and relativity. He was born at Ramsgate, and went to Sherborne School and Trinity College, Cambridge, where he was elected a Fellow in 1884, later becoming senior mathematical Lecturer. He was Lecturer in Applied Mathematics at University College, London, in 1911, and in 1914 became Professor of Applied Mathematics at the Imperial College of Science, a post which he held until he went to America. From a very early stage in his career he had been most keenly interested in the logical foundations of mathematics, and he found a kindred spirit in Bertrand (now Earl) Russell. They went together to a mathematical congress at Paris in 1900, and this was the beginning of an association which led to the publication, between 1910 and 1913, of their great, joint, three-volume masterpiece, the *Principia Mathematica*. Other important books by Dr. Whitehead are *The Aims of Education*; *The Principle of Relativity* (in which an alternative meaning is given to Einstein's equations); *An Enquiry Concerning the Principles of Natural Knowledge*; *The Concept of Nature*; *Science and the Modern World*; *Religion in the Making*; *Process and Reality*; and *Adventures of Ideas*. Whitehead was elected F.R.S. in 1903, given the Order of Merit in 1945, and received honorary degrees from a large number of universities.

BIBLIOGRAPHY

THE following books can be recommended for further reading:

Arnold J. Toynbee. *A Study of History.* (One-volume abridgment by
    D. C. Somervell.)
Arnold J. Toynbee. *Civilization on Trial.*
C. Delisle Burns. *The First Europe.*
Christopher Dawson. *The Making of Europe.*
Christopher Dawson. *Religion and the Rise of Western Culture.*
G. G. Coulton. *Mediæval Panorama.*
H. A. L. Fisher. *A History of Europe.*
John Bowle. *Western Political Thought.*
J. B. Bury. *The Idea of Progress.*
Bertrand Russell. *Power.*
A. N. Whitehead. *Adventures of Ideas.*

ACKNOWLEDGMENTS

FOR permission to include copyright material in this volume, acknowledgments and thanks are due to the following authors and publishers :

To Professor Arnold J. Toynbee and the Oxford University Press for " Civilization on Trial " from the American edition of the book with that title, and for " The Dwarfing of Europe" from the English edition ; to the late Professor J. A. Smith and to the Oxford University Press for " Greek Gifts " from a lecture on " The Contribution of Greece and Rome " in *The Unity of Western Civilization*, edited by F. S. Marvin ; to the Cambridge University Press for two extracts from A. N. Whitehead's *Adventures of Ideas*, " From Force to Persuasion " and " The Business Mind of the Future " ; to Alfred A. Knopf, Inc., of New York and to C. H. Beck'sche Verlag of Munich for the extract from Spengler's *Decline of the West*; to Mrs. H. A. L. Fisher and to Curtis Brown, Ltd., for " The New Europe " from H. A. L. Fisher's *History of Europe* ; to the fifth Earl of Rosebery for his " Outline of Scottish History " ; to the Archbishop of York and the Industrial Christian Fellowship for the sermon on *Christianity and Communism*, published as a pamphlet by the Fellowship ; to Erwin D. Canham for " The Authentic Revolution " ; and to H.M. Stationery Office for the extracts from the *Beveridge Report on Social Insurance*.

INDEX

(Titles of Lectures are in Black Type)

PRINTED FOR THE PUBLISHERS

INTERNATIONAL UNIVERSITY SOCIETY, NOTTINGHAM
PROPRIETORS : CULTURAL PUBLICATIONS (I.U.S.) LTD

BY R. & R. CLARK, LIMITED, EDINBURGH